Initiation

This book builds on the vast clinical experience of Joseph L. Henderson, who became interested in initiatory symbolism when he began his analysis with Jung in 1929. Henderson studied this symbolism in patients' dreams, fantasies, and active imagination, and demonstrated the archetype of initiation in both men and women's psychology. After Henderson's book was republished in 2005 Kirsch, Beane Rutter and Singer brought together this collection of essays to allow a new generation to explore the archetype of initiation.

Initiation: The Living Reality of an Archetype demonstrates how the archetype of initiation is seen clinically today. Divided into distinct parts, the book explores the archetype of initiation in Dr Henderson's own life, as well as suggesting its importance in:

- Clinical Practice
- Culture
- Aging and Death

The chapters in this book amplify and extend the archetype of initiation from the earliest historical periods up to the present day. The editors argue that initiation symbolism often underlies contemporary phenomena, but is rarely recognized; *Initiation* helps to bring a new understanding to these experiences.

This book will be of interest to psychotherapists with an interest in psychoanalysis and analytical psychology, as well as those training at analytic institutes.

Thomas Kirsch is a Jungian Analyst who trained at the San Francisco Jung Institute. He is author of *The Jungians* and has been president of the C.G. Jung Institute of San Francisco and of the International Association for Analytical Psychology.

Virginia Beane Rutter is a Jungian Analyst who trained at both the Zurich and the San Francisco Jung Institutes. She is the author of three books, including *Woman Changing Woman*, that bring art history, archaeology, and psychology to bear on the relevance of this archetype for modern men and women.

Thomas Singer is a Jungian Analyst who trained at the San Francisco Jung Institute. He has written four books including *The Vision Thing* and *The Cultural Complex*.

D1571819

Initiation

The living reality of an archetype

Edited by Thomas Kirsch,
Virginia Beane Rutter and
Thomas Singer

 Routledge
Taylor & Francis Group

LONDON AND NEW YORK

First published 2007
by Routledge
27 Church Road, Hove, East Sussex BN3 2FA

Simultaneously published in the USA and Canada
by Routledge
270 Madison Ave, New York, NY 10016

*Routledge is an imprint of the Taylor & Francis Group,
an Informa business*

Typeset in Times by
RefineCatch Limited, Bungay, Suffolk
Printed and bound in Great Britain by
TJ International, Padstow, Cornwall
Paperback cover design by Sandra Heath

This publication has been produced with paper manufactured to
strict environmental standards and with pulp derived from
sustainable forests.

British Library Cataloguing in Publication Data
A catalogue record for this book is available from the British Library

Library of Congress Cataloging-in-Publication Data
Initiation: the living reality of an archetype / edited by Thomas
Kirsch, Virginia Beane Rutter & Thomas Singer.
　　　p. cm.
　Includes bibliographical references and index.
　ISBN-13: 978-0-415-39792-6 (hardback)
　ISBN-10: 0-415-39792-8 (hardback)
　ISBN-13: 978-0-415-39793-3 (pbk.)
　ISBN-10: 0-415-39793-6 (pbk.)
　1. Psychoanalysis. 2. Initiation rites. 3. Archetype (Psychology)
　4. Henderson, Joseph L. (Joseph Lewis), 1903– I. Kirsch, Thomas,
　1936– II. Rutter, Virginia Beane. III. Singer, Thomas, 1942–
　[DNLM: 1. Henderson, Joseph, L. (Joseph Lewis), 1903– 2. Jungian
　Theory. 3. Symbolism. WM 460.5.J9 I56 2007]
　RC506.I548 2007
　616.89'17 – dc22
                                                    2006102494

ISBN: 978-0-415-39792-6 (hbk)
ISBN: 978-0-415-39793-3 (pbk)

To Joe Henderson – an Initiation Master

Contents

Figures

Contributors

John Beebe, MD, is an analyst member and past President of the Jung Institute of San Francisco, where he is in private practice. He is the author of *Integrity in Depth*. He co-edited *Psychiatric Emergencies* with Peter Rosenbaum; he edited the Proceedings of the 1980 International Association for Analytical Psychology (IAAP) Congress; he edited *Terror, Violence and the Impulse to Destroy*, and he is the founding editor of the *San Francisco Jung Institute Library Journal*.

Thomas Kirsch, MD, is an analyst member of the C.G. Jung Institute of San Francisco in private practice in Palo Alto. He is past President of the International Association for Analytical Psychology and past President of the Jung Institute of San Francisco. He is the author of *The Jungians*, which chronicles the social and political history of the development of the professional Jungian movement.

Betty De Shong Meador, Ph.D, is a non-resident analyst member of the C.G. Jung Institute of San Francisco and past President of the Jung Institute of San Francisco. She is the author of *Uncursing the Dark, Inanna: Lady of the Largest Heart*, and the forthcoming *The Sumerian Temple Hymns*. She has also contributed essays to *The Vision Thing* and *The Cultural Complex: Contemporary Jungian Perspectives on Psyche and Society*.

Neil Russack, MD, is an analyst member of the C.G. Jung Institute of San Francisco with a private practice in San Francisco. He is the author of *Animal Guides in Life, Myth and Dreams*.

Virginia Beane Rutter, MS, is an analyst member of the C.G. Jung Institute of San Francisco and practices in Mill Valley. She is the author of *Woman Changing Woman, Celebrating Girls*, and *Embracing Persephone*.

Dyane N. Sherwood, Ph.D, is an analyst member of the C.G. Jung Institute of San Francisco with a private practice in Woodside. She is the editor of the *San Francisco Jung Institute Library Journal* and a contributor to

The Sacred Heritage edited by Donald Sandner and Steven Wong. She is co-author of *Transformation of the Psyche*.

Thomas Singer, MD, is an analyst member of the C.G. Jung Institute of San Francisco and Chair of the Extended Education Committee. He is the editor of *The Vision Thing* and has also written *Who's the Patient Here: Portraits of a Young Psychotherapist* and *A Fan's Guide to Baseball Fever*. He is co-editor of *The Cultural Complex: Contemporary Jungian Perspectives on Psyche and Society*. He has a private practice in Mill Valley and San Francisco.

Murray Stein, Ph.D, was President of the International Association for Analytical Psychology from 2001 to 2004. He is a founding member of the Inter-Regional Society for Jungian Analysts and the Chicago Society of Jungian Analysts. He has written several books, including *Jung's Treatment of Christianity*, *In MidLife*, and *Jung's Map of the Soul*. He is the editor of *Jungian Analysis* and co-founder of Chiron Publications. Presently he lives in Switzerland and teaches at the newly formed International School of Analytical Psychology in Zurich.

Richard Stein, MD, is an analyst member of the C.G. Jung Institute of San Francisco with a private practice in San Francisco. He teaches regularly in the Institute's Training Program as well as in the Public Programs. He has a particular interest in the spiritual as well as the clinical application of Jungian analysis.

David Tresan, MD, is an analyst member of the C.G. Jung Institute of San Francisco with a private practice in San Francisco and Marin. He lectures extensively and has written numerous articles and book reviews dealing with a variety of issues including neuroscience, the relationship between Martin Buber and Jung, and most currently threshold realms of religious experience including psychological development from initiation to individuation.

Preface

When Joseph Henderson, author of *Thresholds of Initiation*, turned one hundred in July 2003, his friends and colleagues planned a party to celebrate his birthday. A large gathering assembled to honor Dr Henderson's amazingly long, rich, and productive life – even as he continued to see patients and teach candidates.

After the birthday party, the organizing committee found that several thousand dollars had been donated to the C.G. Jung Institute of San Francisco in honor of Dr Henderson. The committee went back to Dr Henderson and asked how he wished the money to be spent. Dr Henderson did not hesitate. He wanted *Thresholds of Initiation* – first published in 1967 and long out of print – to be republished. This original study on the archetype of initiation remains at the center of Dr Henderson's contribution to the theoretical and clinical development of analytical psychology.

A lively debate ensued among the members of the committee. Two different proposals emerged – to republish *Thresholds of Initiation* by itself, or to republish it as part of a larger volume containing new chapters by those who had been influenced by Dr Henderson's pioneering work on this archetype. The second proposal would demonstrate how Dr Henderson's "students" had extended his work into the contemporary theory and practice of analytical psychology. Many analysts continue to understand their work and their lives through the lens of the archetype of initiation. The committee finally decided that the original *Thresholds of Initiation* should stand on its own and be republished with a minimum of editing. Of course, as the archetype of initiation often teaches us, the "final decision" is often not final and unexpected turns can easily lead to another initiatory threshold. Shepherding the book through its next incarnation as republication became one more phase in the unfolding exploration of the archetype of initiation in Dr Henderson's footsteps.

To celebrate the republication of *Thresholds of Initiation*, then, a conference took place in May 2005 – a continuation of the celebration of Dr Henderson's one hundredth birthday party. This event featured presentations by those who had worked closely with Dr Henderson over the years.

These contemporary Jungian analysts spoke about their notions of how the archetype of initiation expresses itself in the early twenty-first century. This conference was an electric event with a high level of focused energy and attention. It was clear that the archetype of initiation was alive and well – and that it remains at the heart of the emotional, psychological, and spiritual identity of the C.G. Jung Institute of San Francisco.

The gestalt of the conference and the quality of the material that was presented led to the idea of collecting and editing the papers for publication. This book is the result of that effort, the next, natural step. As it turned out, the debate about whether to publish Dr Henderson's book by itself or as part of a larger study was moot as the publication of this companion volume represents the coming to fruition of both proposals.

Acknowledgments

Collaborative books are the effort of so many people in so many different ways. A few who have been most helpful are:

Andrew Samuels – who continues to lend our projects his enormous enthusiasm and intelligence.

Kate Hawes – who has given ongoing editorial support to us on behalf of Routledge, a publisher that has treated us with unfailing decency.

Ursula Egli – if Joe Henderson is an initiation master, Ursula Egli is a master of many crafts – spelling, diction, punctuation, eagle-eyed editing and tracking multiple manuscripts simultaneously. Above all, Ursula is a master of good faith who knows how to bring projects to fruition.

The C.G. Jung Institute of San Francisco – deep ties of collegiality through belonging to the C.G. Jung Institute of San Francisco have provided the authors of this volume a solid, professional home for over fifty years. The San Francisco Jung Institute has nourished all of us and we are most grateful.

Introductions

PURPOSE OF THIS BOOK

In the course of preparing his seminal, 1967 book *Thresholds of Initiation* for republication Dr Joseph Henderson wrote that "each generation needs to discover the archetype of initiation for itself. Although the archetype of initiation is as old as human experience, it is always experienced as something 'new' " (Henderson 2005: xv). The purpose of this collection is to help a new generation explore the archetype of initiation in depth by presenting the work of several analysts who have been influenced by Dr Henderson and have discovered for themselves the living reality of the archetype. There are many different voices in this next generation of analysts who have picked up the diverse threads of Dr Henderson's work by investigating different aspects of the archetype, including: how the archetype of initiation expresses itself in women; how modern initiations can be patterned on old traditions; how themes of sacrifice and surrender play a central role in the initiatory journey; how initiation can evolve into the process of individuation; how the initiate experiences being in the presence of an initiatory master; how the archetype of initiation is reflected in contemporary cultural forms, such as movies and literature.

This book introduces the reader to the ongoing, multifaceted, and vital contemporary research on the archetype of initiation. The topic remains central to human experience because, without an initiatory experience, either inside or outside of a psychotherapeutic relationship, modern women and men can find themselves adrift, without a sense of orientation, meaning, or "calling." One can think of the archetype of initiation as patterning and fueling the transitions from one stage of life to the next – or even as running like an underground river from one generation to the next. From birth to death, there are biological, psychological and spiritual transitions which, if mediated by the archetype of initiation, can lead to growth and transformation.

The eighteenth and nineteenth centuries saw tangible fruits of humankinds celebration of reason and the power of the mind to solve problems – from the establishment of democracy to the building of the steam engine. The Age of

Enlightenment and the Industrial Revolution gave birth to new science and its promises for the future of humankind. What a man or woman or a society needed to know in order to thrive in the world could be learned through reason. The twentieth century was ushered in by two world wars and economic collapse, which gave rise to deep unease and widespread loss in the faith in reason to pave the way to creating good lives and good societies. This loss, coupled with the unfathomed dimensions of the newly discovered unconscious, caused people of the early twentieth century to become disoriented, creating more than one "lost generation." Perhaps this is why Dr Henderson rather surprisingly referred to the 1920s as the "nadir of civilization" in the preface to the first edition of *Thresholds of Initiation*. It is of interest that Dr Henderson had his own first encounters with the archetype of initiation at the end of that decade.

The rediscovery of the importance of patterns of initiation came during a time of sequential, global catastrophes which provide a historical context for understanding why this particular archetype captured the imagination of Dr Henderson and the generation that followed him. How were individuals and societies going to orient themselves in an unhinged world in which reason could no longer be relied on? For some – including Dr Henderson – the emergence of the "archetype of initiation" out of the collective unconscious was a godsend because it provided an inner gyroscope or point of orientation that could "guide" an individual. Another, deep part of the psyche offered the possibility of discovering a trustworthy inner compass for navigating essential transformative life events in a world that provided few reliable landmarks.

Since the middle to later part of the twentieth century many cultures as well as individuals have become increasingly receptive to integrating initiatory rituals as a non-rational way of orienting oneself and the community in the world. Rapidly changing cultural patterns and historical vicissitudes have led to a rediscovery of the important role of the archetype of initiation in individual and social development. But, the archetype of initiation – like any other archetype – can be related to in both creative and destructive ways without any guarantee of it being "good" or "bad." Archetypal patterns in themselves have no morality – they simply are. One can just as easily be initiated into a criminal gang or a terrorist cell or a fundamentalist religious community as into a path of individuation.

The psychic energy that can be mobilized by the activation of the archetype of initiation is enormous, even awesome. For instance, the cult of suicide bombers in the Middle East relies on compelling initiatory themes as part of its appeal to young men and women. The call to separate oneself from the ordinary social structure, to undergo purification, to submit to an ordeal, and to offer one's life as the ultimate sacrifice promise the "initiate" a transformed rebirth in an afterlife. Looked at from this perspective, some of the most virulent violence in the Middle East is fueled by the power of the archetype of initiation to mobilize young people to action.

As cultural patterns and historical realities continue to change, initiatory patterns will undoubtedly also continue to change as they draw upon the deep human urge to transform and be transformed which is mediated in the psyche by the archetype of initiation.

Thomas Singer

Reference

Henderson, Joseph L. (2005) *Thresholds of Initiation*, 2nd edition, Wilmette, IL: Chiron.

HISTORY OF INITIATION SCHOLARSHIP

Initiation has long been the subject of great interest to anthropologists and students of comparative religion. As Henderson remarks in his *Thresholds of Initiation*, "Initiation more than any other body of knowledge has suffered throughout history from the fate of continually being forgotten and having to be rediscovered" (Henderson 2005: 1).

In 1909 initiation was rediscovered by Arnold Van Gennep, a member of the Ecole Sociologique in Paris, who wrote the classic *Les Rites de passage* (Van Gennep 1909/1960). Van Gennep recognized that initiation rites were instrumental in helping young boys move from one phase of life to the next. He divided the ritual into three phases: the rite of separation, the rite of transition, and the rite of incorporation. He also saw that many girls needed to be made women by means of appropriate rites which for him began with early menstrual rites and culminated in the marriage ritual. The scholarly consensus of the Ecole Sociologique held that the origins of these rites lay in mankind's innate experience of group identity. The "collective representations," as they were called, originated outside the individual psyche and this view led to a sociology and psychology of social custom. The influence of Van Gennep and Durkheim, another member of the Ecole Sociologique, was enormous for the remainder of the century.

Independently and at approximately the same time in England a group of scholars of ancient Greek religion were discovering the social origins of religion. Jane Ellen Harrison, archaeologist and historian of Greek religion, was driven to include psychological factors in addition to the sociological ones described by the Ecole Sociologique to understand the religion of primitive peoples (Harrison 1912/1974). She discovered an obscure inscription from Crete "Hymn to the *Kouretes*," which described a ritual dance of initiation performed by a group of young men for the protection of the holy child, Zeus, born from the goddess Rhea. There are several versions of this particular myth, but the main point is that the rite signifies a transition from the religion of the Mother to that of the Father. Harrison's intuitive psychological grasp of early Greek religion and its initiatory rituals turned out to be a bridge between the sociological point of view and the newly discovered theories of the unconscious.

Psychoanalysis began to explore the study of initiation in 1912 when Freud published his *Totem and Taboo* (Freud 1950) and Jung published his "Symbols of Transformation" (Jung 1956). Both men looked at the same material and saw a correspondence between myth and ritual of primitive societies and the fantasy material of modern individuals. They each came to the conclusion that in the unconscious there exists an archaic heritage (Freud) or a collective unconscious (Jung). Freud continued to see this material as pathological, whereas Jung saw these same images as representing archetypal patterns to be integrated and as forming the basis of cultural patterns. Freud's emphasis was on the retrospective study of origins of the ritual, whereas Jung developed his synthetic mode and pursued a constructive interpretation of the same material. This difference in interpretation led the two men to go their separate ways and form separate schools of depth psychology.

A few years later Jung wrote the following about initiation in *Two Essays on Analytical Psychology*:

> The fact is that the whole symbolism of initiation rises up, clear and unmistakable, in the unconscious contents. . . . The point is not – I cannot be too emphatic about this – whether the initiation symbols are objective truths, but whether these unconscious contents are or are not the equivalent of initiation practices, and whether they do or do not influence the human psyche. Nor is it a question of whether they are desirable or not. It is enough that they exist and that they work.
>
> (Jung 1953: 229)

Jung's hypothesis of the collective unconscious and its archetypal dominants introduced an inner psychological structure to what previously had been seen as coming from "collective representations" or the "collective conscious." Jung did not specifically pursue the archetype of initiation, and he did not specifically bridge the inner experience of initiation with its manifest cultural forms. This was left to his followers such as Erich Neumann, who occupied himself with the issue of initiation on the level of mythology (Neumann 1954), and Joseph Henderson, who first coined the term "cultural complex" to describe the mediating force between the primordial unconscious and the cultural forms (Henderson 1967/2005).

Henderson has postulated that while the new cultural forms are certainly religious and social in nature, they arise from an interaction between an inner unconscious image and the outer social forms. A reconciliation needs to take place between the primordial (archetypal) image and the collective customs, and it is the conflict between the two which brings many people into analysis. However, for the majority of people, the solution has continued to be a return to a collective social or religious group where initiation is experienced on a group level. This has led to a rise in fundamentalism which can be seen in the attraction of the Christian right, Islamic fundamentalists, and Zionist fundamentalists. For those for whom a collective solution has not been tenable, the archetype of initiation has to be experienced individually and as having both an internal as well as external dimension. Henderson has demonstrated that at nodal points in an individual's life, the archetype of initiation often appears in dreams.

At this point, the story of how Joseph Henderson first came to Jung and then to his interest in the topic of initiation is relevant. Originally from Elko Nevada, Henderson had graduated from Princeton in 1925 and had returned to San Francisco where he wrote book and theater reviews for two local magazines. In 1927, he entered analysis with Elizabeth Whitney, the only analyst of any theoretical persuasion west of the Mississippi at that time. She introduced him to H.G. Baynes, Jung's assistant, who happened to be taking his sabbatical in the Bay Area that year. With Baynes' encouragement Henderson contacted Jung and arranged to spend a year in Zurich. Henderson spent the summer of 1929 with his cousin in Berlin, where he observed first-hand Germany's social and economic unrest. He arrived in Zurich in the fall of 1929, just at the time of the great stock market crash and the Great Depression. He had an intensive year of analysis with Jung, and he attended the Wednesday morning Dream Seminar, which was available to selected English-speaking analysands. The seminar followed the case of a Swiss businessman (Jung 1984). One of the dreams contained a powerful image of a large cauldron filled with metal objects, some of which were crosses and some of which were crescents. To teach the method of amplification Jung divided the participants into two groups, instructing each to research the dream's archetypal symbols. Half of the group was assigned the crescent and the other half the cross. Dr Esther Harding was appointed the leader of the "crescents," which included the young Joe Henderson. Dr Harding's work on the crescent awakened her interest in women's rites of initiation which eventually bore fruit in her classic study, *Woman's Mysteries* (Harding 1972). Joe Henderson and Esther Harding were living in the same pension, and they shared many discussions.

The study of initiation symbolism has been alive in Henderson's researches throughout his seventy and more years as an analytical psychologist. In three major works Henderson describes aspects of the archetype of initiation. The first is a chapter entitled "Ancient Myths and Modern Man" in *Man and His Symbols* edited by Jung (Henderson 1964); second is the book *The Wisdom of the Serpent* co-authored with Maud Oakes (Henderson and Oakes 1963). In both these books Henderson uses dreams from his clinical practice to illustrate how the archetype of initiation appears in the unconscious of modern man. The third is his book *Thresholds of Initiation* which represents the culmination and synthesis of his clinical practice, theory, and wisdom (Henderson

1967/2005). Henderson found that initiatory symbolism frequently occurs in dreams which are archetypal in nature and transformative at their core. His theoretical model of initiation, developed out of his many years of clinical practice, modifies van Gennep's formulation. Following Baynes and Jung, Henderson's experience with initiation has been that after the separation there is a transitional period which he calls the "ordeal" followed by a "trial of strength." These are the core experiences of the young adult separating from the family milieu. These stages are often painful and even "messy." They require the individual initiate to surrender to the process and go with it. Anthropologist Victor Turner has coined the term "liminality" to describe these first two stages (Turner 1967). The third stage, the trial of strength, focuses on that stage of initiation when the process becomes more "rational" while at the same time, the mystery of the archetype is still honored. As this entire process takes place in a "liminal" time and space at the very edges or boundaries of everyday human experience, it is often difficult to perceive if anything is happening at all. During this period, individuals in analysis often complain that nothing is happening. The mystery of the initiatory experience is not visible and yet is so deeply transformative that, for many, life without its unfolding would be unthinkable. The remaking of man requires a separation from the mother and a period of "liminality." For a young man the trial of strength requires a new orientation to the world of the fathers. The process for a young woman is different. The separation from the mother is of a different nature and a woman's relationship to the world of the fathers is also different.

In summary, Jung discovered that initiation symbolism often appears in the unconscious of modern individuals. Following Jung's discovery, Henderson's lifelong study aimed to demonstrate both theoretically and clinically how it actually manifests in an individual analysis. Responding to Henderson's pioneering work analytical psychologists have furthered the research into initiation symbolism, as evidenced by the chapters of this book.

Thomas Kirsch

References

Freud, Sigmund (1950) *Totem and Taboo: Some Points of Agreement between the Mental Lives of Savages and Neurotics*, trans. James Strachey, New York: Norton.

Gennep, Arnold van (1909/1960) *The Rites of Passage*, trans. Monika Vizedom and Gabrielle Caffee, Chicago, IL: University of Chicago Press.

Harding, E. (1972) *Woman's Mysteries*, New York: C.G. Jung Foundation and G.P. Putnam and Sons.

Harrison, Jane Ellen (1912/1974) *Themis: A Study of the Social Origins of Greek Religion*, Gloucester, MA: Peter Smith.

Henderson, J.L. (1964) "Ancient Myths and Modern Man," in C.G. Jung (ed.) *Man and His Symbols*, New York: Anchor.

Henderson, J.L. (1967/2005) *Thresholds of Initiation*, Middletown, CT: Wesleyan; Wilmette, IL: Chiron.

Henderson, J.L. and Oakes, M. (1963) *The Wisdom of the Serpent*, New York: G. Braziller.

Jung, C.G. (1953) *Two Essays on Analytical Psychology*, trans. R.F.C. Hull, *Collected Works*, vol. 7, New York: Pantheon.

Jung, C.G. (1956) "Symbols of Transformation: An Analysis of the Prelude to a Case of Schizophrenia," trans. R.F.C. Hull, *Collected Works*, vol. 5, New York: Pantheon.

Jung, C.G. (1984) *Dream Analysis: Notes of the Seminar Given in 1928–1930*, ed. William McGuire, Princeton, NJ: Princeton University Press.

Neumann, Erich (1954) *The Origins and History of Consciousness*, trans. R.F.C. Hull, New York: Pantheon.

Turner, V. (1967) *The Forest of Symbols*, Ithaca, NY: Cornell University Press.

WOMEN AND INITIATION

In 1973, when studying at the Jung Institute in Zurich, I entered a training analysis with Barbara Hannah. During the extraordinarily productive time that I worked intensively with her, we delved into the mysteries of the feminine psyche. This process arose organically out of the analytic intimacy between a wise old woman, 81 years old, and a young, barely conscious woman of 30 years. Miss Hannah told me that Jung, in response to a question she posed him about herself, had told her that he didn't know the answer, that as a man, he didn't understand the feminine psyche. He said he could not see into psychology from a woman's point of view, from her interior frame of reference, as he could from a man's. Jung said, "You women have to do this for yourselves." Barbara Hannah, Marie Louise von Franz, Emma Jung, Toni Wolff, Esther Harding and many others did just that. Their pioneer contributions and subsequent women analysts' investigations into feminine psychology were clearly enumerated and synthesized in Claire Douglas' book *The Woman in the Mirror* (Douglas 1990). Since 1990, other women have come forward with new perspectives.

In this volume, the work of three women on the archetype of initiation from the feminine point of view are represented, that of Betty Meador, Dyane Sherwood, and myself. Each was written independently, without consultation between the authors. Meador and Sherwood do not address themselves exclusively to feminine psychology, as I do. What the three pieces have in common is that each of our chapters has as a central element a woman in relation to a divine feminine entity. Meador meditates on sorrow and aging, and finds meaning and solace in the words of the first woman poet in history, Enheduanna, whose poems exalt her mistress, the Mesopotamian goddess, Inanna. Sherwood describes her Lakota vision quest under the tutelage of the medicine woman, Pansy Hawk Wing, whose divine inspiration is White

Buffalo Calf Woman. And, finally, I compare the misogynistic initiation rites of classical Greece, under the auspices of the fierce goddess Artemis with the Navajo *Kinaalda* puberty ceremony in which the initiate is said to become Changing Woman, the Navajo creator goddess, as she moves through the ritual. The common thread in the presentations of us three women analysts from our different experiences is a bringing forward of the feminine divine immanent in the human woman, that includes body, nature, and spirit.

My initial work with Miss Hannah and then my work with Joseph Henderson when I returned to San Francisco, coupled with my ongoing clinical development, synchronistically led me to a study of girls' puberty ceremonies and to the overall archetype of feminine initiation. Images of those rites frequently appeared in the dreams and fantasies of my women patients during their psychological journeys. Gradually, I saw broader parallels between the ritual process of analysis and the patterns of puberty ceremonies for girls. Anthropologist Bruce Lincoln defined that pattern as threefold: enclosure, metamorphosis or magnification, and emergence. I have observed this structure in women's psychological initiation in my analytic practice. A woman in analysis with a woman analyst is contained or enclosed in a healing process of ritual relationship – honoring body, ego, and self – that effects a psychological transformation. The psychological unfolding may involve physical, emotional, or spiritual change. The analytic enclosure is naturally suited to feminine development and provides the ritual container for it. Initiation for women is intrinsically body-embedded. Women's blood mysteries – menstruation, defloration, a sexuality laden with the implication of impregnation, pregnancy, childbirth, lactation, and menopause – are defining experiences in a woman's life. Even if she does not have children, a woman carries the monthly rhythm of her menstrual cycle in her body. The experience of her own bleeding and caring for herself during her periods while her hormones fluctuate affects her psychologically, emotionally, and spiritually. Her creativity, both literally and symbolically, is embodied in her monthly ebb and flow. Her spirit is inherent in her biological potential for giving life.

A woman's awareness and valuation of her bodily-embedded identity is greatly affected, however, by the cultural attitude toward women and the feminine. From Aristotle's condemnation of the female as fundamentally inferior to the male of our species, to Jung's definition of strong-minded women as animus-possessed, in the cultural unconscious women carry shame for and confusion about being female. The women's liberation movement of the 1960s sought to eradicate the differences between male and female in the interest of equality which only further split women from the source of their own natural identity and empowerment, from their blood mysteries with their archetypal implications. Therefore, women carry many splits between body, mind, and soul.

Part of the work in any deep psychotherapeutic process for a modern woman, therefore, requires a correction to this deeply held sense of inferiority as well as a healing of these splits. Disempowered by the fact of her birth, from girlhood to adulthood, a woman faces strangely mixed messages about who she is as female, about who she can be in relation to her culture – personally, politically, relationally.

This cultural sense of disempowerment comes to the fore at puberty. Adolescence is an extended initiation in which the intricate web of conflicting messages is acted out in a myriad of ways. Sexuality often becomes the crystallizing metaphor for a girl's difficult rebirth into womanhood. The travesty in our culture is that the media works to sexualize girls long before puberty; there is no respect and protection for the archetype of the maiden. This rape of the innocent results in a girl becoming a sexual object to the exclusion of her whole person. If she adopts this role, her feminine development is aborted.

Working with adolescent girls in my practice, I see a girl becoming sexual, more conscious of herself, and finding herself both attracted to boys and attractive to them. Then she discovers that her attractiveness is also negative and threatening. Her societal disempowerment, the subtle sense of her inferiority to men, her sexualization by the media which reduces her to Barbie doll beauty and thinness, and her confusion over her own sexual power overwhelm her. A girl may then act out with sexual promiscuity, withdraw from the field in horror, or muddle along miserable and lost. This toxic environment is responsible for the self-destructive epidemic of middle school and high school girls starving themselves, dropping out and losing their voices, or resorting to primitive bloody rituals of cutting their bodies to express their pain and to feel alive, instead of dead, inside. The pressure of the conflict in the psyches of young women erupts in initiations of their own makings, as they struggle to express the internal legacy they have inherited. Many girls carry the war against their bodies into adulthood.

On the positive side, those girls who find their way through this morass become more differentiated and are able to claim their intelligence, competence, athleticism, and overall self-worth, as well as their sexuality. Adolescent girls exhibit the empowerment that is being born of the inner battle to right the cultural imbalance between men and women. At the healthy end of the spectrum, they express themselves through dress, speech, music, and body art. The girls' movement since the early 1980s continues to liberate girls from restrictions in the world as never before. Along with this have come a plethora of books on the subject of raising girls with a sense of healthy self-esteem. We continue to see many of these mothers and daughters in our analytic practices where we work with the intergenerational struggles of this evolution.

In classical Greece, although young girls patronized Artemis, her function in their initiation was to deliver them into the demeaning position of being wife and mother to the men who ran the state. They had no recourse within the social system but to submit; some chose to take their own lives instead (Chapter 3). My observations in my clinical hours, as well as those of others, of the loosening of this old patriarchal hold in women's psyches are evidence that Jungian analysis is a laboratory where the awareness on the part of the analyst can further or inhibit the dissolution of this cultural and archetypal struggle. Overt betrayal or denigration of the feminine obviously occurs when an analyst of either gender sexualizes the relationship with the patient. But when an analyst has personal needs that prevent her or him from giving the initiate the profound caring attention that she requires, or when the analyst misses the initiatory signs in the work, that cultural blindness becomes a subtle betrayal. If the analyst, male or female, consciously or unconsciously, holds the position of exclusively serving the patriarchal system, he or she is bound to thwart a woman's development and inhibit the initiatory process. Then a woman, now re-wounded, has no recourse but to abandon the container, or submit to a false process, and, either way, die a psychological death.

When, instead, the analyst holds a position of awareness for both the cultural problem as well as the personal history and internal conflicts of the individual woman, she or he can further the initiation as well as support the cultural revolution of empowering women. The archetype of feminine initiation will emerge organically, often in the image of a female deity to contain all the levels of the work. The intra-psychic and interpersonal shift in feminine consciousness that is slowly percolating through individual women's efforts to free themselves from this legacy is as radical as the discovery of atomic energy.

Virginia Beane Rutter

Reference

Douglas, Claire (1990) *The Woman in the Mirror: Analytical Psychology and the Feminine*, Boston, MA: Sigo Press.

STRUCTURE OF THIS BOOK

There are many different ways that the chapters of this book could be organized as there are many different cross currents that link the various chapters to one another. But, an organic structure emerged as the co-editors discussed how best to arrange the material.

Part I: The archetype of initiation and Joe Henderson

- Thomas Singer
- Neil Russack

The most natural place to begin this book is with the man who introduced the reality of the archetype of initiation to the Jungian tradition. But, rather than presenting his theory, our authors chose to show the man and his work through his early experience of initiation and their later experience of him. There are two chapters in Part I.

In the first chapter, Thomas Singer documents Dr Henderson's own early experience with the archetype at a critical juncture in his development. An initiatory drawing that Dr Henderson produced at a time of personal crisis is the focus of this chapter. The second chapter comes some seventy years later in Dr Henderson's life when he is seen as the initiator through the eyes of an initiate, Neil Russack. Dr Henderson neither seeks this role nor indulges it. He simply is, and the initiatory process is perhaps best understood through what happens to Neil Russack, who experiences him in this way.

Part II: The archetype of initiation in clinical practice

- Virginia Beane Rutter
- Richard Stein

Two of the analysts who have done the most to track the archetype of initi-ation in their clinical work, Virginia Beane Rutter and Richard Stein have contributed fine examples of the living reality of the archetype of initiation in contemporary individuals.

Virginia Beane Rutter explores two contradictory threads of the feminine initiation experience through her original researches into ancient Greek rites associated with Artemis and ongoing Navajo rites associated with Changing Woman. Drawing on her extensive clinical experience with women in the midst of transformation, she demonstrates the paradox of denigration and empowerment that are two sides of feminine initiatory rituals.

Richard Stein traces the development of a profound journey in a man who suffers greatly the ordeal, trial of strength and sacrifice that are the hallmarks of masculine initiation, whether it be in a primitive or modern society.

Part III: The archetype of initiation in culture

- Murray Stein
- Dyane N. Sherwood
- John Beebe

The archetype of initiation does not occur in a vacuum. Not only does it appear in the context of individual stage of life transitions, but also it is responsive to changing cultural needs and attitudes. Three analysts speak to the cultural manifestations of the archetype of initiation in different con-texts. Murray Stein addresses contemporary manifestations of a spiritual calling, even when a postmodern age declares the need for meaning and its mythological underpinnings dead. Dyane Sherwood describes how an ancient tradition of the American Plains Indians has found new meaning for American Indians and non-Indians alike. Finally, John Beebe explores how one of film's greatest directors, Alfred Hitchcock, plumbed the archetype of initiation in a most deliberate and ironic modern way with his classic film, *North by Northwest*.

Part IV: The archetype of initiation in aging and death

- Betty De Shong Meador
- David Tresan

The final stages of life inevitably circle around the physical, emotional, and spiritual realities of death. Two senior analysts take on this final threshold of initiation with strikingly individual and clear voices. Betty Meador, long a student and scholar of the goddess Inanna, presents an unflinching consideration of the central role of sorrow, separation, and loss in the initiatory preparation for death. David Tresan also places painful loss at the center of his emotional and philosophical meditation on death as it relates to initiation and individuation in the "late style" of life.

Part I

The archetype of initiation and Joe Henderson

Chapter I

In the footsteps

The story of an initiatory drawing by Dr Joseph Henderson

Thomas Singer

This chapter tells the story about a drawing – about its creation and its meaning to the man who drew it, Dr Joseph Henderson. The narrative unfolds on many different levels simultaneously. A few of the levels that the reader may want to keep in mind about this remarkable drawing and its even more remarkable creator are:

1   This is the story of a young man's search for meaning, orientation, and even the renewal and transformation of his life at a critical moment in his development.
2   This is the story of the making of a special kind of drawing – a drawing based largely on the inner reality of the psyche rather than the outer circumstances of a life – although the outer circumstances are essential to the inner events.
3   The "language" of the drawing comes from the world of dreams, of the imagination, of myth, and it is expressed symbolically. The drawing itself tells a story just as there is a story behind the making of the drawing.
4   This is a story that takes place at a particularly "ripe" time both in modern history and in the early development of the Jungian tradition – just between the two world wars and at the peak of the Great Depression – 1930 and 1931.

The telling of this story best begins with a recounting of how the drawing first came to my attention – just about seventy-five years after it was drawn. As part of celebrating Dr Henderson's one hundredth birthday in 2003, a fund honoring his remarkable career and life was established. A committee was formed to decide the most fitting way to use the fund's generous contributions and it became clear that republishing *Thresholds of Initiation* – Dr Henderson's seminal book – was the perfect tribute. About the republication, I wrote in the Foreword at the time:

> For many, *Thresholds of Initiation* became the **landmark**, the **talisman**, and the **model** for both analysis and for analytic training at the C.G. Jung

Institute in San Francisco. Based on Dr Henderson's work, the process of analysis was often framed in terms of the archetype of initiation. The book *Thresholds of Initiation* became a "threshold of initiation" on which both analysis and the analytic training program were patterned – not in the sense of prescribing a course of treatment or in designing a curriculum but in establishing an underlying purpose, value and meaning to the analytic endeavor.

(Henderson 2005: xiv–xv, original emphases)

Shortly after writing that description, I received an email from Dyane Sherwood, the committee member who first suggested creating a fund in honor of Dr Henderson's birthday and one of the contributors to this book. Her message contained a PDF image of a drawing that Dr Henderson had made in 1931 (Figure 1.1, in the color plate section). Dyane thought the drawing might make a good cover for the reissue of *Thresholds of Initiation*.

When I opened the computer file, I was dazzled. Something inside me literally vibrated in response to the image on the screen. I don't know if anyone has made a study of the phenomena of "PDF files and the numinous" or "emails and the archetype of initiation" – but, based on my experience of seeing Dr Henderson's 1931 drawing on the screen for the first time in 2003 (Figure 1.1), I can testify to the fact that the numinous and the archetype of initiation can be experienced in cyber space.

Although I had seen the drawing on the wall in Dr Henderson's home office before, I had not really taken note of it. Suddenly – in Dyane's email – it came to glowing life on my screen. It seemed so fresh and full of energy – even brand new – although it had been drawn three-quarters of a century before. It spoke directly to my soul – as if I had known it all my life. I became an ardent advocate for this image to become the cover of the new edition of *Thresholds of Initiation*. Ultimately, Dr Henderson made the decision in favor of another image, which represented to him a coming to fruition of his initiatory journey, whereas the image of this chapter was more at the beginning.

Dr Henderson and I began a year-long discussion about the drawing of this study which I jokingly referred to as "the cover not chosen" – the subject of this chapter. Those talks in themselves became a journey between Dr Henderson and myself. As the chapters in this book demonstrate, many have followed in the footsteps of Dr Henderson – in their unique ways. This chapter tracks Dr Henderson's own footsteps in his reminiscences of this drawing, leading us back to the origins of his experience with the archetype of initiation.

Joe Henderson was born in 1903. He was 27 years old when he drew this image in 1931. It would be another thirty-six years before the material of his own personal experience would ripen into his professional account of the archetype of initiation, *Thresholds of Initiation*, first published in 1967. He would begin telling me the story of the making of the drawing in 2004, in his one hundredth and first year. This image, then, is a living symbolic bridge between Dr Henderson's own initiatory journey in the early 1930s, his clinical portrait of the archetype of initiation in *Thresholds of Initiation* in 1967, and the writing of this chapter in 2006. Over the years, Dr Henderson has shared many parts of this story with others, although this is perhaps the first time a narrative has been put together as a coherent story about this drawing which laid down the footsteps for one man whom so many came to love and to follow. Of course, there was no real following in Dr Henderson's footsteps and none of the authors of this volume would either claim to be able to or want to follow too closely in his tracks because our tradition is fundamentally about finding one's own way. Still, we are all interested in Dr Henderson's footsteps.

The centerpiece of the story is an image that might best be thought of as a psycho-spiritual map that anticipates and guides the archetypal initiatory journey of Joseph Henderson – a kind of inner compass. It is not easy to stay oriented to person, place and time – the stuff of ordinary linear development and narrative – while simultaneously tracking an inner life in its archetypal unfolding. It is not easy to remain oriented in multiple dimensions simultaneously. In telling the story of this drawing, we are tracking biography, psychology, symbology, iconography – all in the context of the archetype of initiation as it unfolds in the life of an individual. Teasing these layers out and interweaving them has been the "ripening fruit" of my conversations with Dr Henderson. Every time I thought I had developed some sense of where we were in the narrative of the drawing – or thought I knew what a particular part of the picture was about – Joe would surprise me with new information that added incredible richness and texture to the story. For instance, at one point, Dr Henderson told me additional details about the upper right quadrant (which I will discuss later) and I remarked to him in some amazement, "I never knew that." He replied simply, "How could you? I never told you about it before." The image became richer and richer. The story is told mostly in Dr Henderson's own words and the interpretations of the drawing are exclusively his. It was not my role to interpret his drawing; my role was simply to ask questions.

Here is some context and basic chronology. Dr Henderson traveled from America to Zurich in the fall of 1929 to study and to analyze with Jung. He remained in Zurich until June of 1930. He settled in London to begin his pre-medical studies in the fall of 1930 which continued through the academic year into 1931. As he was completing these studies in the spring of 1931, Joe had two big dreams on consecutive nights in the midst of his premed course exams:

> The dreams made me think I needed an analytic hour or two to talk to Jung. I booked travel to Zurich as soon as I could, and I went to see Jung in the early summer of 1931. Jung was not very helpful. All he said was that he was leaving in a day or so for summer vacation.

Jung was not there for Joe when he needed him.

> I went to Zurich because I was in trouble. I needed to talk to Jung about myself. I needed someone. So, I decided to interpret the dreams myself and do this drawing – which took about three weeks. At stake was whether or not to go to medical school.

Joe never talked to Jung about the details of this drawing, but – at the age of 101 – Joe said, "I activated the archetype of initiation within myself and realized that I could interpret my own dreams."

Here are the two dreams that Joe had in the spring of 1931. These two dreams find abstract, symbolic expression in the top and near the bottom of the drawing. (The rest of this chapter will isolate parts of the drawing with close-up images, each of which tells a separate part of the story. To see these parts in relation to the whole, please refer back to Figure 1.1.)

> A white horse (white circle in Figure 1.2) is running along the surface of a gray sea. An eagle flies down from the sky and bites the horse in the back of the neck where there is an exposed artery. Blood spurts up from the pierced artery and the horse dies. I awoke and knew that I was going to fail my premed course exams on the following day.

Even as we look at the image of the dream, as it appears in the top of the drawing today, the spurting blood seems fresh – as if it just happened this instant – which underlines the timelessness of archetypal reality. To some, the outer events and circumstances of Joe's life at the time of this dream might not suggest an "ordeal," but to those who know the reality of the inner world, this dream and its symbolic representation in the drawing convey grave danger and the onset of an ordeal.

Dream Two is represented in the drawing near the bottom and is shown in detail in Figure 1.3.

> The dream of the following night is set in the depths of the ocean. A snake with a red head comes up from below – from the depths – and bites a flat, black fish. The snake bites the fish in exactly the same way that the eagle bit the horse on the back of the neck the night before.

Joe elaborated on the meaning of the dreams over time in the following way:

> The dreams seemed very complicated to me. The "eagle" bite (Figure 1.2, Dream One) was a "bad one" – a killer. It said to me that I was going to fail my examination on the next day. The red headed snake bite of the second night (Figure 1.3, Dream Two) suggested a renewal of life – life giving rather than death dealing. That surprised me and suggested

that I was going to pass the examination somehow, but I didn't know how. The dreams seemed to be two pairs of opposites and I knew I had something to work on:

- There was the snake coming up from below, biting the fish.
- And there was the eagle coming down from above, biting the horse.

The pair of opposites above was matched by a pair of opposites from below. It presented to my eye a double vision, or two pairs of pairs.

While Jung was away on vacation, I told the dreams to one or two women. One woman especially reacted to it – Linda Fierz David who wrote a book about women's initiation in Pompeii (Fierz David 1988). She said that the dreams were "interesting" and she saw me as dreading the whole process of becoming a doctor.

In that sense, the eagle was the medical profession itself. I was putting myself through something that was a trial of strength. The white horse symbolized my natural enjoyment of life and my not wanting to inhibit it. The serpent with the red head symbolized life energies coming from below and bringing new life. The flat fish lying on the bottom of the sea was like inertia itself, just heavy and unable to move. So there was a threat from above and a bite from below.

In medical school my body was heavy, like the fish on the bottom of the sea. I had to kill my inertia and the wish to remain a white horse instead of a red snake. I had to give up my passive identification with heroic youth (white horse). Both the inertia (the flat fish) and the passive identification with the heroic phase of life and its enjoyment (the white horse) needed to die. Linda Fierz pointed out that the white horse carried natural instinct and the enjoyment of life – it needed to "die."

In a way, all of the animals in the dreams were ambivalent. For instance, the black eagle of the first dream became – in subsequent dreams – blue and white rather than black and white. I saw that as more "favorable." The drawing that I made from these two pairs of opposites (the two pairs of animals) became dynamic. It's complicated, but its complication is what makes it interesting. I came to think that the bite of the eagle showed my fear of failing – that's why it was so negative to me. Not just failing the examination, but failing at the whole process of becoming a physician. I was afraid that I would be unable to go through with a medical career.

The first dream said that I was convinced I had failed. The second dream suggested that there could be a positive meaning to this failure. The snake dream was hopeful to me, that I might still be able to proceed. The hope for renewal really came from the snake bite from below.

I also told the dreams to my great friend Cary Baynes. Cary wouldn't interpret the dreams at all, but she would listen to me "informally." She made me get an appointment with Jung when he returned at the end of the summer, after I had completed painting the image. We went to Bollingen and had supper with Jung. After supper, I showed him my painting. Jung said that it showed I had "unusual decorative ability." He also said that the left side or the feminine side was more finished and the right side, the masculine side, was less finished and I should get to work on my masculine side. He saw the right side as "breaking up" with different images. He didn't comment on the central area. I had already interpreted it to my own satisfaction.

Let's take a closer look at the iconography of the drawing as elaborated by Joe, keeping in mind that this is an interior story. The initiatory ordeal portrayed in this drawing is happening in the psyche – not outside in the world.

The symbolic rendering of the two dreams at the top and bottom of the drawing that Dr Henderson has already described in his own words can be seen as both stating the precipitating inner problem at the archetypal level and as framing the drawing.

At the very center of the drawing is a gold circle of "peaceful resolve." It is surrounded by pieces of blue turquoise and red coral (Figure 1.4).

This inner core was the first thing that Joe painted after going to an art supply store in Zurich and carefully picking out a piece of parchment on which he could work comfortably. He started drawing in the center using gold, coral, and turquoise. Joe told me that drawing the center first "put it all in motion." Just beyond this core of brilliant light that "centers" the drawing is an area of intense black about which Joe said the following:

> This is the black obsidian mirror of Tezcatlipoca. I was very taken up with Mayan and Aztec art and archeology when I was drawing this. It is said that if you look into this mirror, you can see your essential Self.

About this god, I found the following:

> Tezcatlipoca was the Aztec god of war. He carried a magic mirror that gave off smoke and killed enemies, and so he was called "god of smoking mirror." Whoever would gaze into this black mirror of obsidian might perceive the meaning of his soul.[1]

Joe said to me: "Looking into the black obsidian mirror symbolizes the ability to focus on the inner life."

Directly encircling the black mirror is a series of masks, some of which brought to my mind Donald Kalsched's archetypal defenses of the personal spirit. But, Joe noted particularly the one at the top: a "hermaphroditic" figure with feathers in the hair representing the "fullness of life" and the one opposite to it at the bottom, a skull figure that represents "death."

Beyond the golden, turquoise, and coral core, and beyond the black obsidian mirror and then beyond the encircling ring of ritual masks, the central drama of this initiatory tale is played out in a progression of four panels that move from the lower left quadrant, to the lower right quadrant, to the upper right quadrant, to the upper left quadrant. These four panels tell the story of the snake's journey and/or of the transformation of the psyche's libido.

One can think of what happens to the snake in these four panels as being a picture of a transformative process along the instinctual-spiritual poles of the psyche. Joe never told me if he considered himself a member of a snake clan – but the esoteric narrative of this drawing is told through the snake's development. The snake at the lower left is, as Joe said, "OK with itself – at rest" (Figure 1.5).

Joe said, "Its movement hasn't happened yet in reality, but it signifies the beginning of the initiatory process of snake undergoing a whole new cycle of transformation." The ordeal – begun by the white horse being killed by the eagle above and the renewing serpent with the red head emerging from below to kill the flat, black fish – hasn't yet mobilized the snake at the bottom left. But, Joe went on to describe the snake at the bottom right as "manic, chaotic, agitated" (Figure 1.6).

Joe explained, "He's really being worked over!! He's in motion (the red balls) and he may be suffering." The snake's ordeal has begun. The snake in the upper right quadrant comes up and, according to Joe, "Out of itself into a new spiritual place and takes on the form of a plumed serpent" (Figure 1.7).

I asked Joe if the plumed serpent of the upper right hand quadrant was a coming together of the feathers from the eagle of his first dream (at the top of the drawing) with the red headed snake of his second dream (at the bottom of the drawing) – and that out of this coming together of feather from above and snake from below there emerged the figure of the "plumed serpent." Joe agreed with this as a possible origin of the plumed serpent, but said that putting the feathers of the eagle together with the serpent biting the fish to make the plumed serpent was not something he thought about consciously when he made this drawing. Joe said that the upper left hand quadrant showed the resolution of the initiatory ordeal in a mandala that takes the form of a plant (Figure 1.8).

In another telling of the story of the snake's transformation (the time when Joe told me a piece of the story I had never heard before because he had never told it to me before), Joe talked more about the symbolism of the upper right hand quadrant (Figure 1.7).

The additional story about how this part of the drawing developed reveals how deeply interwoven in the initiatory process can be the role of dream, of active imagination, of outer life circumstances, and inner psychological development. Looking closely at this part of the drawing, one sees that the plumed serpent emerges out of a sun that is divided into two. This imagery comes from another dream that Joe had during the period that the drawing was taking shape. The dream itself had been further elaborated in an active imagination that Joe had about it.

> I saw myself dead in a dream. There was a sarcophagus with a statue of me on its cover. As I looked at the sarcophagus, I began to come to life. Then, I saw a priestly figure with a staff in his hand – on top of the staff was a sun symbol divided into two halves. It meant that I was going to come to life instead of remaining a corpse in the sarcophagus.

Joe continued his explanation of how the drawing formed itself: "The plumed serpent coming out of the divided sun in the drawing is an imaginative elaboration of the divided sun dream."

In creating the progression of panels to tell the story of snake's transformation, Joe decided that he wanted the drawing to have a "counterclockwise movement" (see Figure 1.1). He said to me, "The whole drawing begins and ends in the center, but its narrative moves counterclockwise." This was a conscious and contrarian decision by Joe. Jung and others had observed that conventional mandala movement, such as those in stained glass windows, emphasizes clockwise movement. Joe's dilemma was how to get it "to turn around and to rotate, but in a different way from the mandalas that others around him – including Jung – were drawing and studying." He didn't want his drawing to look like a replica of works by others who were presumably following Jung's lead. Henderson knew that Hitler's swastika also goes counterclockwise which gives it an aspect of witchcraft that invokes a magical dimension.

In addition to the counterclockwise movement of the snake's development, there is another feature that gives Joe's drawing a dynamic quality. Joe decided to leave the entrances to the center more open – thinking of them as "open windows, in direct contrast to the formal gateways of the Tibetan mandala which guard the entrance to the center." Joe wanted to leave "a way for all the major symbols to move freely in and out instead of their being closed in." Joe said this was a message to himself that said, "Look inside, but don't avoid looking outside as well."

Perhaps it was the counterclockwise movement and the "open windows" that led Toni Wolff to take note of Joe's drawing hanging on the wall when, a few years later, she visited his apartment in London. Wolf was accompanying Jung on his October 1935 trip to England on which occasion Jung delivered the Tavistock lectures. She said that Joe's drawing "was unlike any other mandala she had seen." Wolff found the other Jungian mandalas "too geometric, too regular – they had their own design – but didn't say anything beyond that." She liked the dynamic openness and asymmetry of Joe's drawing and that is what has excited me as well.

Looking closely at the drawing, there are many other details that one can focus on. Every element has meaning and one is meant to travel around the picture participating in a symbolic journey that orients, transforms and initiates. However, there is insufficient space to discuss every detail of this intricate and elaborate symbolic image. But I do want to highlight one additional comment by Joe about the "sacrificial knife" in the lower right hand quadrant (see lower left portion of Figure 1.6).

"What had to be sacrificed?" I asked Joe. At the age of 101, he replied: "The tendency to identify with the Self as if it were my experience." On another occasion, he said that his "inertia" (the flat fish at the bottom of the sea) needed to be sacrificed, as did his identification with the "white horse," a kind of identification with the "hero" and with a life of pleasure. Or "sacrificing inertia can be another way of saying that the ego's identification with the Self needs to be sacrificed." Finally, at the age of 101, he said: "It is an ongoing experience."

Without much help from Jung on the occasion of his urgent visit to Zurich, Joe returned to London at the end of the summer of 1931 – renewed and initiated from within. He was permitted to retake the premed exams in Botany and Physics which, as his dream predicted, he had in fact failed. He was not required to take all the courses over again. He passed the exams and entered medical school at St Bartholomew's in the fall of 1931.

Part of the architecture of initiation that Joe was to later sketch in *Thresholds of Initiation* was what he in fact experienced personally in returning to London and entering medical school. An essential aspect of the archetype of initiation is to rejoin the world in a new way as a natural expression of the initiatory experience – to get, as Joe put it, "more connected to life and the social order." Joe found himself developing an outer relatedness which was particularly difficult for someone as naturally introverted as he had always been. Of this, Joe said:

> I was beginning to know what it is to be socially minded – to read the newspaper. I had not been at all interested in politics or anything related to it. As I began to get into the medical world, I thought I should join the human race and be more socially minded. Part of my initiation was to develop a social attitude – to join the world. All of the people around Barts hospital and Cambridge were extremely liberal . . . I dutifully read the *New Statesman* and the *Nation* every week because everybody I knew did that. The study of Medicine and becoming a doctor was an initiatory experience.

Henderson's "joining the human race" can be seen as an outer manifestation of the "open windows" in his drawing – the ability to move more freely in and out of the inner world. This attitude resulted in a new readiness to take an interest in some of the great traditions of the political, social, and scientific world of his day:

1   He felt a political connection to the New Deal of Franklin Roosevelt through his Uncle Charlie's presence in Washington, DC as a Senator from Nevada and as a leader of the Finance Reconstruction Corporation.
2   He participated in an illustrious social and scientific tradition in England through his relationship to his future wife, Helena, and the Darwin family of which she was a member.
3   He joined one of the oldest and finest medical traditions in the world by studying at St Bartholomew's which dates back to the eleventh century and could claim William Harvey – the discoverer of the blood circulatory system – as one of its own.

The drawing was a wonderful initiatory link between my premedical world and my plunging into medical school. As in the drawing, medical school brought me into the presence of death and its opposite, rebirth. Initiation in medical school brought about both the feeling of being small and insignificant and of being large and part of an important world. I felt very small and yet part of a big tradition. Of course, those feelings of being big and small go along with the archetype of initiation because there is the experience of one's personal "puniness" in the presence of something big, important and meaningful. One is very small and *IT* is very important.

It is with a final reflection on the dynamic between "small/big" that I want to bring this narrative of Dr Henderson's drawing to a close. (Much of the drawing, by the way, is very small while the overall impact is very big.) During the year of interviewing Joe and listening to the many stories associated with the time around the making of his drawing, there were pregnant silences between us in which no words were exchanged.

On occasion, I found myself gazing out the window of his office pavilion at the clouds passing overhead with a heightened awareness of the fact that they have been coursing the sky long before human consciousness of them. Observing the low hanging, swift moving clouds in the shared silence with Joe filled me with wonder at the fleeting miracle of life on this planet – and wonder at the puniness of our everyday lives and concerns in the face of timeless mysteries – such as the mystery of initiation.

Learning – over and over again – about the right proportions between small and big;

Learning about a healthy tension between this "smallness and bigness"

in the psyche,
in the social order,
in the natural order,
and in the spiritual realm;

This Learning is at the heart of the ongoing experience of the archetype of initiation and its mystery of death and rebirth about which Dr Henderson has taught so many so much.

Finally, if you look carefully, you will see his "footsteps" in the drawing.

Note

1 http://en.wikipedia.org/wiki/Tezcatlipoca

References

Fierz David, Linda (1988) *Women's Dionysian Initiation: The Villa of Mysteries in Pompeii*, Jungian Classics Series 11, Dallas, TX: Spring.

Henderson, Joseph L. (2005) *Thresholds of Initiation*, 2nd edition, Wilmette, IL: Chiron.

Chapter 2

Sitting with the old master

Neil Russack

A true master guides you into and through the dark places, oversees your initiation and encourages you to have your own unique life, with its fierce taste and its riches. This is the story of a few meetings with Joe Henderson in which the context of our connection was simple: he is very old and close to death. And he seems unafraid, and linking with him was frustrating and exhilarating and full of kindness and love and led me deeper into my own life. This is what an initiation master does – leads you into your own life. And even when you think he's past his prime, he uses that material too. Here's what happened for me with Joe Henderson.

Sometimes I just follow the image that the world gives me. Late one afternoon in fall, as I was thinking about love again, a spider ran across my desk, moving fast. Instead of killing it, I watched to see where it would go. It went over the side, underneath. The spider's way seemed gentle, subtle – the dark is the spider's element, the place of incubation and secret ways, of waiting, web spinning, killing and mating. A spider is prepared and the world comes to it.

I first got the idea of sitting in the quiet from my ancient 101-year-old analyst. I still see him from time to time and the spider led me to go and talk with him about a new book. His suggestion about my first book was: "Leave out the personal material." I didn't actually take his advice. This new book is even more personal than the first, and I was curious to find out what he would say.

We sat together in the garden. "What questions do you want to ask me?" was his opening. This took me by surprise because I had written a cover letter outlining my concerns. He had responded enthusiastically to the first chapter and said he had read the book twice. He had broken his ankle since I had seen him last, and he looked older, his face more sunken. This physical deterioration however was balanced by a greater degree of quiet. Deeper than the formal composure he has always been known for, was a tremendous stillness. I wasn't even sure he was noticing me. It was as if he had broken through to a secret known only to him – perhaps as death moved a step closer. In fact, he looked so different that in one sense I didn't recognize him; the animal in me seemed to be facing a creature I had never met before. While quickness had been his hallmark, his body was now inert, there was no energy emanating from him. And though he was still well groomed, he seemed indefinably less meticulous in appearance than his custom has been. Is he losing it? I wondered, as one does with the very old. No, he wasn't, it turned out. We discussed my new manuscript. He had a clear idea of what was happening in the book and went through my concerns one by one. He seemed to be following the energy of my interest at the time, rather than the letter I had sent ahead. I needed to ask my questions again so he could feel what was going on *now* as I asked, not *then*, when I wrote the letter. That's just how he works.

"You're moving from the animal realm to the human realm and I am interested to see you use the name Sophie for the heroine. How did you decide to use that name?" he asked.

"Should I explain more about her?"

"No," he said, "let the readers discover her on their own. How you write about her in your own way is much better than explaining her theoretically. Fiction comes naturally. You can trust people to have their own response. Finish the book and I will have more to say about this. The book is simple but deep; too much intellectualism won't work."

I wondered about a publisher.

"Books do get published. Find the kind of publisher who likes unusual works that wouldn't otherwise be seen – the little known, but much appreciated works. This book reads like a mystery story but with a sensitive assessment of feeling."

Then he spoke *as* me, something slightly uncanny that he does sometimes. When he does that my body warms up, I feel a touch, a real connection to him. He said, "Let it be the book I want to write."

I found myself treating him as an oracle, someone in touch with the rhythm of the universe. I began asking him whatever came to me. "What about my next book?"

Again he spoke as me, "See what happens, let it be something that intrigues me." He went on then, in his own voice, "The value of this book is that it introduces the unconscious, and how it works in people's lives. It is open and revealing and keeps you guessing. It begins with frogs, and that makes you want to keep reading."

I wrote the book because I was fascinated by a story a friend told me about a woman who had a childhood ritual in which she hurled her sacred frogs down the cellar stairs into the dark to die and be reborn. Hearing that story had made me want to keep reading too.

Then my mentor shifted his point of view once more, into the voice that he uses for an aerial view, a thinking voice that offers no personal connection to the one he is talking to, in this case me.

"Sophie, being an aspect of the feminine, has a spiritual quality and that also keeps people interested. Sophie suggests an anima figure and has her place in relationship to the unconscious. She demonstrates how the unconscious is important in understanding women and their mystery."

The questions kept tumbling out of me: "What do you think about the role of childhood trauma in this account?" I asked.

He turned into me again in his completely natural way, "Writing helps me through the family and away from them. It is a good reason for writing. The book is asking to be written. Let fantasy speak more loudly than my thinking."

It occurred to me for the first time that my mentor had an effect on me like that of the frogs who died and were reborn. He led me into the realm of magic. He shifted shapes and became different people. This was a matter of course for him. In his company I became more free, more open to my imagination, more willing to follow the lead that was being given to me. Though he understood theory, and even invented theories, he rested in the mystery of life and was always tuned into the aliveness that was likely to break out at any second. Sophie led me into a world of magic without knowing that that was what she was doing. This very old man lived in that world.

And it made him fearless. "Why do you worry what people will say about you? Let them think whatever they want." I felt suddenly released from a cage, a burden was lifted from my shoulders; I could be free, and without the slightest hesitation I took these words as his blessing.

We were outside, by a table on the patio of his garden in back of his house. The garden is huge and calming with a view over the valley. It has had a lot of care spent on it, and has a big California live oak in the middle; he and his wife used to hold outdoor theater and dance performances there in summer, one Sunday afternoon each month. These festivals were called "Sons of Art" after the title of a work by Henry Purcell.

He was in his wheelchair on a patio and I was sitting close in because his hearing was not good. In the past we had always met in his little garden studio, so things had changed; this time was informal. He began to get restless and I wondered if I had overstayed my visit. "I'm getting cold," he said, "let's go inside." I took hold of his arms to get him up to his walker but failed, and he fell back into the chair. I was trying to gauge how much support to offer. When he was still a fiercely independent 90, he had fallen from the last brick step onto the sidewalk outside our office building, crashing on both knees, bang! His head almost hit the pavement and his briefcase flew into the street. "No," he said at that time, "I can manage on my own," and up he got as if nothing had happened.

Now we sat side by side in front of a blank TV in his living room. I didn't know what to expect. On the way in I thought to myself that he had been so affirmative of everything I was trying to do because of his years – that he is probably supportive of everything anyone does. That was the second time I thought that he was losing it because of his age. He must have read my mind because he spontaneously told me that he was trying to find a way to discourage a man from writing about Jung. "It's embarrassing," he said. So for the second time it was me not him; I was the one off balance.

After a little silence, he asked if I wanted a glass of wine, then asked Kenny, his attendant, to get us that good Chardonnay. With our glasses filled to the brim, we sat back and talked of ordinary things. He said how grateful he had been for the recent birthday party given for him:

"It was good to see friends around and feel life going on in a positive way rather than getting bogged down in all the problems of old age. I can't go anywhere now, but I don't mind and anyway all my colleagues are dead so I wouldn't have anyone to visit, but I am appreciative to be able to still have the house where people take care of me and do the things I used to do myself."

Then, almost as an afterthought, he mentioned a little sheepishly that he had made friends from some of his patients, acknowledging that life's necessity now took precedence over his previous formality.

I wanted to take things deeper so I asked about his dreams.

"They have been very strange lately. I've been surprised by them and don't know what to make of them. I dreamed of many people passing before me, people of all kinds and ages, people I had never seen before, with whom I had no relationship, just passing through night after night."

He looked quizzically both at me and himself, but didn't ask me what I thought. Rather the dreams were just left there on the table to be themselves. I listened without commenting, but wondered again about the aging process; I'd never seen him bewildered by his dreams before and the dreams seemed collective, impersonal. Had he lost touch, I asked myself, with that deep, scholarly, interior life that always had nourished him? I remembered when, thirty years earlier, I mentioned to him that I needed my house in Inverness as a retreat; he said that sometimes he would sit quietly on his garden wall and things would come to him. He seemed almost overjoyed about my relationship to Sophie, the heroine of my new book, and her frogs.

As the wine began to take effect, I glanced over at him. He was utterly peaceful and I realized I had never been with another human being who was so quiet and still. No ripple of energy came from him. We were both staring straight ahead and withdrew into silence, that thing I had sometimes been afraid of in the analytic hour. Now I felt no need to interrupt it and neither did he. Then, inexplicably, I experienced an immense space opening and the exhilaration of entering it. In that space things could take their own natural shape. Afterwards I remembered I had wanted to ask him what he thought about death and had forgotten. I was beginning to kick myself when it occurred to me that perhaps this silence and spaciousness was my answer. It was so entirely beautiful and sufficient. We were both sitting side by side, facing forward. I was to the left. I felt relaxed and close to him. He has marvelous big hands and I can clearly see them at rest on the arms of the chair. I remember all the details very clearly.

When I was in the garden with him, and he didn't bring up any particulars from the book, I realized he couldn't help me with the book any more, and that I was on my own. I thought it was because of his age, but it's not. I had changed. I didn't need him that way any more and that freed me to be myself and the pressure to ask him more or make the most of our time dropped away. In a relationship with a mentor there is always a little bit of trade going on. You help me and I'll be your child or admirer or take a certain role. Now nothing was needed. Consequently we became closer, there was a simpler kind of appreciation and love in the room. I had the sense that he wanted me to stay, that he was giving me something now that he couldn't find a way to do before, that he was finally accepting me as a man, who like him, had found his own way. Perhaps he always did, but now that I had changed and didn't need a father any more, I trusted him and I could love his old man's wildness. I could meet him in that wilderness. He talked about *his* life and I wanted to hear.

The conversation swerved toward ordinary life again. Whether or not he picked up my slight concern about how long to stay, he mentioned that he liked to eat around six, watch the news after dinner, and go to bed early, after eight o'clock. Earlier in his life, he would write at night. He added, "Sometimes I just wake in the middle of the night and lie there."

For me the middle of the night is a sweet time in which I feel the permission, the absolute freedom, to think whatever I want. I look forward to waking in the dark, and I imagined that this might be true for him also.

"It must be nice for you to have that time to yourself," I responded.

"No," he was adamant, "I have too much alone time during the day as it is."

As I was wondering how to relate to him now, he began talking about *his* relationship with Jung. As a young man he had done a formal analysis with Jung and then the war intervened. After the war he would go back from time to time and spend a few precious hours with his mentor. He said that he was careful to prepare his questions because Jung's time was so limited.

> "Of course Jung was complicated and extremely unpredictable, you knew he was a genius, so you never knew what to expect, and even though his temperament would change without warning in a moment, one forgave him for that, because his response was always so interesting."

He was loosening up and told me a story about Jung chopping wood. It was one of his shamanic stories that showed me how he and I had changed and how our relationship was different now:

"You know who Ruth Bailey was, don't you? She had gone on the Africa trip with Jung and was never a patient of his the way other colleagues had been, rather she treated him as an ordinary man. So it was decided that she would take care of him and live with him after Emma Jung died. One day, he was outside chopping wood and she flung open the kitchen window and called out, 'Don't you know you are too old to be chopping wood, you old fool?' and slammed the window shut before he could respond. Jung would smile because he loved someone treating him as an ordinary person."

I couldn't resist asking him if he was worried beforehand what he would write as his chapter in the book *Man and His Symbols*.

"No, I wasn't worried because it was all laid out for me. It wasn't interesting either because it didn't come from me. It wasn't something I wanted to write for myself."

We both lapsed into that magic silence again, and I felt his answer hit my chest; what people thought of you wasn't the important thing – in this case contributing to a famous work – it was being yourself, your true self, that was crucial. That's where the life was. This infinite empty space was full to the brim with whatever arrived when I occupied it. With his silence, this old man was leading me into the unfathomable richness and mystery that, with Jung, he had learned to rely on. And this silence had magic wherever I encountered it; it had magic, whether it appeared in Sophie's frogs, in some ancient, green tiles that had seized my imagination recently in Seville, or in many unnamable and uncountable little things that happen every minute.

At this moment I think of a dinner party thirty years ago, when I asked my mentor where dreams come from. He said, "No one knows, it is a mystery."

Now the old man was facing death, and I had joined him, and we sat, side by side, no longer analyst and analysand, no longer even colleagues, simply two human beings looking at a blank television screen viewing this mystery together.

It must have been late when I left that afternoon, but I don't remember leaving. It is as if the parting were swallowed up in the silence. And the strange thing was that before and during the parting, it was the first time that I didn't worry that this might be the last time I would see him. Even when he was younger and healthy, I sometimes had those thoughts. But now, paradoxically, I didn't. I didn't worry when he would die or when I would. Somehow it didn't matter. I can't really explain it. It is as if this newly discovered space extends into death, and my relationship to him transcends death. Normally, I would wonder whether to shake his hand or give him an awkward hug, but that didn't matter now. Wherever I walked, the magic would be there, in a bird song, say. I remembered a marvelous moment when Lear, after his night on the heath, with the first sunlight, pretends to take an arrow from his quill to shoot game. For a moment he had the joy of life itself. I felt bigger after my visit.

This led me to remember all the other times I had experiences of the world opening in such a way. The marker of entering that space for me is an indescribable peace that I had otherwise felt only with animals.

I entered such a moment years ago walking on a beach with a sharp drop-off at Point Reyes. For no apparent reason, my chest seemed to expand to infinity, and a moment later a man high up on a dune yelled, "Whale off-shore." I turned and watched a dark shadow pass not a hundred feet from me. This expansiveness, inviting and warm, made me feel as if I were part of something larger than myself, and more welcoming that anything I had ever known.

I have had the same feeling lying next to my dog, with my head resting on his belly, in front of the fire. Also when I was standing close to a deer among the trees and neither of us moved.

The arrow of Eros struck Sophie and her frogs. There, the magic was in relationship to heat and fire, and now I'm experiencing this arrow myself, a piercing connection with my mentor, but the arrow isn't moving, it's not darting from him to me and back again – instead it's floating, it just is. Eros has transformed into a silent, all encompassing space and something that was localized had escaped and become available everywhere. My dog, my mentor, I, and all living things are in this together. Robert Hass captures it in his poem, "Happiness," when two people view a pair of foxes looking up at them "long enough to symbolize the wakefulness of living things" (Hass 1996: 3–4).

I remembered another such opening in the deep caves of the Dordogne in France when I saw the Paleolithic animal paintings. Confined underground with no easy way out, I thought I might be claustrophobic, but the drawings of early hunting magic woke up my imagination. I became a horse, my hooves kicking up, my mane flying, as I ran with other horses turning with the arc of the world, our hoof-beats in tune with our heartbeats. I had dropped into a world older than time.

The Lakota murmur their ritual blessing "*Mi taku oyasin*," or the English equivalent "We are all related," as they enter and leave their sweat lodges. Once, in the woods of Montana, having murmured these words myself, I took my place in just such a confined hut of sticks, blankets and hot stones. We were led by the Blackfoot healer Buster Yellow Kidney. During the first round of chanting, suffocated with the sage smoke and overwhelmed with heat, I feared a heart attack, but crows in great numbers came to my rescue. The dark space of the lodge opened into a vision of a plain wooden room. A simple wood bench – as in a sauna – ran around the perimeter.

Instead of people, crows, black as night, filled the bench, and they were cracking up, laughing, uproariously, bent over in uncontrollable hilarity, slapping their legs with their wings, knocking each other off the bench. The idea I might die was the funniest thing they ever heard – as if I could get off the hook that easily. I had more work to do in this life, much more, and who did I think I was to think I was in control of my own life? The crows were not taking things so seriously, and their raucous laughter infected me and reversed my fears and this also seemed a way to touch the vast peace I felt in the silence with my mentor.

And now, for me, the curve of Eros had entered the silence as I sat with this old man. "Your book is an introverted man's vision," he said as if I had forgotten my own nature. Now, I could sit in my cave, like a spider in the dark, waiting to be fed.

> "That night I dreamed I was building a new house, my own house, a house of silence and openness, where life simply is as it is. Instead of reaching out, I can be receptive to what comes, as I once was as a young man when I was painting murals during the day and at night slept out-doors alongside rows of chardonnay vines. At that time I befriended a Lakota Indian woman, who could walk at night across twigs without making a sound. Once she said, 'The spirits are talking tonight, can you hear them?' "

I wrote up this encounter with my mentor and then I went back to see him. I didn't really know why, though I did show him the paper, which I intended to present at a conference in his honor.

"If my health is good," he said, "I'll attend."

"Should I read my paper to you or do you want to read it yourself?"

"My hearing is not good, so let me have it." He held the paper close to his face, and read line by line, taking half an hour. Then he blurted out, "My hands aren't large, look." He put the paper down and lifted his hands, turning them about, as if the two of us were performing a medical exam. "That is a small point, nothing to fault you about."

Of all the things I had hoped he might address, I never could have imagined he would bring up the size of his hands. He was more inscrutable than ever. The marvel of this ancient man waving his hands about seemed itself to be like a Zen koan and broke the tension of my waiting. By reducing his hands to normal size, he was bringing his largeness down to meet me at a human level. It's a good thing I didn't mention his large Buddha ears, which in my mind, matched his big hands. If I had, he might have taken one off and handed it to me.

Studying his hands, I tried to make them smaller, like Alice did in Wonderland, with her drink. I managed to see them through his eyes – I saw them do something I knew was impossible, which was to shrink. His fingers stayed the same, large and puffy like those of my childhood piano teacher, but the hands actually got smaller. It was amazing, really. My mentor had a gardener, a practical person who didn't seem to think of him as someone special, and I asked her for a second opinion. "His hands are enormous, the biggest hands of anybody I know." Then I asked my mother-in-law. "Yes, he was always so fastidious, and then he had those big farmer hands," and she laughed.

My mentor made one other comment about my paper. "It will get people to ask themselves, 'How does it feel to lose your analyst?' It is a subject many people think about."

So, as usual, I didn't discover whether he liked my piece or not. He did say, "What you wrote fits your nature and you are writing in your own voice," but gave not a word about what for me was the most charged thing happening during that silent half hour – he was reading a paper, prepared for an audience, about how he himself was facing death. Would they be shocked? Would he be embarrassed sitting there? He was just matter of fact and didn't comment further. So I asked him more about death. He responded with a story:

> "When I went to Zurich to work with Jung, I was 26 and he was in his early fifties, and wasn't sure he could work with someone so much younger. Jung said, 'Do you know that I have to think about death everyday?' I was delighted with that response. I could see that he was not afraid of death. And he gave the impression that there was nothing for me to fear about death either. He showed me what I would have to do to catch up with him."

"Do you think about death often?" I asked.

"It is something always there that I move into as I go along."

"Do you think the soul lives on?"

> "Of course, I think that, but I have no vision of this mystery. I hope I have some indication of an afterlife, but I can't be sure that will happen. What we know about death is going on in life. I think of people who came to see me who have died. When they were approaching death, they saw the same thing; they lived their life and then they were ready to die. But you haven't answered my question, have you finished your book?"

"Yes, I feel finished." While I wanted to have finished it, as I said this, I had to acknowledge to myself that I hadn't quite completed it.

He then spoke in his elevated voice, "Sophie evokes ongoing and beautiful passages. As an archetype she is so knowing and wise, a spiritual anima. She usually comes later in life and leads to a credible ending."

"Why did you ask if I had finished the book and what does it mean to have finished?"

"It means that you will have finished a page in your life experience."

Then I did something I hadn't planned; I told him a dream. It was one of those pieces of unexpected magic that happen when I am with him. It was late, he had taken so much time reading my paper and had given his blessing, then, unexpectedly, I launched into a dream and he listened. I really wanted to know what he thought about the dream:

> "In the dream I'm in a cave with other people settling down for the night. We are waiting for something when a bear with two cubs comes crashing through. She lies down next to me, and begins to nibble on my left hand. She leans on me, with her good, warm, substantial body, and I feel taken care of until her weight becomes so oppressive that I can't breathe. On the way in, I had seen the jacket of a dead colleague hanging on the wall."

My mentor helped out with the dream:

> "The bear came to mother you, to companion you during this time, to bring me back to my normal self, and to women again. (He was reverting to his way of becoming me in his speech.) You can feel the weight of her presence in your life. The bear reveres life. She has come to rescue you from being drawn into dangerous relationships. You are in danger of giving yourself over too much to this muse. (He circles a dream the way a hunter might circle an animal in the grass. He passes over the same ground more than once as his – and my – understanding accumulates.)
>
> The bear in your dream is not a wild animal. She comes charging into a cave with people. She has come to get me out of the animal world into the human world. The bear represents the power of the feminine, not in the animal world. The mother symbol in Greek mythology is the bear. She is Artemis and represents the world of wild things, all giving and all loving. She leans against me, for me to feel her, to feel the warmth of her presence. But she, the bear, is half human, close to the animal archetype. There is a danger in that. She lets you know not to get too close to her.
>
> This takes a place in a cave that, like all caves, is an initiatory place. She follows animal nature telling you, 'Don't get into trouble.' The bear mother and her cubs are the symbol of human life. She is an initiatory symbol. You are to be happy to have met her. You are in the realm of Artemis."

About the analyst, whose jacket was hanging on the wall, he said:

> "In the last two or three years of his life, he gave himself too freely to people who interested him. You don't have to make a human sacrifice. The bear is informing you that there is no further danger. You have stories to write and you are free to write them."

I remembered that the image of this jacketed colleague came up early in my own analysis. My mentor said, "He has too much anima and you don't have enough." What my mentor meant was that he lived his outer life only as it reflected his inner interests, his dreams and his writing; nothing else mattered. He went after ecstatic experiences wherever he could find them. At that earlier stage of my life I had trouble pursuing things that interested me. Now I had become more like my colleague.

My book and the mystery about the frogs who died and were reborn had fired up my imagination to such a pitch that living outside the inner fire seemed bland. I knew I had to finish my book and my business with the frog. I had sat with my mentor in front of a blank TV observing a mystery, yet the story of death and rebirth still haunted me.

I noticed that even though my mentor had opened me, he hadn't shared his own experiences of the mysteries of life. This was the one thing I had really asked him about. He had shared dreams along the way and even shared their interpretation with me and with others, but what he drew from them to form his own larger view, he kept to himself. My mentor wasn't prone to disclose his secrets.

He was like a *Tai Chi* master, who maintained around himself an energy field that no one could penetrate. And like the *Tai Chi* master, he would respond only to what was brought to him. Sometimes he used examples from his own life, but when he did, it was always in archetypal or symbolic language that was difficult to interpret. I would have to puzzle it out for myself.

The next time I saw my mentor I still hadn't given up pressing him about death's mystery, and this time he got angry with me.

"That is not something I think about. I will learn about it when it happens."

But I wanted him to think about it. I wanted to know what he knew about death, I wanted to see what he saw. Why couldn't he tell? After all, his secrets would die with him. Why would this be something he would hold onto? He said, "I'm not like Jung who was more interested in death. He talks about it in that last chapter of his autobiography."

I told him, "I read Jung's introduction to *The Tibetan Book of the Dead*."

"That's a book I haven't consulted much," he said.

Undeterred, I reminded him what Jung told him when he first went to see him as a young man: Jung, not sure he could work with someone so young, said that he thought about death every day. My mentor looked directly at me and said, "That was meant for me. That is what he said to me. He would have said something different to you."

My feelings were hurt until I remembered how he had greeted me when I came into the room to meet him. He was asleep in his chair and when he woke, he seemed at first to be confused, then smiled and said, "Neil, how nice you are here." He wanted to know what was going on in my life. He didn't want to answer abstract questions. They seemed to him irrelevant to the fact that I was alive.

"No, I'm not interested in what will happen to me when I die," he said.

"I will wait to see what happens. You will be ready when the time comes. I fell last night, and I thought that might be it. But no, here I am, and with a little nap, I am upright just as you see. But when I get sick, I will go quickly, in two or three days."

Now it was my turn to get irritated. I put him back into being the teacher again. I didn't want reassurance. At that time I thought he was trying to help me to face death, when now I think he was just saying how it is for him. I wanted to know what he had gleaned from his dreams, from his work with Jung, from his own research and reading, about the mystery of death. I do know that he had been interested in the mystery religions throughout his life. He read widely and remembered everything he read.

Whether my mentor was pushing me into life or whether he wanted to enjoy his remaining days, I don't know, but the message I was getting was clear. There is a richness about relationship and love that has to do with mortality. It is puzzling and it is what led me to want to know more about death. But I was going about it in the wrong way. My mentor was also helping me. Like a Zen master, he blocked me, he told me "No." I had to live in the world, with the passion I had been given by the story about the frogs, and informed by the knowledge from my mentor.

Then I looked down at my own hands. I have never really worked with my hands but I thought that now I needed to make something physical the way God, in Michelangelo's painting, brought Adam to life. I sat down and began to write this account of my time with the old man whom I loved.

Reference

Hass, R. (1996) "Happiness," in *Sun under Wood*, Hopewell, NJ: Ecco Press.

Part II

The archetype of initiation in clinical practice

Chapter 3

The archetypal paradox of feminine initiation in analytic work

Virginia Beane Rutter

Approaching the threshold

The archetype of feminine initiation has been expressed in women's ceremonies for their blood mysteries: menarche, defloration, pregnancy, childbirth, nursing, and menopause. The feminine self seeks realization in this body-embedded archetype that is reflected in her mind and her soul. Women's initiations, however, are colored by the cultural bias of 2500 years of patriarchal social and political domination. As a modern woman develops, she encounters the external barriers in the culture to her empowerment in the world, and simultaneously struggles with a psychological paradox. This paradox can be seen in both ancient and modern puberty ceremonies. Therefore, in analytic work a woman's psychological initiation often partakes of the field of consciousness and the symbols and myths of these rituals. Cultural denigration versus celebration of women at those crucial thresholds are encoded in the archetype and come forward under the stress of analytic work. Each woman's psyche takes up the ancient paradox and creates new meaning for her individuation and for an emerging cultural paradigm of feminine empowerment.

To demonstrate this paradox I will compare two archetypal feminine deities through their puberty ceremonies: the goddess Artemis in Classical Greece (fifth to fourth centuries BCE), and the Navajo creatrix goddess Changing Woman in the *Kinaalda* ceremony (practiced to this day on the Navajo reservation in Arizona). The two cultural practices reveal different attitudes toward women and illuminate how this paradox manifests in a woman's psychological initiation. Both these ceremonies have the objective of socializing women for their cultural roles, but the classical Greeks devalued being female, while the Navajo value femaleness.

The issue of gender – like those of race, religion, and sexuality – seem to constellate polarization in people. My intention is not to polarize but to bring the reader into the feminine experience. I offer this material with the intent of rebalancing the opposites of masculine and feminine. Consider the following dream I had in August 2003, while staying on the island of Ydra in Greece.

> I am approaching the side entrance of a temple through a sunlit court-
> yard. The temple resembles the Blue Mosque in Istanbul. I am a young
> girl, perhaps 7 or 8, walking with my mother, who is holding my hand.
> She is taking me to be dedicated at the temple. As we move toward the
> steps, there is a quality of "resistance" or "hesitation," a feeling of
> impending loss, in her? Or in me? Or in the situation? But we both walk
> calmly, slowly, with unswerving purpose toward the entrance, silently
> sharing the knowledge that this is an enormous step, full of awe. Once
> through the doors, will she leave the temple by herself? Without me? Will
> I be alone? Will we ever see each other again? The feeling quality is of
> approaching the threshold, the mystery of an interior, dark unknown.

In the wake of the dream, my associations unfolded. I had just traveled to
Istanbul and had kneeled in the Blue Mosque, lost in time, struck by the
diffuse light and an eastern grace. There, I had also visited the Monastery
Chora, where one of the early Christian mosaics depicted the birth and life of
the Virgin Mary. One scene showed St Anne bringing her daughter to be
presented in the temple.

The dream, therefore, brings together Islamic, Jewish, and Catholic faiths.
But the sense in the dream is that once at the doors, my mother would leave,
that I am to enter a place she cannot follow. The intimate feminine dyad of
mother–daughter is meeting the masculine powers that prevail in this temple.
In me, the child, the known sunlit world of my mother's realm is facing the
dark unknown mystery of the interior of the temple. Known vs. unknown,
dark vs. light, feminine vs. masculine, warring faiths – all these opposites are
held in the container of the dream, as we pause at the threshold.

On a personal level, I was approaching another initiation in my life that
meant a new internal separation from my mother. Her advanced age also
heralded our final physical separation – eighteen months later, she died. In
the dream, there is no question that I, the child, will enter the doorway and
proceed with the initiation. Why the possibility of losing my mother forever?
After an initiation, there should be the possibility of reuniting as adult
women. What does the feminine self want to fulfill with this dream? Certainly
one intention is to support my individuation in an atmosphere of holding the
opposites.

Why is the threshold of initiation or of analytic work so delicate for a
woman? The words *threshold* and *initiation* are related. The ancient Greek
word for *threshold* is *bathmos*, the step, up into a doorway. The Greek word
myo, from which our word mystery comes, means "to close oneself after
seeing the secret" (Kerenyi 1967: 45–47). In the ancient mysteries, there were
two kinds of secrets: those that were forbidden to be told, *aporrheton*, that is,
"those kept secret under the law of silence," and those that were un-tellable,
arrheton, "the ineffable secrets." From Greek, *mysteries* evolved by means of
the Latin verb *ineo* meaning "*to go into,*" *initium*. Hence our word *initiation*

with its layers of meaning: mystery, secrecy, and moving or crossing over a threshold. The first step over a psychological threshold holds the intention to accomplish the ritual. But there may be many retreats along the way, leavings and re-enterings of the sacred space.

The ritual is the ordered set of acts that leads to the induction of the initiate into another state of being. The twisted paradox at the heart of a woman's struggle to individuate originates in the worldview in which, as Jung (1982: 55) said, "woman stands always in the shadow of man." The western origin of this psychological condition is seen in Aristotle in the fourth century BCE, who taught that woman is an incomplete form. For example, he declared, "The male is the more perfect in all species," and "Woman is a deformed man" (King 1983: 112).[1] That classical Greek cultural prejudice still obtains. In 1971, two millennia after Aristotle, this view was actively opposed by a woman attempting to right the social wrongs based on female inferiority in the law. Ruth Bader Ginsburg, then the Director of the ACLU's Women's Rights Project, asked the Supreme Court to invalidate an Idaho law that she said commanded the "subordination of women." Her brief stated: "American women have been stigmatized historically as an inferior class and are today subject to pervasive discrimination . . . a person born female continues to be branded inferior for this congenital and unalterable condition of birth" (Greenhouse 2005).[2]

This cultural archetype of woman's inferiority continues to evolve as culture evolves. While women still carry the shadow for men, the feminine value inherent in traditional ceremonies of women's blood mysteries is alive and active in women's psyches. Denigration and celebration vie in the psyche of each woman, whose dreams and unconscious material reach back and down to pluck the symbols necessary for transformation. Each woman's way is individual, yet partakes of the archetype of initiation.

This archetype is particularly amplified in the relationship between woman analyst and woman patient. The female dyad potentiates a feminine mystery and supports a woman in her individuation. The work generates other entities: archetypal feminine figures, aspects of the feminine self who guide the two women in the work. The self may take many forms during an analysis – divinities, animals, or numinous symbols, to mention only a few. During that initiation the woman struggles with the paradoxical feelings engendered by the classical Greek designation of a woman as *kalon kakon*, literally, a *beautiful evil*, a necessary evil. She was both needed for reproduction, yet her beauty and seductiveness undermined a warrior's strength. She was considered undisciplined, licentious, and lacking in self-control (King 1983: 110).[3]

A woman is often unconscious of her psyche's innate capacity for bearing this archetype of initiation. During the clash of the paradox in herself, in the intensity of the initiatory process with another woman, she awakens to her own meaning and empowerment. She moves into a strength and wholeness that has a profound inductive effect on the men and women around her.

Artemis: ambivalent goddess of initiation

The first threshold of initiation is the female body. Ironically, as the eternal virgin, the classical Artemis does not shed her own blood in the hunt, in sex, or in childbirth. Yet she sheds the blood of others as huntress, and as the divinity present at all the transitions in a woman's life which involve blood-shed. Artemis is *Eileithyia*, the midwife, the protector of childbirth. She earned this epithet because when her mother Leto bore the twins – she and her brother Apollo – Artemis was painlessly delivered first. Then Artemis helped her mother deliver her brother (Graves 1992: 55–56).[4] Greek women approached labor in fear because death rates of both mother and child were high; girls' bodies were often too immature to give birth. They prayed to Artemis *Eileithyia* for an easy birth or for release from the pain of childbirth with an easeful death.

In analysis, the birth of new life comes up in dreams as the symbol of pregnancy and delivery. A 25-year-old single woman, Carmina, who was struggling to develop herself as an artist, dreamed:

> An obese woman I know is pregnant and about to give birth. I am amazed she can do this. She disappears in order to give birth to her baby. In her absence I experience her labor pain, as if I'm sampling it. I'm shocked; it's so painful. I never realized it could be that painful. I am impressed that she is able to go through with it. I see how far I have to go to reach that point. I think how fortunate I am that I live in this century, because I can ask for help when I give birth. Otherwise, I would surely die.[5]

Although she had a difficult relationship with her personal mother, Carmina was well on her path; she was negotiating both separation and reconciliation while she was analyzing her own development. Death always hovers at the threshold of birth. For a woman in analysis whose mother has been psychotic and destructive, these thresholds become even more frightening and prob-lematic. After suffering an unwanted abortion, Beatrice, a woman in her mid-thirties, had this nightmare:

> I am seeing inside my own womb. It seems like a universe. There are all these children shrieking from inside me, hundreds of faces inside my womb, cowering in terror from my looking. They are not born, and they are never going to be born. The womb is a place of death, not life.

There are periods in analysis in which a woman of any age, at any stage of life, is seized by the initiatory archetype and becomes vulnerable, confused, resistant to change, and sometimes despairing. In this liminal space, she struggles with both her personal complexes and with the cultural force that tells her that she is "less than a man." A man encounters obstacles along the path to his individuation, but manhood, including becoming bigger and stronger at puberty, is inherently valued. Becoming a woman is suspect and fraught with both inner and outer contradictions. Women often describe seeing their first blood and being told to hide signs of it in the bathroom, that it is shameful, disgusting, in other words, to hide becoming a woman.

Nancy, a 35-year-old woman suffering from isolation and depression, told me her story:

> I took great care to wrap each Tampax in toilet paper. But my father said to me, "You should hide it better than that. I was totally mortified." Then I dreamed that a shark was coming after me in the water because I was having my period. It could scent the blood.

Nancy's brothers were held in high esteem in the family. She and her mother were lower in status. Nancy said, "I feel neutered."

If she was not initiated, a woman has remained a girl and learned to hide the essence of who she is, even from herself. In order to begin to transform, to cross the threshold and engage with her development, she must bring to consciousness the archetypal paradox of being inferior, yet valuable as sexual object or childbearer, and then feared or made dangerous for even those limiting roles. This intricate process of sifting through inner and outer influences takes courage and perseverance.

As a girl approached the steps to enter Artemis' temple at Brauron or Mounichia for her service to the goddess, it is likely she felt fear and resistance. She came there knowing that she was to be married off as soon as possible after menarche, that her prospective husband would probably be a stranger, and that she would be separated from her mother, family, and friends. Artemis' title, *Kourotrophos*, "nurturer of youth" referred to her as the protective patron of pre-pubescent girls. The following epigram provides a list of a Spartan girl's offerings in the temple on the threshold from girlhood to adulthood:

> Timarete, the daughter of Timaretos, before her wedding,
> has dedicated her tambourine, her pretty ball, the net
> that shields her hair, her hair, and her girl's dresses
> to Artemis of the Lake, a girl to a girl, as is fit.
> You, daughter of Leto, hold your hand over the child
> Timarete, and protect the pure girl in a pure way.
>
> (Neils 2003: 153)

The Navajo girl, on the other hand, approaches the threshold of her puberty ceremony with trust in Changing Woman, the chief deity of the Navajo people, who presides over the four days in which the initiate is said to be

"walking into beauty." The Navajo concept of beauty includes an harmoni-
ous environment, both natural and cultural. The girl's participation in the
ritual restores the balance of the tribe. Womanhood is valued for the Navajo,
who are both a matrilineal culture in which property passes from mother
to daughter, and a matrilocal one; when a girl marries, her husband comes to
live in her home.

By contrast, a Greek girl being consecrated to Artemis at menarche knew
that her bleeding was associated to being a sacrificial offering. She was seen as
a wild animal who needed to be tamed or broken in, after which she would
marry. She knew that menarche indicated that she was ready for her role in
reproducing, and that she was forbidden to shed the blood of others. She
therefore prayed to Artemis, who did not bleed, asking the goddess to prevent
the onset of menarche.

The desperation of classical Greek girls under these repressive circumstances can be seen in a gynecological text of the fifth to fourth centuries
BCE, from the Hippocratic corpus, called the *Peri Parthenion*, or "On the
Diseases of Virgins." The text describes the phenomenon of pre-pubescent
girls exhibiting a desire for death (*epithymia thanatou*). Girls often attempted
suicide by means of hanging or strangulation. The text says: "The girl is ripe
for marriage," ready to bleed, to enter the transition to womanhood. Then
she shows symptoms of delirium, a fear of darkness, and has visions which
compel her to jump or throw herself down wells or to strangle herself. Or she
shows an erotic fascination with death (*erao*) and she welcomes death as a
lover (King 1983: 113–114).

Bloodless suicide in Greek thought was associated with avoiding rape or
unwanted defloration. These girls avoided the model of marriage shown in
the nuptials of Hades and Persephone, the bride's abduction by death, by
choosing to take their own lives. This so-called "disease" of self-strangulation
shows virgins (*parthenoi*) clinging to their virginity, to their childhood, when
it was time to accept becoming a woman (*gyne*). Once a girl begins to bleed,
the treatise states, she recovers and dedicates her childhood toys to Artemis.
Marriage and childbearing are recommended as the cure for her disturbance.

After her marriage, there was yet another hurdle for a girl to cross in the act
of childbirth. Artemis is also called *Lochia*, the name of the afterbirth dis-
charge. And a Greek woman did not realize her status of womanhood if she
died during childbirth or just after, unless she delivered the afterbirth before
she died. In the Hippocratic texts the *lochia* are analogous to menarche; both
are normal, "like the flow of blood from a sacrificed beast." Menarche and
first *lochia* thus seem to complement each other, forming the opening and the
completion of the transformation of *parthenos* to *gyne* (King 1983: 121–122).
Positive values accrued to the self-sacrificing *gyne*, negative to the *parthenos*.

A Greek girl acquired a girdle (*zone*) that she put on at puberty and dedicated to Artemis. On her wedding night, her spouse untied it. Later, when
delivering her first child, the girdle was also untied and rededicated to

Artemis. Artemis is therefore called *Lysizonos*, the Loosener in this aspect, because she releases the *zone*, releases the virgin to cross the threshold of bleeding into the further status of woman. When a Greek girl resisted her fate and sought death, she used this girdle to hang herself (King 1983: 120–121). Artemis herself embodies contradiction: protecting maidens from violation, receiving the dedication of their childhood toys, yet calling them to become women once they begin to bleed.

Sacrifice was central in Artemis' worship. A fierce image of the goddess from her temple at Brauron (Figure 3.1) shows her in an aspect that suggests both her raging at the rape of maidens and simultaneously demanding bloody sacrifices in her honor. This effigy was rubbed with the blood of sacrificed animals (Graves 1992: 435–441).[6] In one sculpture of a young girl at Brauron (Neils 2003: 152), a girl holds her pet rabbit that she had to sacrifice when she began to bleed. I have seen this motif in women's dreams at times when they were being asked to give up a regressive pattern or behavior. For example, a woman named Clare, in her forties, feeling the empty nest after her only child, her daughter, left for college, dreamed:

> I am at the ocean on the beach. I see huge eagles perched on a raft coming in on the waves. I know I am expected to collect the fuzzy little animals, hamster or rabbit like, from the beach shed and feed them to the eagles.

Unlike a Greek girl, Clare's sacrifice promised to bring her autonomy, not enslavement. This is a powerful example of how a modern woman's dream uses the ancient ritual on behalf of her individuation. The unconscious selects the essence of the sacrificial symbol and uses it to show what is required for Clare's development.

Artemis' function as a goddess spans the two temporal aspects of "woman": strangled, non-bleeding girl; and released, bleeding woman. Yet, she herself stays firmly on one side. She who sheds the blood of others is "strangled"; she who releases others is "bound." This raises the question of how a girl can become a woman in a culture in which her initiatory divinity or companion is one who never crosses the threshold herself. Psychologically, might the initiate stay frozen at the crossroads too?

In addition to self-strangulation, other symptoms of the pre-menarchal "disease" of the virgin were a sudden loss of voice, coldness, grinding of teeth, and a feeling of suffocation (King 1983: 116). In the psyche, women approaching this initiatory ground often find themselves in a strangled state. These are the moments in analysis when a woman says, for example, "*I feel there is something in my throat blocking my speech . . .*" or "*I have a strange feeling in my throat . . . there is something trying to come out . . .*" or "*I feel constricted in my throat*" or "*I feel like I can't breathe when I'm trying to speak up for myself . . .*" or "*I think I'm making myself clear, I want to be heard, but*

I can't get the words out . . ." or "*I can't find words for the feelings I'm having.*"
Clare was simply dumbfounded after her eagle dream. These feelings of
strangulation during a woman's process often reflect a need to recover herself,
to withdraw from a relational field, and find her own voice. Otherwise she
becomes desperate to escape from the conflict between what the self is
demanding and the needs of the people or circumstances of her life. But there
was no escape for a Greek girl.

The young girls selected to live at the temples of Artemis participated in
races to honor the goddess. These ceremonies have elements that reflect the
intentions of both education and preparation for menarche (Marinatos 2002)
and of a substitute sacrifice to appease a dangerous goddess. In the com-
munal aspect the sacrifice of a goat warded off the anger of Artemis, the
bringer of plague; in the personal aspect the self-dedication of girls warded
off death in childbirth (Faraone 2003: 61–62). A fragment of a krater from
Brauron, 430–420 BCE, shows girls running with forearms extended and
hands cupped like the paws of a bear (Reeder 1995: 322–326). The ritual was
known as the *Arkteia*, "playing the she-bear," and the girls were dubbed
"bears" after Artemis' animal. The story underlying the *Arkteia* is as follows:

> There once existed a tame male bear which lived in the sanctuary at
> Brauron. One day a young girl teased the bear, who then scratched her
> and drew blood. Several boys, friends of the girl, killed the bear. Artemis
> was so angered at the sacred bear being murdered that she ordained that
> henceforth young girls should serve her as Little Bears there.
>
> (Reeder 1995: 321)

The girls were regarded as a form of the bear that had been slain. The word
"teasing" in the story has sexual overtones; her bleeding from the scratch also
suggests defloration. Artemis disapproved of young girls' premature sexual
exploration. In one myth, when her nymph Kallisto lost her virginity to Zeus,
the furious Artemis cast her out of her hunting circle, changed her into
a bear, then shot the bear-maiden with her own arrow (Reeder 1995: 328).

In the racing images on the vase fragments, some girls are nude, others
wear a short garment, the *chitonistos*. Nudity may indicate the girls' wild
pre-marital state. The girls probably ran around an altar. They appear to flee
from a bear, apparently in alarm; they "acted the bear" by pretending to be
bears in flight from the pursuing bear. Their pursuit acted out the metaphor
of the male pursuit of the female in which the capture of the female was
equivalent to domestication. Girls probably also danced with tame bears who
were kept in sanctuaries as late as the second century CE. The girls both
encountered the bear as maleness or sexuality, and identified with the bear as
the goddess Artemis herself.

I imagine Greek girls also internalized the bear as the mother they were
about to leave when they married, and the mothers they hoped to become

(Henderson 2005: 229–239, Appendix). One woman in analysis, eight months pregnant with her second child, who had a distorted body image, dreamed:

> I am in the corner of a swimming pool, resting. I feel something slimy and look down. I recognize one of several mother bears marching in a circle around the pool at the bottom, hands on one another's shoulders. There was a friendly, ritualized feeling.

A few weeks later this woman delivered twin baby girls, little sisters to her son. This woman gave thanks to Artemis, who had delivered her well and easily. Here, the unconscious chose Artemis as a positive midwife goddess. Yet these are mother bears, not Artemis as virgin goddess. The unconscious creates an individual blessing for this woman that allays her anxiety about the forthcoming birth.

Ruby, a 40-year-old married woman and the mother of a two-year-old son, was working in analysis to shed the patriarchal patterns in herself that plagued her mothering. During an active imagination:

> The bear came to her, saying, "You need all the nurturance you can get." In another, Ruby was dismembered as a bear tore her apart. When she reconstituted, she found herself sucking the she-bear's milk, feeling full of peace. In another, she became a bear and mated with a male bear to become pregnant and undergo a psychological hibernation. "Bear is in my body," she said. In the cave another bear and her cubs snuggled around her to protect her.

When Ruby came out of hibernation, having given birth to cubs in her active imagination, she was able to be with her son in a new way, follow his energy, and join him in expressing a love of life. Ruby's initiation through the bear was both violent and nurturing, both aspects of Artemis.

The priestess of the Artemesian sanctuary was known as a bear. The girls had a lengthy absence from home in the care of priestesses, who imbued the girls with mythical and ritualistic guidance appropriate to her future domestic role. The priestesses were celibate, in honor of the goddess. On the vase fragments, the girls run while older women attendants with baskets and branches coordinate the activity. A change in clothing played a part in the rituals. A *krokotos*, a garment dyed with the herb saffron, was featured. Saffron was traditionally associated with women, especially with their menstrual ailments. This chiton is thought to have been changed for a long garment suitable for a marriageable maiden. The bride then wore a saffron-colored veil on her wedding day.

The time in service at the temple prepared girls to give up their animal aspect. Yet the marriages they would enter were arranged for the explicit

purpose of reproduction, an animal function. How could a Greek girl reconcile these contradictions? And how does a modern girl or woman, carrying
this internal conflict today, psychologically reconcile them to emerge with a
whole sense of self?

In her wildness, the pre-menarchal Greek girl was an undisciplined threat
to the social order in contrast to the controlled reproductive woman she was
slated to become. The word *hysteria* was used medically in a non-derogatory
way, *hysterike pnix*, for the tendency of the womb to run wild if not allowed
to conceive a child (King 1983: 116). If she was wild she could be chosen for
sacrifice like a wild beast. The vase fragments also show bounding fawns, the
quarry of Artemis' hounds; the girls are both prey and sacrificial victims
(Reeder 1995: 324).

The sense of being a sacrificial victim is reflected in Carmina's experience
of menarche. She described her state of mind at age 12, as she travelled in
Spain with her family, as follows:

> There had been no allusions to menstruation in my family. And I didn't
> want breasts or femininity. We were looking at all this bloody art in
> museums and churches – martyrdoms and crucifixions. One day I got my
> period. That night in my hotel room I was looking at the stars through a
> glass cupola and I suddenly disappeared, dissolved into the starry space
> above me. I realized that religion was all a big lie, that I was going to die.
> It felt like cosmic death. I went screaming into my parents' bedroom.

The shocking associations of Catholic bloody martyrdom with the appearance of Carmina's first blood had a profound consequence. In that terrifying
moment, she was resonating archetypally to herself as the bloody sacrifice.
As Carmina developed, however, the reality of her corporeal feminine mystery supplanted that of the church. Her body consciousness and her spiritual
awareness were inextricably intertwined. And her symbolic inner world was
vividly available in her psychological work.

The image of the goddess Artemis as the eternal virgin, free to roam in the
purity of nature, also comes up in the dreams of women in analysis. A woman
who is drowning in conventional womanhood and collective demands can be
renewed by the energy of this independent, solitary, free spirit of the woods.
Artemis has control over the wild aspects of nature. With animal instinct,
her nymphs hunt, dance, and play in meadows and groves beyond the fields
cultivated by men, inviolate and inviolable. Women dream of lions, leopards,
bears or supernatural dogs, who call them to their own wild natures. But the
shadow of the bear chase or the sacrifice always lies in wait, as Artemis
hovers at the threshold of psychological initiation.

The mystic southwest painter Meinrad Craighead encountered the power
of Artemis in a vision in Greece at Brauron. In her painting *Initiation
at Vravrona 1998* (Craighead 2003: 251). Artemis is shown as a brooding

bird-like figure, her wings outstretched over her gray wolf dog and two figures. One of the figures appears to be a girl child just emerging from a cocoon; the other, an older woman shrouded. The whole tableau creates a temple diorama in blood red, black and white. Artemis has claimed both child and woman for her own.

Artemis is one of Meinrad's spiritual guides. Meinrad is a woman who individuated from a very young age through her devotion to her art, her Catholicism, and to the great mother in her many aspects. This artist chose to live a celibate life, never marry, never have children; yet she plumbs the depths of feminine mystery in her paintings. Meinrad's way has been to stay with Artemis on the wild side of the threshold. Each woman in analysis must find her own way.

The Greek girl appealed to Artemis to prevent her menarche and receive her into her band of nymphs, perhaps through lifelong service in the temple. Failing that, she looked to Artemis to shepherd her through the thresholds of marriage and motherhood. The threat of sacrifice loomed over both paths.

Changing Woman: walking into beauty

In the Navajo *Kinaalda* we have a living tradition of a celebratory initiation for girls at puberty. The Navajo girl looks to Changing Woman, her people's chief deity, as a creator, as the originator of Navajo culture: an independent divinity and a woman who bleeds, conceives, and bore twin sons. Changing Woman gave her people the *Kinaalda* ceremony in the form that she herself had experienced it: a four-day ritual of coming into womanhood. She also created corn and gave it to the tribe. In the course of the *Kinaalda*, the girl becomes Changing Woman and is imbued with her power.

When a Navajo girl begins to bleed, her family begins preparation for the summer ceremony (Begay 1983).[7] As part of her preparation, the girl chooses an "ideal woman" to sponsor her in the initiation. The Navajo girl chooses a woman whom she admires; the requirement is only that she not be a member of the family. This choice of a sponsor in the Navajo tradition is a compelling parallel to the choice of a woman analyst.

Each Navajo girl ritually follows in the footsteps of Changing Woman, is dressed as Changing Woman, goes through the prescribed ritual that Changing Woman is said to have gone through – and is re-created as Changing Woman, with the complete support of the people around her. Each woman's path in analysis is different and initially she may feel isolated. It may be many years before she has a community that appreciates or understands what she has undertaken. And while her conscious goal at the outset may be to resolve a conflict or disturbance, she is often surprised and dismayed to find, as the work progresses, that her deeper nature demands a submission that she had not envisioned. If she listens to her unconscious, it soon yields the symbols that usher in her initiation.

As a feminine archetype of transformation and fertility, both physiological and spiritual, Changing Woman's energy permeates the work of psychotherapy between two women. Early in her analysis, Carmina dreamed:

> I am talking to you. Your face keeps changing, the proportions changing. I ask, "Why do you do what you do?" You say, "I do it to get my heart back." The color green is somehow important. Then suddenly you get really old, wrinkled, aged. Your face cracks as if it were made of dried mud. I'm shocked awake, then fall asleep again quickly. I say that I am not close enough to you. We are standing with bellies touching, facing. You are much younger, my age. How could you have been so old?

The Navajo myth says that when Changing Woman walks to the east, she becomes a maiden, when she walks to the west, she becomes a crone; then she turns and walks back again, to her own youthfulness. She is earth; green is the color of renewal, plants, spring, life, new growth. In the dream, my face is like dried mud, the earth in winter. During the *Kinaalda*, the sponsor renews her relationship with Changing Woman's divine energy through the initiate.

Something like that is happening in this dream. My heart is meaningfully engaged: I, also, have an investment in the work. The unconscious chooses the figure of Changing Woman to mediate the analytic relationship, to lend the heart connection necessary for Carmina's maturation process.

On the first day of the *Kinaalda* ceremony, a blanket is hung in the hogan door to indicate to Talking God and the other gods that a ceremony is taking place. Hundreds of people come from miles around to share in celebrating the girl. The blessing that she embodies by undergoing the ceremony extends to the whole community. Men and women participate in creating her ritual.

The sponsor washes the girl's jewelry and dresses her in the traditional woven dress (*biil*) and moccasins with leggings (*kentsaai*). This is the attire that Changing Woman wore (Figure 3.2). Ocean salt and red ochre are mixed and placed in a buckskin pouch that she wears for a secret purpose (*chii dik'oozh*). Then her sponsor adorns her with the jewelry. Some of the jewelry is gifted to the girl, some loaned; it is made of mixed semi-precious gems – turquoise, white beads, jet, coral, and obsidian.

Initiatory themes of bodily adornment routinely come up in women's analytic work. A woman's dreams and memories frequently return to the time of her menarche and the extended adjustment to her monthly cycles into her teenage years. These are a series of Carmina's dreams, showing different ways in which the symbol of jewelry adornment furthers her realizing her feminine identity.

> There is a spiky silver necklace made of hollow pods. The necklace is taken away from me. Children fill each bead with something. My mother takes it. I take it back and say it's mine. It's heavy and warm.

I am sorting through my jewelry. I can't seem to find anything that I want to wear. Everything is too plain or too cheap or doesn't match what I am wearing. Where is my jewelry?

I'm wearing a necklace of beads around my neck, orange and yellow, associated with my childhood. You come up and break it off my neck. I'm shocked at the violence. I say, "You've been wanting to do that for a long time!" You say, "Yes, I just couldn't stand it anymore."

Carmina said, "I feel like the awkward teenage I once was. I rejected my mother, and in so doing rejected myself." Themes of separating from her mother, finding her own individuality, and breaking a regressive childhood bond appear clustered around the initiatory motif of adornment. In the unconscious, jewelry also represents the enduring value of the feminine. Through the dreams, Carmina became conscious of her denial of her femininity.

The Navajo sponsor then washes the girl's hair and brushes it with a yucca brush. One of the taboos the initiate must observe is that she must not look in a mirror, nor look at her own reflection during the ceremony. Carmina dreamed:

I'm an in-between age person, trying to grow up but also aware of stunted qualities. I'm washing my hair, and I realize it has grown. It has grown very fast and I let it down to my knees. My mother is either skeptical or she does not like it.

I'm following a blonde woman with beautiful hair. Her hair is up in a tortoiseshell comb. I'm like a slug behind her, doing everything wrong.

In the liminal space of the analytic work, Carmina is being initiated into her womanhood. As she examines her self-image by washing and dressing her hair, she is differentiating from her mother and dealing with her shadow in the figure of the blonde woman.

Sarah, a woman in her early thirties, married with a 4-year-old son, dreamed: "I have a vision of myself in the midst of other people. I am going bald. The top of my head is bald. In the front and the back there is still hair." Sarah said, "I associate hair with femininity, and losing it with revealing the shadow." Invested in a "good daughter" identity, Sarah's challenge in the work was to acknowledge her shadow; balding is beyond her control.

Beatrice dreamed:

I can see strands of my hair and a pair of hands tying it up into granny knots. I feel great anxiety.

I am holding a cellophane package. In the package is a long silver hairpin with Kuan Yin's face and sleeves. I put it in my hair.

Beatrice had an affinity for Kuan Yin through her mother's devotion to this goddess. There is a dissociative quality to the first dream connected to Beatrice's traumatic loss of her mother as a young girl. In times of deep suffering, Kuan Yin appeared to soothe her. The initiatory elements of haircombing and hairdressing are expressed ambivalently. Each woman's unconscious uses the initiatory imagery to address her unique consciousness.

The Navajo sponsor ties the girl's hair back preparatory to the molding ceremony. Wearing her ceremonial attire, the initiate lies on a pile of blankets, while her sponsor massages her body. The Navajo believe that at the time of menarche, a girl's body becomes soft again, as it was at birth. She is therefore susceptible to being literally reshaped, molded, and massaged into womanhood. She is also considered psychically susceptible, so the women around her give her continuous instruction during her tasks throughout the four days. By massaging the initiate, the sponsor also directly renews her relationship with Changing Woman's divine energy.

Marta, a 40-year-old woman in analysis, had experienced her mother as "crude, disgusting, and unboundaried." She had internalized that feeling toward herself, other women, and the feminine. She preferred her father who was "dry, clean, and neat." Although she had sought out a woman analyst, Marta was anxious about our relationship. A year after beginning analysis, she had the following series of dreams over the course of a month:

> A woman and I exchange caressing massage. It feels so good. My boyfriend glances at us in passing. I think he will not understand that it is important, not frivolous, and is about caressing and loving our own bodies.

> I learn a new kind of research done naked, so you can notice the changes on and in the body when something else happens.

> A huge fat woman gives us pictures of herself naked and shows us into a small room to look at them. I am with my "real" mother, not my birth mother; she feels like my chosen mother, the good mother. In the photos, the naked fat woman is totally exposed. There are close-ups of her face and skin. My initial horror of her body changes into awe, gratitude for her gift, which is union with her flesh.

> I go for a special session with Virginia. I am to lie on a couch with her on one side and a young woman on the other, who is to help her. They will massage me at the appropriate time. I begin to cry deeply. It is understood that this time I am going to let go of a key piece of holding or fear.

Marta talked about the women giving new life into each other's bodies. She was doing acupuncture, and had begun talking walks. She said,

I have had a prejudice against the heart and love. It's a shattering experience to direct love and attention toward myself. I am reinhabiting my
body; it has always been an unsafe place to reside in. I was both attractive,
therefore seduced, and ridiculed and abused.

In the dream, as she submits to the work in relation to me and a younger
version of herself, her tears prepare her to let go of her fear. Marta's sense
of herself was being re-formed in the intimate woman-to-woman container
of the work.

The ritual reflection of the vulnerability that invariably precedes the
emergence of a new identity is found in the molding ceremony. There are
periods in analysis when the only thing a woman knows is that she is
profoundly changing. She doesn't know who she is becoming, or what the
next step will be in the process. There is a long period of disintegration, where
her old assumptions, attitudes, and ideas, and sometimes relationships, begin
to crumble, dissolve, and fall away. During this process of disintegration, a
woman feels exposed and raw. A dissolution of old patterns and vulnerability
accompany all the biological and psychological stages in a woman's life.

The Navajo girl is sung into beauty. The repetition of the songs and prayers
both restores their efficacy and effects the girl's transformation. When the
sponsor sings, massages the initiate, and helps her to dress, and to comb her
hair, it is said that "she is being adorned with a song":

A woman is being formed
With turquoise shoes she is being formed . . .
With turquoise leggings she is being formed.
With turquoise visible all over her body, she is being formed . . .
With turquoise shirt, she is being formed.
With turquoise beads on her body she is being formed.
With turquoise clothes, she is being formed . . .
With turquoise bracelet, she is being formed.
With turquoise neck piece, she is being formed . . .
With her face being turquoise, she is being formed.
With her voice being turquoise, she is being formed.
With a perfect turquoise on the top of her head, she is being formed.
With a turquoise headplume, she is being formed, at its tip
    a very beautiful female cornbeetle appears, she is being formed.
As her words are brought forth her voice is beautiful, she is being formed.
With turquoise, in blessing she is being formed.
With white shell, in blessing she is being formed.
With various jewels, in blessing she is being formed.
With various fabrics, in blessing she is being formed.
With these ever increasing, never decreasing, she is being formed.
With long-life happiness, she is being formed.

Behind her it is blessed, she is being formed.
Before her it is blessed, she is being formed.
                    (Rutter 1993: 58, taken from Wyman 1970: 515–516)

When the *Kinaalda* girl returns the blankets on which she was massaged to their owners, the covers have absorbed the power of Changing Woman. Everything the initiate touches during the ceremony becomes charged with the Blessingway energy and that of the deity. The benediction is transmitted back to the owners. The initiate also uses her hands to transmit this grace during a ceremony in which she stretches the younger children in order to encourage their growth.

Because her body is a vehicle for this powerful earth energy, the girl must observe certain taboos to keep herself pure and apart in order to concentrate on her purpose. For example, she has a taboo on eating sugar and her hands may not come in contact with blood. Therefore, she does not participate in preparing the meat from the sheep that are butchered for the feast.

The bodily mutation that the initiate undergoes – adornment with jewelry, washing and combing of her hair, dressing, pollen or clay painting of her skin, and molding her body – represents a set of receptive elements in her ritual transformation. Psychologically, this receptivity is mirrored in analysis by a woman's willing submission to the process and her receiving and engaging with the unconscious and the relational field in the container. Like the Navajo initiate, her femininity is also expanded and intensified.

In the *Kinaalda*, an active set of elements are equally important. They emphasize endurance and strength, which empower the girl in a different way. With these tasks, she must challenge herself. The first of these is the race. The girl must race twice a day, running toward the east, where the sun rises. This represents the girl's pursuit of sun, as she emulates Changing Woman, the divinity impregnated by Sun and Dripping Water, who bore twin boys, the heroes in the Navajo Enemyway cycle. The initiate's father instructs her in tying a cord around a bush to mark her distance. Each race she must run a little farther, setting her own pace and distance. Others may run too but are forbidden to pass her, threatened with premature death if they disobey this taboo. They are directed to shout while they are running to attract the attention of Wind People and Holy People. Only positive energy is allowed for the Blessingway ceremony. Positive thoughts, actions, and prayers are required for the ceremony to be accomplished.

Psychologically, new kinds of discipline are needed for a woman to cross the threshold into a more mature stage of life or consciousness. Carmina had the following dream:

I'm with a group of women. We're running a race somewhere in the mountains. A big rude woman pushes past us all. At one point we've collapsed on the ground. I get into an altercation with her because I don't like her. I say, "Your spitting on the ground spreads germs. I don't like it." It is a big risk, because I am not sure I am right. Two women, one on either side of me, put their hands on my arms in a gesture of solidarity. I feel it was right to confront her. I see a group of women runners, Amazons. They have a red piece of cloth held as a banner in front of them. A coach, a man, arrives. My group is still sitting on the ground, collapsed. He says, "We need another group of women to run like them." I am the first one to volunteer. And I think I can't do it, but I do do it.

Carmina was standing up to her self-denigrating shadow, and coming alive. The dream also reveals the contra-sexual archetype, a positive animus, in the figure of the coach. Like the *Kinaalda* girl's father, the coach challenges Carmina to go beyond her fatigue, and she rises to the occasion. Carmina felt elated after this dream.

As a woman gradually separates from her internalized patriarchal view of herself, men in her dreams, representing her inner partner, become more positive and differentiated. An early dream of Carmina's shows the patriarchal wound that women and men share:

I am living in an apartment with a woman friend who is in love with a man. She has the stereotypical, perfect Barbie and Ken attitude. I'm sitting in a window seat, cross-legged with her. Two men walk by, gross fraternity types, drinking beer. I hate them, flip them off. My friend says, "That's not good; you're going to cause problems." They come in, offended. A big fight ensues, screaming, hassling. A man is standing against the wall. I take a beer bottle and throw it at his head, which splits open. At the same moment, the identical wound appears on my head, but my wound doesn't hurt. Then he is going to kill me. I go down on my hands and knees and say, "Please don't kill me; don't rape me," knowing I hate him and hating myself for apologizing.

Carmina associated the dream with her feminist philosophy which included a lot of anti-male vengeance. She realized that the wound that she had yet to feel was from her father. Instead, she was living the wound in projection, in uncontrollable rage toward men. As she explored lesbian relationships, she gained weight, cut her hair short, and wore clothes to disguise her body. Her parents' gender roles of dominant patriarchal male and female victim had left her feeling angry, neutered, and damaged. Many years later, having shed her negative self-image, the inner man, like the coach in the dream above, encourages her feminine identity:

I wake up in bed with my lover. I've lost an earring in the bed. I look down and find many earrings and other jewelry in the bed. Then we're outside digging a hole in the ground, finding potshards and bones, doing archaeology.

In the course of our work, Carmina stopped the flight from her father and faced the pain. She became involved with a man who later became her husband. In the dream, her relationship with him contributes to her retrieving the symbols of her womanhood. Cooperatively, the two are recreating a male–female relationship.

The second task of endurance that the *Kinaalda* girl must perform is that of grinding corn for the cornmeal cake.[8] The girl uses a *mano* for grinding and brushes the cornmeal from the *metate* using the same yucca brush with which her sponsor has brushed her hair in the combing ritual. The girl's body is considered to be one with the fruits of the earth. After the grinding, she blesses the cake with the powder of a ground aragonite stone.

When the cornmeal is ground, the women make the batter and stir it in multiple tin tubs. Although not a task assigned to him, the father may spell the girl in stirring when she becomes fatigued. The men dig the pit in the earth, which is then lined with corn husks before the batter is poured in. The women smooth and bless the cake with the corn pollen that has been used to bless the girl's body. The girl lays corn husks on top and her father adorns her with a pendleton robe before she performs her special blessing of the cake.

On the third night of the ceremony, a man tends the fire, keeping it stoked during the all-night sing in the hogan. The sponsor blesses the girl's body with the corn pollen one last time, and does a final haircombing, during which she pulls her bangs up and back. Inside the hogan, the initiate is expected to stay awake all night, another challenge of endurance.

The cake is baked by the next morning. It has a complex symbolism. Sacred corn represents life for the Navajo. Round, yellow, fire-baked, it evokes a solar masculine image, yet it is baked within a subterranean pit, within the feminine body of the earth. Both men and women cooperate in making it. The placement of the corn husks on top provides a sacred orientation to the six directions. Sharing and eating the ceremonial cake on the fourth day is a communion for the participants with the Holy People, the gods, and with one another (Lincoln 1981: 32). The cake is feminine nurturance as sacrament. The initiate cuts the cake and gives the center cut to her sponsor or to the medicine man. She is forbidden to eat her own cake, as if it is her own body that she is offering.

When the cake has been shared and the ceremony formally concluded, the girl enters a four-day seclusion, a time of reflection, during which she can absorb her induction. This is considered the beginning of her maturity, when the Navajo say, "One begins thinking for oneself" (*ada nitsidzikees dzizlii*). Accomplishing her puberty ceremony, the *Kinaalda* initiate restores unity and balance to her tribe. Through becoming Changing Woman, she garners and dispenses the benedictions of the deity.

Just as the blood mysteries of women's bodies are enacted ritually in her body, women are predisposed to the ritual expression of those transform-ations. Each process of feminine development or psychological change inher-ently calls for a ritual response that acknowledges its meaning. As a woman's inner guides emerge, they spontaneously enact rituals through her dreams and fantasies that fall into a pattern leading to the initiatory goal. Late in her analysis, Carmina dreamed:

> I am painting squares of women's rituals. In the painting there is a line of women going down to the water. I decorate them with jewelry in a gold pen. I dream that I am one of these barbaric women with gold lines coming off me.
> I see my cousin with her hair blowing, and it strikes me how beautiful she is. All her clothes have minerals and metals sewn into them . . . now I'm in a room with strange creatures, all women, primitive Venus figures, almost spherical, breasts, bellies, no personality, all sexual. Beads are sewn into their skin/hides.

In one tale, Changing Woman is said to have white beads in her right breast; turquoise in her left (Reichard 1950: 114–115).

> I am enacting a ritual with my three girlhood friends, now women. A group of people are standing in a circle watching. One of the women is nude. Another is bathing her with precious liquid. The liquid is cham-pagnelike. Each one of us undergoes this ritual. I am talking with the three of them. We are talking about the problems going on in their lives. One of the women says, "Carmina is the one who does this work for us." It is like the child in the family who has the therapeutic role. I feel good and proud. It is true. There is nothing unusual about it.

Holding the opposites

Like the sponsor in the *Kinaalda* or the priestess at Artemis' temple, the woman analyst becomes the patroness or midwife, the presider over the threshold. She welcomes the patient in the waiting room, ushers her across the sill into the consulting room, stands at the door to her dream world, guides her in self-reflection, or into the mysteries of alchemy.

The Greek rites of Artemis at Brauron and the *Kinaalda* rite of the Navajo have opposing impacts on a girl's psyche. But there are similarities in the elements of the ceremonies: adornment with special clothes; the taboo on touching or shedding blood, instruction by a priestess or sponsor, hair styling or cutting, and racing. Both serve a cultural purpose of valuing a girl for her fertility, and for her role as a childbearing wife in the community. The critical difference between them lies in the Navajo's valuing of women, their high status in the society, and the close affiliation between mother and daughter which is fostered from one generation to another. Specifically, the honoring of the girl's body as beautiful and as having a beneficent effect on her surroundings is empowering to her. If a young Navajo woman individuates away from the collective ideal, she begins from the ground of feeling her intrinsic value as a woman, for she has "walked into beauty."

In analysis, women often make this symbolic return to menarche through dreams and fantasy that find expression in part through the imagery of puberty ceremonies: bathing, cleansing, hair styling or cutting, adornment with jewelry or new clothes, racing or other challenging physical tasks, and instruction or guidance by women elders. In all these dream processes, bodily mutation effects a transformation from girl to woman.

In the Artemisian initiation, girls were separated from the family in order to enact a ritual of leaving the childhood maiden state, and to be prepared for the role as wife and mother. Sacrifice was inherent in both refusal and acceptance. This was a feminine mystery under the auspices of Artemis, a divinity who herself stays on one side of the threshold, even as she mediates womanhood for girls. There at Brauron, the masculine took the form of a bear or the spirit of a bear. In the Navajo girl's initiation, there are secret feminine aspects, and the whole is orchestrated under the sponsorship of the "ideal woman" as the medium for the deity Changing Woman. But men also play a cooperative role in accomplishing the ceremony, the girl's induction.

A woman must be initiated into her own selfhood before she can meet a man equally. Her initiation is the purpose of the feminine mysteries. This parallels a boy's challenge to manhood through his ordeal, trial of strength, or vision quest. We all can learn from the Navajo model of respect for honoring a girl's emerging identity as a woman.

Men and women analysts alike must help bring to consciousness the persistent residues of Aristotle's judgment on women in both the women and the men we treat. The psyches of women continue to bring forth dreams and unconscious material, motivating a woman to step into her empowerment and exercise her individuality in the world. Each acknowledgment by the analyst of the working of the archetype of feminine initiation in an analytic hour, each recognition of the motifs that further a woman's sense of developing selfhood, each opening into the spontaneous ritual expressions that arise in the course of deep psychological work, are part of the positive evolution of the archetype. These subtle awarenesses bring women, and the feminine, out of the shadow into the light.

Notes

1 See Aristotle, *De generatione animalium*, 737a.
2 In Reed vs. Reed, Justice Harry Blackmun gave automatic preference to men over women for selection to administer an estate. Ginsburg's goal was to persuade the

Supreme Court to accept a new paradigm, to see sex discrimination as analogous to racial discrimination and to declare that under the Fourteenth Amendment's guarantee of equal protection, official policies that discriminated on the basis of sex were presumptively unconstitutional.

3 See Hesiod, *Theogony*, 585.
4 Hera persecuted Leto for Zeus' infidelity by forbidding Leto to give birth where the sun shone. Leto fled, carried by the South Wind, to the island of Ortygia and gave birth to Artemis painlessly. Blown on with the newborn girl, Leto arrived on Delos, a floating island, where, after nine days of labor, Artemis helped her mother deliver Apollo. Henceforth, the island became fixed and no one is allowed to be born or to die on it; instead, people are ferried from Delos to Ortygia to begin or end life.
5 See Rutter (1993) for an in-depth exploration of the dreams, histories, and analytic journeys of Carmina, Beatrice, and Sarah, three of the women whose dreams appear here.
6 The original wooden effigy was said to have been stolen by Orestes and Iphigenia from the Taurons and brought to Brauron at Artemis' instruction. Ancient worshippers rubbed the image with the blood of sacrificed animals.
7 Begay's (1983) book was written for the Navajo Curriculum Center. It outlines the girl's puberty ceremony in detail with both Navajo and English text.
8 Currently, the girl grinds a designated amount of corn and the rest of the ground cornmeal is purchased. Thirty pounds of cornmeal for one cake is not unusual.

Further reading

Burkert, Walter (1985) *Greek Religion*, Cambridge, MA: Harvard University Press.
Frisbie, Charlotte Johnson (1967) *Kinaalda: A Study of the Navajo Girl's Puberty Ceremony*, Middletown, CT: Wesleyan University Press.
Keuls, Eva (1985) *The Reign of the Phallus: Sexual Politics in Ancient Athens*, New York: Harper & Row.

References

Begay, Shirley M. (1983) *Kinaalda: A Navajo Puberty Ceremony*, revised edition, Rough Rock, AZ: Navajo Curriculum Center.
Craighead, Meinrad (2003) *Crow Mother and the Dog God: A Retrospective*, San Francisco, CA: Pomegranate.
Faraone, Christopher A. (2003) "Playing the Bear and Fawn for Artemis: Female Initiation or Substitute Sacrifice?" in David Dodd and Christopher A. Faraone (eds) *Initiation in Ancient Greek Rituals and Narratives*, London: Routledge, pp. 43–68.
Graves, Robert (1992) *The Greek Myths* (complete edition), London: Penguin.
Greenhouse, Linda (2005) "The Evolution of a Justice," *New York Times Magazine*, April 10.
Henderson, Joseph L. (2005) *Thresholds of Initiation*, 2nd edition, Wilmette, IL: Chiron.
Jung, C.G. (1982) *Aspects of the Feminine*, Bollingen Series, Princeton, NJ: Princeton University Press.
Kerenyi, Carl (1967) *Eleusis: Archetypal Image of Mother and Daughter*, Princeton, NJ: Princeton University Press.

King, Helen (1983) "Bound to Bleed: Artemis and Greek Women," in Averil Cameron and Amelie Kuhrt (eds) *Images of Women in Antiquity*, Detroit, MI: Wayne State University Press, pp. 109–127.

Lincoln, Bruce (1981) *Emerging from the Chrysalis: Studies in Women's Initiation*, Cambridge, MA: Harvard University Press.

Marinatos, Nanno (2002) "The Arkteia and the Gradual Transformation of the Maiden into a Woman," in Bruno Gentili and Franca Perusino (eds) *Le Orse di Brauron: Un rituale di iniziazione femminile nel santuario di Artemide*, Pisa: Edizioni ETS, pp. 29–42.

Neils, Jenifer (2003) "Children in Greek Religion," in Jenifer Neils and John H. Oakley, *Coming of Age in Ancient Greece: Images of Childhood from the Classical Past*, New Haven, CT: Yale University Press, pp. 139–161.

Reeder, Ellen D. (1995) "Pandora: Women in Classical Greece," in *Women and the Metaphor of Wild Animals*, Catalogue, Section 3, Princeton, NJ: The Trustees of the Walters Art Gallery and Princeton University Press, pp. 299–372.

Reichard, Gladys A. (1950) *Navajo Religion: A Study of Symbolism*, vol. 2, Bollingen Series 17, New York: Pantheon.

Rutter, Virginia Beane (1993) *Woman Changing Woman: Feminine Psychology Re-Conceived through Myth and Experience*, San Francisco, CA: Harper.

Wyman, Leland C. (1970) *Blessingway*, recorded and translated by Father Berard Haile, Tucson, AZ: University of Arizona Press.

Chapter 4

Initiation as surrender

A twelve-year analysis

Richard Stein

If each phase of life can be pictured as the expression of a major archetype, then the archetype of initiation may be viewed as the process of transformation from one archetypal phase to the next. The following clinical material is an example of the working process of this archetype in a mature patient during the course of a twelve-year analysis. This case focuses on the later stages of the initiation process as a path of individuation, in the sense that C.G. Jung used that term, that is, becoming conscious of the many parts of oneself. For this to happen, the heroic attitude towards life must give way to an openness to previously unconscious aspects of the personality.

Henderson's thesis, that when an appropriate initiation ritual is not provided by family or culture, the psyche may devise an internal compensation for it, is central to the understanding of what follows. The patient had some knowledge of both Jung and Henderson's work, but was not specifically familiar with *Thresholds of Initiation* (Henderson 2005) nor was he aware during the analysis how well his dream process demonstrated the premise of that book. The material shows the importance of the intellectual ego's surrender to something beyond itself, and much like Jung's early insight into the death of the hero, this surrender makes space for an experience of "the reality of the psyche" to emerge.

This case is in the spirit of Henderson's clinical approach, as it allows for the unfolding of a deep process without overanalyzing it. With intelligent patients who have suffered neglect or trauma in childhood, too much interpretation may reinforce intellectual defenses against emerging memories, emotions, and imagery. I regard this kind of analysis as "implicit work in the transference," in contrast to more explicit interpretation of the interpersonal dynamics. While attending to subtle interactions in the analytic relationship, my focus was to foster a holding environment in which his unconscious could find a safe and empathic container to reveal itself. As the dream process took shape, it seemed to confirm the rightness of this approach.

For myself as the analyst, this creative holding means sacrificing the cloak of analytic certainty, but it also serves as a model for the patient to sink deeper into less familiar and more irrational experience. Jung describes his discovery of a similar analytic attitude after he broke with Freud, a break which he anticipated in 1911 while he was writing "The Sacrifice," at the conclusion of "Symbols of Transformation" (Jung 1956). Reflecting on that change nearly fifty years later, he wrote:

> Above all, I felt it necessary to develop a new attitude toward my patients. I resolved for the present not to bring any theoretical premises to bear upon them, but to wait and see what they would tell me of their own accord. My aim became to leave things to chance. In regard to their dreams he said, The interpretations seemed to follow of their own accord from the patients' replies and associations. I avoided all theoretical points of view and simply helped the patients to understand the dream images by themselves.
>
> (Jung 1963a: 170)

This surrender on the part of the analyst creates a more open field for exploration, but the patient must do his part if an initiatory process is to take hold. Initiation is, after all, fundamentally an expression of the archetype of death and rebirth, the sacrifice of an old attitude in order for a new one to emerge. For surrender to be a transformative experience, there must be a letting go of a part or symbol of the self, which may feel like an involuntary death imposed by fate. As Jung wrote late in life, *"the experience of the Self is always a defeat for the ego"* (Jung 1963b: 778, italics in original). In the material that follows, the sacrifice of the supremacy of the intellect and of a highly rational standpoint is pictured in the dreams as suffering and crucifixion. Many eastern practices, however, view surrender as a voluntary self-giving on the path to awakening from an illusory world, a theme also visible here. Heinrich Zimmer (1951: 4) writes, "The primary concern (of the East) has always been, not information, but transformation, a radical changing of man's nature and a renovation both of the outer world and of his own existence." The psychoanalyst Emmanuel Ghent suggests a similar distinction in analytic approaches "in the schism between analysts whose emphasis is informational (insight is what cures) as against those for whom the focus is transformational (with cure comes insight)" (Ghent 1990: 112). If deeply felt surrender is to accomplish something resembling a cure, there must be a connection with some transpersonal factor in the psyche, by whatever name we call it. Here the initiation archetype brings about a break from the old status of being (a rite of separation), which may feel like either submission to an external authority or surrender to an inner process. The transformative experiences take place in a liminal state shrouded in mystery, represented in the material that follows as dreams and visions within the dreams. Finally, the rite of reentry is often well defined and expressed symbolically as a rebirth and return to ordinary human conditions. The whole process may be seen in three steps: death, transitional state, and rebirth. This initiatory drama dissolves strongly held religious or intellectual beliefs, opening the patient to previously unknown possibilities in the psyche. The archetypal energies are freed from religious dogma and express themselves in new and startling images that speak uniquely to the individual.

There is often a tension in the psyche which is expressed in the analytic process as being pulled in two different directions, one resembling a return to an earlier state of development, a regressive return to the world of the mother. The other is seen as a more forward-looking development, which in the language of initiation is either the trial of strength or the ordeal, or some combination of both. Henderson reflects that the heart of his book "focuses on the first essential element of initiation, the ordeal. This stage is often painful and even 'messy.' It has an element of surrender to it" (Henderson 2005: xv). In the dreams that follow, we shall see the ordeal in the form of the Crucifixion, which is the central image in Christian culture of the ego's submission to transpersonal factors. The ordeal and the trial of strength are followed by, or alternate with, images of descent, baptism, and return to the mother. The tension between these two patterns finally resolves in a third initiatory process, the rite of vision, as deeper wisdom is revealed. This represents a profound revelation of the reality of the psyche, which brings healing to the separation of mind and body, the ego and the unconscious.

Case discussion

The patient came to analysis as a man in his late forties seeking help for chronic pain, marital and family conflicts, a tendency to overwork, and his own desire for personal growth. He had a longstanding interest in his dreams and some familiarity with Jungian psychology, but he also had a strong skepticism about New Age ideas, woolly thinking, and religious dogma of any sort.

Chris grew up in a poor family in the rural South. His father was a miner and a severe alcoholic, who had lost the family farm because of his drinking. In contrast to his father, Chris's mother was a strict Southern Baptist. The children suffered physical abuse from their father and severe neglect, scanty food, inadequate winter clothing, and poor medical and dental care. Chris was sheltered by his mother's religious beliefs until he was a teenager and began to think for himself. Around age 12, he went through a crisis of faith and an adolescent depression; he put his reliance in his own emerging intellect and his desire to get away from his early family experience. He applied himself academically in high school and won a scholarship to a state college, where he found new intellectual horizons and was a part of the 1960s subculture. Then he was drafted and went to Vietnam.

Chris finished college after getting out of the Army and worked at a number of manual jobs before coming to San Francisco. A casual conversation with a friend about his lack of direction led to a referral for Jungian therapy. During the decade of that treatment, he got a well-paying job in the hightech industry and married a middle-class Jewish woman. Many years later, when he came to me as a middle-aged man, he had been through a career change and was a licensed health professional.

The early months of our work dealt with his marital problems and a serious physical injury that required multiple surgeries and ongoing pain management. Tensions in his marriage had increased during the stressful time he was out of work because of a recent operation. Although admitting to thoughts of suicide because of the pain, he claimed that he was not depressed. After about two years of treatment, suffering physically and emotionally, he dreamed of the Crucifixion for the first time. Subsequent appearances of Christ were often months apart, and interspersed with other powerful dreams about animals, initiatory ordeals, and more personal material. This dream came as a total surprise to both of us and led to an emotional breakthrough in the session:

> Something about the Crucifixion. I'm with a man, shorter, Greek looking, like a portrait of Alexander the Great, behind billowy light blue curtains. We're on the backside of Golgotha, so we can see the backs of the crosses. The two crosses on either side are raised and set in place. For some reason, I think they're suffering less than Christ will suffer. The cross with Christ is raised and the long vertical pole falls into the hole dug for it. It's a terrible sound and I imagine the pain in the places where nails hold his body to the cross. The vertical pole makes a loud "thud" sound and a groan goes up from the crowd.

His association to Alexander was the heroic attitude. He realized that he'd been trying to keep up his life as though the pain would not interfere with it. He admitted, when he registered my wince at hearing the dream, that he had been hiding the extent of his physical suffering from me. I told him that I could see it on his face at times as he came up the stairs and into the office. I didn't tell him that I felt sympathetic pain in my own body at times when he shifted awkwardly in the chair. He said that he was afraid that talking about it would only make it worse, but he did proceed to tell me about the nightly ice packs, the insomnia, and his memories of childhood sufferings that came in the wee hours of the morning. His wife had a lot of work-related travel, and he would lie there alone with the pain thinking, "I have nobody." Then, very slowly, in a lot of pain, "No body." After a silence, I repeated it as a question, "No body?" "Well, she's not there and between the pain meds and the ice I can get pretty numb." We both realized he was thawing out a bit, giving in to suffering it consciously with me rather than alone. There were tears in the silence.

The next dream, which referred to the Messiah, came a year and a half later:

> It seems that I'm in Jerusalem. It's the time between the Crucifixion and the Resurrection. The Messiah is recovering in someone's home. He's lying in bed, writhing in pain. Later it seems he's in a large walk-in bath. Someone says, "Messiah, you need to be careful of your wounds." He walks out of the tub. There's blood in the water. He touches the blood and crosses himself. I go over and touch a drop of blood and do the same. He walks past a boy who's blind. His eyes are completely white. As the Messiah passes, the boy's eyes change slowly to a beautiful blue. The boy sees. Then it seems I'm on a stage talking to the audience about this story. All the while Gorecki's Third Symphony is playing. The strains are getting louder and louder. I wake up thinking, "What is this?"

Chris realized that the boy was a part of himself blind to the healing mystery he was being shown in the dream. He hated the childlike attitude of religious thinking, which he said was just "wish fulfilling fantasy." It reminded him not only of his mother, but also of his wife's family and their New Age ideas. He remembered the fights he had with his own mother when he quit the church and decided not to believe anything he did not get for himself. The music was the most powerful part of the dream, as though it contained all the emotion that he was not feeling. There was a sense of awe.

In spite of his intellectual bias against religious dogma, the dreams are showing Chris that his early experience of faith has some important meaning to him as an adult. Based on church tradition and ritual, Henderson writes that the time between the Crucifixion and the Ascension "was essentially a return to the Mother for the sake of rebirth, represented by the living water of the baptismal font" (Henderson 2005: 75). It seems that the dream is restoring a basic childhood faith he shared with his mother before he broke with the church. He is also discovering a new feeling for the archetypal psyche as an adult. This return to the mother is followed by an upwelling of masculine forces in the next dream.

> Later I'm watching a band of gorillas. The males are fighting over a harem. The females and the young are watching, trying to stay out of the way. The Messiah appears and sits among them. The gorillas stop fighting and return to eating. The Messiah says, "These are my faithful. They are content." In the distance on a mountain top a wild storm suddenly appears. I can see the silhouettes of some gorillas grunting and dancing against the backdrop of the storm. One raises his arm as if to point. They all howl and dance. I look for the Messiah but he is not here now.

Chris was fascinated with evolutionary theory, especially the ongoing studies of the higher apes and recent discoveries in paleo-anthropology. He had utter contempt for the creationist view of the Bible that he had been taught growing up. He put his trust in science, so he felt a bit confused by the Messiah's strange words to these gorillas. "These are my faithful. They are content." The imagery was vivid, moving, and real to him. He felt a sense of awe as he saw the gorillas' dance in the coming storm. I commented on the juxtaposition of nature and religious imagery, which he agreed was important. The fighting male gorillas with the backdrop of a wild storm suggests a thunder rite in tribal cultures, and it shows the eruption of strongly competitive masculine forces, mediated at least temporarily by the Messiah (Henderson 2005: 154).

A few months later he dreamed of me:

> I am with you. You are exasperated with me about Jesus. "Let go and get God," you say. I can't believe you're saying it. You're saying it about my mother-in-law. "If you forgive her," you say, followed by something from one of the Parables. I have this experience that the Parable feels like bubbles going up to the sky. Then a voice is

saying, "If you had the faith of a mustard seed." Later, I'm on a train going through the Swiss Alps, moving through beautiful vistas. The train stops. We all gaze at the wondrous peaks.

Chris imagined that I didn't like his dreams about Jesus. He assumed that I was Jewish, and he suspected that I shared his negative attitude towards Christianity. But he himself was ambivalent about Christianity. He didn't like his Jewish mother-in-law's anti-Christian prejudice or her irrational New Age ideas. He hoped I wasn't supporting "that kind of shit." He made jokes about one of his friends who was always talking about "BuddHA" and a friend of his wife who was into "the goddess." I gestured to a statue of Kwan Yin near him on the windowsill. He laughed uneasily and said, "Oh, that's just Jungian stuff." "Really?" I asked, and we both had a good laugh. He went on to the mustard seed parable, citing the passage in Luke 16, and joked that I probably didn't know the Bible that well. I agreed that I did not know the exact reference. He went on to say that the vistas in the Alps were something he could see with his own eyes. He knew I loved the mountains and felt a connection with me about them. Then he said that the dreams were just as much a fact of nature, that they were his direct experience. He wasn't sure what they meant and sometimes wanted to hear more of what I thought, but basically he was glad I didn't try too hard to interpret them.

I silently wondered if the appearance of the Messiah might help him to heal the split between his childhood faith and his adult skepticism. I also considered that the words said by *me* in the dream, "Let go and get God," suggested a fear that I wanted him to surrender directly to God. Could it be, I was thinking, that God was far too abstract and impersonal for his surrender, perhaps an object too dangerous? He knew the *Book of Job* as well as the parables. Given his negative father wound, I thought that he needed a human intercessor closer to his personal experience, the Messiah who appears as the wounded healer, yet also points to an archetypal dimension of the transference.

Eight months later came a longer dream, which I will summarize in part. Chris walked into the office with the dream, paper in hand, gave it to me with a shrug, and said laughing, "What's a modern Christian to do? Why do I keep getting dreams like this?"

This dream takes place in Europe, in the ruins of a beautiful church in the forest, with parts of walls, blue stained glass windows, and a road leading into the deep forest.

I hear a group singing the old gospel song, "The Golden Crown":

"As I went down to the river to pray
Studying about the Good old way
And who will wear the robe and crown
Good lord, show me the way.

Oh sisters, let's go down
Let's go down,
Come on down
Oh sisters let's go down
Down to the river to pray."

Later, I'm above the tree line in the mountains. The road has gotten steep and rocky. I look back and there's nothing but steep road. There are spots of blood on it ahead of me. My back hurts so much that I want to lie down by the side of the road, want my back to sink into the road. I watch the clouds drift by. Up the hill further I can hear noise. There's a public execution going on! Then I get hot and sweaty, and I realize it's the Crucifixion! There are groans and awful noises. Then it's all quiet. I'm actually awakened by the quiet.

"The Golden Crown" was a hymn he loved as a child, and he enjoyed the scene where it was sung in the film *O Brother, Where Art Thou?* (Joel Coen and Ethan Coen 2000). Yet the shift to the hard climb, the pain, and another dream of the Crucifixion was a different matter. I was struck by the feeling quality of the hymn, with its images of descent to the river and his positive childhood memories, in contrast to the difficult climb, which represents a trial of strength leading to yet another ordeal. He said, "I know I'm hurting, so why do I need dreams like this? It's really hard stuff to deal with." The time was up, and I had no ready answer. It was an awkward moment, a silence not unlike the quiet that awakened him at the end of the dream. After the session, I thought that this quietude had the effect of a Zen koan, stopping not only his mind but mine as well. That silencing of the mind made space for some new awakening in the psyche.

Within a week came two powerful initiation dreams, one more spiritual and the other purely instinctual. The initial one anticipates the visionary experiences that follow. The first dream within-a-dream in the series is an indication that the ordeal and trial of strength are giving way to a new phase of development, the rite of vision:

> I'm lying on the ground near my old cabin in the woods. I fall asleep by the creek and start to dream, knowing I'm dreaming. In the dream, I've just finished up in the outhouse, and I'm looking at the beautiful view of the mountains off in the distance. I'm wondering if I'll wake up in the dream and write down what I'm dreaming. Later, I walk past the cabin, through the forest to where I see another house above the creek. As I get closer, I see it's a castle with a light in one of the windows. It's a bit strange. As I get closer, I realize it's Jung's castle and he's inside. I walk around to the entrance and he's sitting in a chair reading with his glasses part way down his nose, looking a little silly. We both laugh, as he knows he looks silly. It seems like we talk for a long time. I want to ask him if he was really a Christian, but before I do he says something about Christ that I don't understand. At the same time I can feel his answer, something like, "We are what we are." But it's not in words or sentences. I struggle with his answer because I know what it is but can't say it. It's symbolic feeling? He puts his hand on my shoulder and says, "It will be alright." I want to ask him more questions, especially about evolution. He looks at me intensely, with his eyes ablaze. He seems to be saying in the same fashion, that is, without words, "That is your problem." Then he says he has to go. Later, I'm walking back through the forest to my cabin. When I look back, the castle isn't there anymore. Then I'm lying on the ground near the creek, and my old girlfriend Meg is waking me up. "We could hear you snoring all the way up the hill," she says. Then we take off our clothes and go for a dip in the creek. As I'm getting out of the water, I look across the meadow at Black Dog Peak. The sky is bright with color though it's midday. Then I really wake up.

Chris wished he could remember and understand what Jung said about Christ. He knew he was dreaming, so he thought he could be more conscious about what happened. It was like the Grail castle, a place where you could find the truth. I pointed out that it might be seen as an initiatory dream, that the outhouse and the snoring grounded him in ordinary reality, markers that he is a natural man; it seemed to me that they were like rites of entering and exiting a deeper imaginal realm. He agreed and said he appreciated that Jung could laugh at himself. I was aware of the warmth and the felt sense of connection that had developed between us, and that his sense of humor helped him keep a better perspective on the serious pain he still suffered. I never knew if he associated the dream Jung with me at a conscious level, but I did not raise the question. What I did ask was what he meant when he said it was "symbolic feeling." He answered that it was "pre-logical," like knowing something directly, without knowing how you knew it. That kind of knowing felt good, just like the dip in the creek after he woke up. The color was very moving, like dawn or sunset, but in midday. He was very moved by how real it was.

It occurred to me that for a man with such a terrible father history, Chris had come a long way in accepting help from male authority figures. He had other dreams of Lincoln, Eisenhower, F.D. Roosevelt, and Churchill, and it seemed to me that Jung was a logical inner father to help him in the process of finding the right psychological balance between the scientific and religious attitudes. Jung's responses in the dream reminded me of a Zen master, who points the student to his own experience rather than trying to provide explanations. "We are what we are" is like a Zen koan, and his answer about evolution puts the issue right back where it belongs, as a psychological process inside Chris. I thought of Jung's visions in his near death experience; when he was about to enter the rock temple, he too sought answers to ultimate questions about his life but was turned back to the direct experience of it.

Chris's cabin suggests the initiation hut in shamanic cultures. Henderson writes about the rites of purification which lead from public ceremonies to an individual vision. "The little hut thus serves the function of providing a transitional stage of containment between the purificatory rite and the transforming encounter with the animal" (Henderson 2005: 158). Having bathed in the creek after his individual meeting with Jung as master of initiation, Chris is ready for the animal encounter which follows. The next dream seems important as an instinctual compensation to the spiritual experience in the Grail Castle:

> I am on a high desert plain overlooking a plateau in an ancient time. As I look down over a series of valleys, I see great herds of reindeer surging through the valleys. I notice some of the animals are white,

only a few. Their antlers are different too; they glow with color. As the herds come together and drift apart the white deer move into different positions, all done in a synchronized way, purely instinctual, the herd probably unaware it is taking place. It's so rhythmic, hypnotic, and beautiful. Then suddenly Cro-Magnon men that I know jump out of the bushes and rocks and bring down a deer. It's very intense. The weapons are not as advanced as you'd think, so they have to get much closer, and it's much more violent. One of the men with a short spear finally gets it into the deer. The deer goes down on its front knees and makes a pitiful noise. Then it's over. The men are eating the liver raw. There is blood everywhere, on them, on the ground, everywhere. I start to get sick. I wake up feeling I'm going to vomit.

Chris thought that the scene was from thousands of years ago, at a time when animals were plentiful and the hunt was good. There was a contrast between the white deer, the leaders, and the red blood after the kill, which was accomplished with a short stone pointed spear, three or four feet in length. He said, "I guess you have to kill to eat." I felt that he had to surrender to his aggression as well as to his religious impulses, and that the dream was a partial answer to his question about the meaning of life in the castle dream. At a cultural level, a similar compensation was at work during the first centuries of early Christianity. Roman soldiers flocked in great numbers to the Mithraic mysteries, whose central symbol was a man with a knife slaying a bull. Chris's experience of the primitive hunt forces him to recognize the primitive need to kill in order to survive, the very opposite of the Crucifixion, which symbolizes man submitting to a higher, transpersonal force.

The dream that follows has a complex reference to a wild bear as the animal master of initiation; the bear is then replaced by a humorous version of Henderson:

I am going up a mountain with a wild bear and a man who has trained him. Perhaps the man is you. The bear is trained but not tamed and will always be wild. The man throws black spots on the ground, making a whoosh sound, then a thud. If you look into the spots of blackness, it's a long way down. We continue to climb, and the bear acts threateningly but becomes less ornery when the man throws the black spots on the ground. We reach the top at sunset, and there are bears dancing to music around a fire. We laugh and join in. I think I must be dreaming. The fire burns down, and we all go to sleep. In the morning the bears are gone, and I feel an aching, a deep longing, knowing I'll never see them again. Someone behind me says, "Come on in." I turn and see that it is Joe Henderson, looking like a hobbit with his hair very long but neatly combed. He is at the entrance to a cave where he has been painting black spots on the walls. He tells me that I'll never see the bears again, but he says, "You can do this." He picks up a paint brush and it goes "swoosh," through the air, and then "thud" as it hits the wall. The dream continues with a descent down the mountain with the other man, me feeling overwhelmed, almost like I've been on an acid trip; the image of the swoosh and spots of blackness reminds me of black holes in space, but are also still spots on the ground.

Association: The black holes are some shadow element. It seems that by making use of them in a conscious way, you can keep the dangerous aspects of the bears in check.

Much like Jung in the castle dream, Henderson is a father figure and mentor at the cultural level. His book concludes with an Appendix (Henderson 2005: 229–239) about the symbol of the bear in ancient mimetic rites of initiation, so it is fitting that the wild bear leads Chris and me to a meeting with Henderson. The dream seems to be integrating the spiritual initiation of the meeting with Jung and the wild aggression of the primitive hunt. As Jane Harrison puts it, "But bears, alas! retreat before advancing civilization" (quoted by Henderson 2005: 236). Here the aggressive energies of the bear are transformed by the master of initiation (Henderson) into the creative act of cave painting, which shows the acculturating process of "advancing civilization" and serves the function of a shamanic rite. This process reminds the dreamer of the deep mysteries of creation and destruction in the physical universe, the black hole.

The psychological implications of bringing that blackness down to earth, that is, to ego reality, with artistic expression are enormous. The sound of throwing the blackness, a whoosh followed by a thud, brings to mind the "thud" sound of the first Crucifixion dream when the vertical pole fell into place, and with it the horror of meaningless pain and abandonment that Christ suffered on the cross. In the present dream, Chris's psyche uses an image from modern psychics to convey the terror of the void, of non-being, which he had experienced as a primal agony in childhood. With this integration of the dark and primal affect, the analysis is providing him with the means of symbolizing unbearable suffering (affect) to the ego in the form of an archetypal image.

Sometime after the dream of Jung's castle, I noticed that Chris was capitalizing the pronoun "He" in the typewritten dreams when the Messiah appeared, but neither of us commented on it. This wild bear dream was followed by another involving orca whales and then a dream about dancing "bear people" and cave art.

In another long dream:

> I fall asleep on a train in the southwest and dream of Christ recovering from his wounds, his ordeal, needing rest and water. He walks past people on the train, and everyone who looks up changes for the better, their skin is brighter. Many, many people want to follow Him, but it's not the time yet in His life. Then I wake up and want to tell people about my dream, but everyone is asleep. I hear someone playing an old Hank Williams song from another car.

It seems that the powerful animal dreams are related to the healing of the Messiah, and that there is an interplay between the instinctual and spiritual poles of the psyche.

A few months later, Chris dreamed he is traveling by boat down the Nile River in Egypt when the captain warns them of the crocodiles in the river. Chris falls asleep in a deck chair and dreams that someone is bringing him a container of several scraps of metal.

> At the bottom of the bucket there's a crucifix and a figure of Christ bleeding on the cross. His hands are bleeding and so are his feet. I touch the blood and think it's holy. "Jesus wept," I hear someone say. For some reason I say, "It's the shortest verse in the Bible." It dawns on me as I dream that this is no ordinary boat. It is on a mythical Nile River which is a river of dreams. "I'm unclear about its meaning," I say, "but it's something about traveling on a river that still has man devouring beasts. It's unlike real life because it's the buildings and cars and pollution and saw mills and mines that are devouring men in real life." Later, I realize that the person I've been talking with will ask me to interpret his dream when we are awake again.

Chris was struck by the fact that once again the deeper meaning was carried by the dream within-the-dream, and he wanted to know what I thought of that. I said that he seemed to be relaxing in the dream when he fell asleep on the deck chair, which was a deeper surrender of conscious control. He wondered about the fact that the person he was talking with will ask for a dream interpretation from him. I asked if he thought it might be me, and he said, "Well, you always ask me what comes to mind when I tell them to you." It seemed as if something of our dialogue might be getting incorporated into the dreams, but in a more significant way, this dream anticipated his need to leave analysis and find his own way with the unconscious. Just as he was handed the bucket containing the blood of Christ to touch and hold for himself, he might be preparing to work more directly with these numinous experiences on his own.

The next dream occurred while Chris struggled with his dislike of his Jewish mother-in-law. After his father-in-law died, Chris wanted to support his wife and be respectful of her family's grief, but he was annoyed by his mother-in-law's comment about being reunited with her husband in heaven – "not to mention the family dog," he told me sarcastically. Yet it genuinely pained him to feel like an outsider with her relatives because he disliked their religious attitudes, and he had said Kaddish with the family at the gravesite, moved by the genuine feeling in the prayers. In the dream:

> Chris leaves his wife on the sidewalk in New York after expressing disgust with a religious looking older Jewish couple. He goes alone into a library built like the Guggenheim Museum, in a spiral shape. Trying to take the elevator up to the twelfth floor, he is involuntarily carried down to a church in the basement; here he finds Jesus in one of the pews and kneels to pray with him. Jesus has dark curly hair and looks Jewish. He is holding a Rosary in his hands, but the Hebrew prayer he says is the Kaddish.
>
> As he goes through the Kaddish, he's also going through the Rosary beads. Then He says something to me about David. I realize that the old couple I saw on the sidewalk was David and someone else. He gets up and I see that he's undergone the crucifixion. I say, "Messiah, you must be careful." He walks past a young boy who is sleeping on the benches. The young boy wakes cheerful and follows Jesus. He goes to the elevator and I follow him in. He pushes 12. I wake up.

His musings about the dream point to an acceptance of his own shadow.

> I woke up confused, not knowing which way is up. King David is the one who gets away with everything in the Bible, and God still loves him. He can do no wrong. In contrast, Jesus is from the house of David, but he is humble in how he suffers. I remember sleeping on the back pew of the church when I was a boy. Twelve is a complete cycle of time, and it feels as if something's coming full circle now. At age 12 I went through the worst crisis of faith. After that I decided I had to make it on my own, and that I wasn't ever going to rely on anything I couldn't see or touch or think for myself. It's been changing lately, and I have a new feeling about it all – the dreams, this work. My life isn't so stuck.

He went on to say that he was reading a literary biography of Christ, and that he realized there was a more symbolic level of meaning in the story. He was sure that there was some reason he was being given these dreams, and that it might take the rest of his life to understand them. I agreed that they were big dreams, and added that whatever they meant to him over time, his attitude towards them had certainly changed during our work together.

This dream of Jesus saying Kaddish is laden with archetypal symbols. Let me say briefly that the central theme is the reconciliation of opposites: Jewish/Christian, up/down, knowledge/faith, age/youth, skepticism/belief, and the vertical and circular images of initiation which resolve in the spiral. Chris has taken to heart the advice that Jung gave him in the Grail Castle in response to his question about evolution. As you may recall, Jung replied, "That is your problem." What was an intellectual interest for Chris, a scientific problem to be investigated, has taken on an inner, symbolic meaning, conveying the paradoxical nature of the initiation process. The spiral shaped library with a church in the basement is a cultural symbol uniting the desire for learning with a religious attitude. It is also an indication that the initiatory process is both vertical and cyclical; that is, the maturation of consciousness involves movements backwards as well as forward in time.

Henderson writes, "In contrast to [the] stepladder or evolutionary view of initiation, our material has shown a distinctly cyclical character in which a return to old patterns is of no less significance than a sense of progression to new ones" (Henderson 2005: 178).

The final dream of Christ recapitulates old themes of submission as baptism, the trial of strength, the threat of an ordeal, and finally a new and more profound visionary experience.

Chris is swimming in a warm pool of clear, delightful water. The scene changes:

> Later it seems I'm on a journey on a road in high desert country. I'm following a procession of some sort. Up ahead someone says this is Emmaus Road. I hear a whip crack in the air. Maybe someone is being whipped? I'm scared. The thought of being whipped is terrifying. Then I realize that everyone who takes this road sees a vision of Christ. It doesn't matter who you are or what you're doing. Up ahead, at a specific place, everyone in the procession falls into a trance. They seem to stop. You can hear them speaking in tongues, some weeping and some laughing. I walk to that place and hear something. Then it seems that I'm further down the road. I turn back and look. I'm amazed that it happened so fast. Then it seems I'm speaking in tongues with someone. We talk for a long time and then I step to the side of the road and into a modern building. Patients are waiting in the waiting room. I think, "What the heck was that?"
>
> I'm swimming in the pool again, this time nude. The water is soft, luxurious, relaxing and healing. I hear someone say, "This is heaven." For a moment it seems like they said it in tongues. At the shallow end, the minister is baptizing people. He's speaking in tongues. I get in line. Later I'm back near my cabin swimming in the creek. It's a warm summer day and I feel I've come home.

He thought about his suffering at the hands of his father, and told me that he had heard speaking in tongues in church; once as a child, he had almost fallen into that trance. He knew that Emmaus Road is the Road to Damascus, where the conversion of Paul took place. Saul was the skeptic who became a believer, and Chris mused out loud, really free associating in the hour for the first time, wondering if there was an inner place where everyone can have a vision, where everyone heard and spoke a different language. I was struck by the way he was letting go to a stream of inner ideas and images, settling into a deeper place in himself. Apropos of this stream of consciousness, it seems important to add that he had been writing poetry for some time, hearing and speaking another language, but it was during this period that he first began to get some of his work published.

Chris had conflicted feelings about whether to have another surgery to correct a problem from the previous one, as he had been getting differing opinions from various specialists about what to do. He was coming to the realization that there was no clear, scientific answer and that he didn't know whom to trust, when he had a powerful dream about his surgeon which helped him decide to go ahead:

> I am at a large stadium where a convention of doctors is taking place. Groups of them are operating on people. . . . The scenes of sawing and hacking are very bloody. Then I see [my doctor] operating on someone. I feel that it's wonderful when it's over and the person will live.

He would need to take time off from work again and told me he was thinking of leaving analysis. He wanted to rest and heal, work on his poetry, and have more time with his family. He also thought about how to work on the dreams on his own. A few weeks later he had a different type of dream, one that points to the connection between Christianity and alchemy.

> I am watching an ancient Egyptian woman standing in a partly framed house, 2 × 4″ studs, no sheetrock or walls. She is dressed in a floor length, white linen dress, outlined with sparkling gold. Her face and eyes are outlined with gold as well. Then I see that she is peeing. The curious thing is that as she's peeing I see that she has a penis. The penis is sparkling gold as well. Then I say, "Hey!" She turns and pees towards me, but she's too far to reach me. Her penis is very golden, very sparkling. In another possibility, everything is the same but her dress is black, outlined by gold.

The Egyptian woman reminded him of the dream of going down the Nile; he felt that she was some presence from the past or from another dimension in the new house under construction. He liked the aesthetics of seeing her dress in white and gold, then black and gold. I commented that Egypt was the birthplace of western alchemy.

In "The Psychology of the Transference" Jung writes that the hermaphrodite often appears at the beginning, not at the end of a process

(Jung 1946). Chris's decision to leave analysis marked the end of one phase of his life, but it also represents the beginning of a deeper experience of himself. Henderson comments on the "compactness of image or brevity of statement" that he's noticed in the dreams of people who are approaching the end of analysis, when individuation has become a way of life (Henderson 2005: 203).

We followed Chris's material closely to see what the psyche had to say about his decision to end our work. He dreamed of a beautiful woman offering him a red apple from which she'd taken a bite. Through her small bite in the apple he could see another world, teaming with life. He hesitated and then bit into it. Later it seems that someone in his family is interested in analysis. In a subsequent dream,

> He comes to the end of an arduous journey with an old African chief, perhaps a shaman, who gives him a special gift when it is time for him to go on alone. Traveling ahead, he meets a young boy with a message for him; the message is, "Through Christ our Lord."

In a final dream:

> He is in a beautiful southwest canyon and sees a herd of wild mustangs race by. Later, a single horseman rides up to his camp fire. The old cowboy's face is wrinkled with age and battle scarred; as he rears his horse in the sunset, he waves his cowboy hat in a gesture of goodbye. He's magnificent, glowing with life. Chris gulps and starts to cry as he waves back.

It seemed to both of us that he was on the right track, and he set a date for ending.

It has been several years since the completion of almost twelve years of analysis. I contacted Chris for his permission to write about his material, and he was quite interested to hear what I have been thinking about it. He told me that he has continued to engage his inner life and to work on the major dreams about Christ, most recently stimulated by his reading about early Christian Gnosticism. From his description of a recent trip abroad, it appears that he is doing much better with his physical limitations and getting more enjoyment from life. Is it possible that the analytic experience of initiation, imaged so powerfully as the Crucifixion and Baptism, has helped to alleviate some of the historical and emotional aspects of his suffering, despite his ongoing physical condition?

At the conclusion of *The Vision Seminars*, Jung writes, "Such an experience of the unconscious leaves – if nothing else – a definite and everlasting mark upon the inner man, an awareness of the deep recesses of the soul, which never vanishes" (Jung 1976: 1379).

In the early stages of life, initiation serves the function of helping the young person to leave the parental home and get established as a responsible adult. Once these major challenges have been faced – work, career, relationship, family, and commitment to a community – other demands for maturation appear. In the face of loss, illness, declining powers, and finally the approach of death, the nature of initiation becomes a far more introverted process, one which may reveal rich inner meaning and sustain the outer life. The material presented here extends into spiritual questions far beyond the psychological developments discussed in this paper, yet it powerfully demonstrates the vitality of the archetype of initiation and the validity of "the reality of the psyche."

References

Ghent, E. (1990) "Masochism, Submission, Surrender: Masochism as a Perversion of Surrender," *Contemporary Psychoanalysis*, 26 (1): 108–136.

Henderson, Joseph L. (2005) *Thresholds of Initiation*, 2nd edition, Wilmette, IL: Chiron Publications.

Jung, C.G. (1946) "The Psychology of the Transference," *Collected Works*, vol. 16, Princeton, NJ: Princeton University Press.

Jung, C.G. (1956) "The Symbols of Transformation," *Collected Works*, vol. 5.

Jung, C.G. (1963a) *Memories, Dreams, Reflections*, New York: Pantheon.

Jung, C.G. (1963b) "Mysterium Coniunctionis," *Collected Works*, vol. 14.

Jung, C.G. (1976) *The Vision Seminars*, Princeton, NJ: Princeton University Press.

Zimmer, Heinrich (1951) *The Philosophies of India*, Princeton, NJ: Princeton University Press.

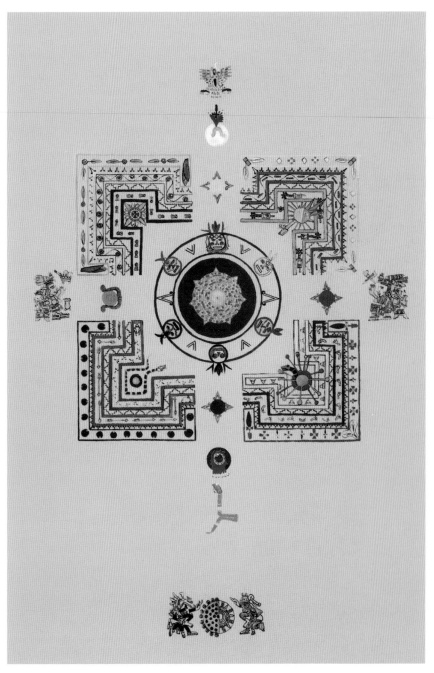

Figure 1.1 (Plate 1) Dr Henderson's 1931 drawing

Drawing reproduced with Dr Joseph Henderson's permission.

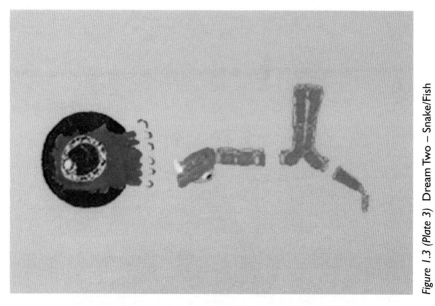

Figure 1.3 (Plate 3) Dream Two – Snake/Fish

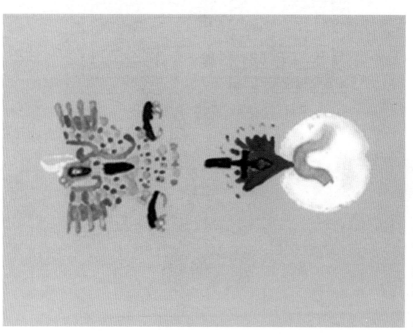

Figure 1.2 (Plate 2) Dream One – Eagle/Horse

Figure 1.4 (Plate 4) Inner Core

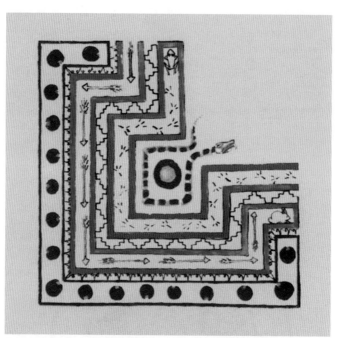

Figure 1.5 (Plate 5) Snake at Rest

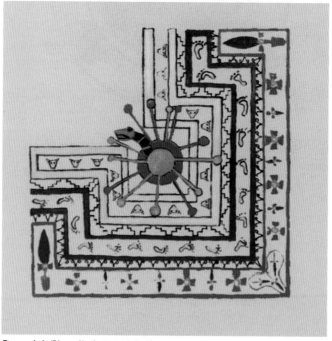

Figure 1.6 (Plate 6) Agitated Snake

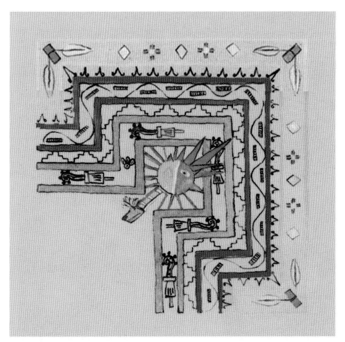

Figure 1.7 (Plate 7) Plumed Serpent

Figure 1.8 (Plate 8) Plant Mandala

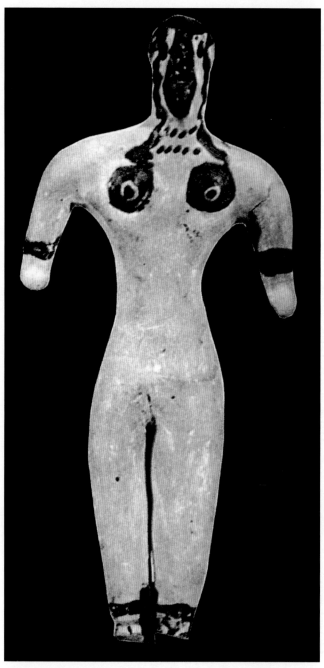

Figure 3.1 (Plate 9) Artemis of Brauron: Statue carved of wood

Photo: Meinrad Craighead.

Figure 3.2 (Plate 10) Changing Woman and Corn: Drypainting

Photograph by Peter George, from Leland C. Wyman (ed.) (1970) Blessingway, Tueson, AZ: University of Arizona Press, Figure 8. Copyright © The Arizona Board of Regents. Reprinted by permission of the University of Arizona Press.

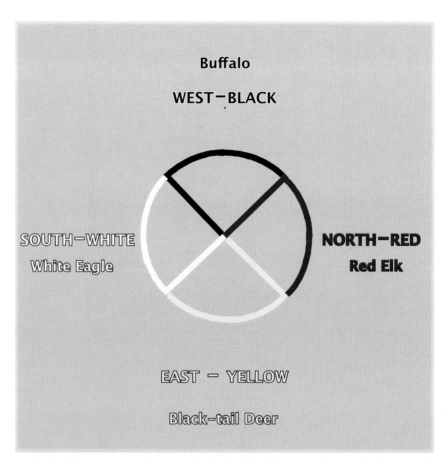

Figure 6.1 (Plate 11) The Lakota medicine wheel, showing the four directions, their colors, and the animals associated with each direction, as taught by Pansy Hawk Wing. The animals associated with a direction vary among groups and holy people. Depending on their visions, the animals may change over the course of someone's life.

Part III

The archetype of initiation in culture

Chapter 5

On modern initiation into the spiritual

A psychological view

Murray Stein

Reading "My Name," a poem by Mark Strand (2005), reminded me of a similar experience I had when I was struggling with vocational questions in my early twenties. Strand lyrically captures the astonishment when, within the natural and familiar world that seems to be running along steadily on a continuous track of time and space, one receives a most personally addressed "signal of transcendence":

> One night when the lawn was a golden green
> and the marbled moonlit trees rose like fresh memorials
> in the scented air, and the whole countryside pulsed
> with the chirr and murmur of insects, I lay in the grass
> feeling the great distances open above me, and wondered
> what I would become – and where I would find myself –
> and though I barely existed, I felt for an instant
> that the vast star-clustered sky was mine, and I heard
> my name as if for the first time, heard it the way
> one hears the wind or the rain, but faint and far off
> as though it belonged not to me but to the silence
> from which it had come and to which it would go.
>
> (Strand 2005)

In keeping with the muted spiritual tone of modernity, the speaker's intimation of immortality when his name is called, "faint and far off," is only a hint of eternity but profoundly moving nevertheless and no doubt deeply inscribed thereafter in his consciousness. What should one make of this? These lines offer a poetic rendering of a spontaneously induced initiation into the spiritual, a point of entry into individual Gnosis, which however is housed and maintained with the domain of the psychological as are all Gnostic dreams and visions. Initiation into the spiritual is one of the varieties of religious experience that today we interpret as psychological.

The key element of this initiation is the profound experience of being personally addressed by the archetypal. In the poem, the speaker's name is called by a "voice" that emanates from the deep psyche, from the stars, nameless and timeless. What seems to be one's most personal and intimate possession – a name – is instantly transformed into something quite impersonal, belonging to the ages, not to an individual "me." It transcends the individual and transient bearer. The personal is thus lifted to the impersonal, the individual to the sublimely archetypal. Likewise, one's time-limited existence within the frame of human life becomes extended infinitely beyond all space and time. One is immortalized.

The Bible is replete with such astonishing initiations through a sudden transforming appearance of the unseen powers and the infinite[1] – Moses addressed by Yahweh at the burning but unconsumed bush on Mount Sinai; Jacob wrestling through a memorable night with the Angel of the Lord; the Holy Spirit speaking from on high as Jesus of Nazareth is baptized by John in the River Jordan. These are for us standard and traditional images of spontaneous and unscripted initiations into the spiritual. Whether this introduction into the spiritual extends beyond a single moment and results in a radical transformation of identity and vocational direction – that is, in a generalized Gnosis that gives an individual's life a whole new sense of ultimate meaning and purpose – depends on the subject's further conscious engagement with the transcendent Other, the Speaker of one's name. In the case of the modern poet, one does not know how far this revelatory moment will take him, since the poem concludes with the initiatory experience itself. The biblical figures do show dramatic change. Jacob is renamed Israel by the mysterious opponent of the night,[2] clearly a stand-in for Yahweh; the timid Moses accepts his divine commission and becomes the bold leader of the Hebrew people; Jesus is divinized and enters his ministry thereafter with a mission based on identity with the Father. Such transformational engagement with the irrational process that begins and flows from this initiatory moment is surprisingly identical with the psychological process that Jung named individuation.

Initiations introduce and induce people into a new stage of life or level of consciousness, and they answer specific questions that are related to a person's identity. An initiation sponsored by and dedicated to the social world – such as a baptism, a bar mitzvah, or a wedding ceremony – answers questions about who one is with respect to one's community and what one's social location is at the present stage of life. It offers what Jung called a persona, the equivalent of what Erik Erikson (1950) named a psychosocial identity. A social identity serves as well to alleviate social anxiety by granting a defined status with respect to other people. The question that is addressed and answered by an initiation into the spiritual, on the other hand, is quite different. It tells of *why one was born*. The questions answered here are not "Who am I?" or "What is my name?" or "Where do I stand in relation to other people?" They are rather: "What is the meaning of my name from the perspective of eternity?" "What is my immortal destiny?" The answers to these questions come from the vertex (a term much used, as I observed, and with fond reference to Wilfred Bion, by Michael Fordham) of transcendence. The social vertex is horizontal; the spiritual vertex is vertical and cuts through linear time at every (or any) moment. Initiation into the spiritual happens in the event that Chronos (linear time) meets eternity and produces what Paul Tillich (1963), following the Greek tradition, named *Kairos* (an opening in time that is pregnant with potential meaning). The result of receiving an initiation in the spiritual vertex is "Gnosis," a type of knowledge that both intimates why one was born into this life, as regarded from the perspective of the archetypal, and offers a transcendent identity to match this knowledge. In this initiation, one's name is both called and changed in significance. Such Gnosis directs one to a sense of identity and meaning that is grounded in the archetypal, in eternity. This is not rational knowledge. It is noetic (from the Greek *nous*), by which I mean that it is derived from what Aristotle called "something within . . . that is divine" and that therefore partakes of eternity.[3] This is the perspective, or vertex, of the Self (in Jung's terminology), not of the ego. Initiation into the spiritual unites the time-bound and the timeless, the ego and the Self, and by this conjunction may serve to put existential anxiety to rest.

The question is: does this make sense in a modern cultural context? Throughout the recent period in western cultural history that goes by the name of modernity, people have speculated that humans were possibly growing beyond the need for the spiritual, and most certainly beyond their childish dependence on traditional religion. As the scientific worldview takes hold more firmly in culture at large, it has been thought, the importance of religious faith will fade and then disappear altogether along with all other superstitious beliefs that claim to explain the nature and purpose of the universe. Science will eventually explain concretely and materially what religions have sought to account for with their mythologies and theologies. What Aristotle referred to as "something within . . . that is divine" will be discovered in a set of neurons that can be measured and photographed. Scientific logic will ease myth out of the picture altogether.

Following upon the provocative line of thought put forward by Francis Fukuyama (1992) in *The End of History and the Last Man*, the German Jungian analyst, Wolfgang Giegerich (2004) has applied to psychology a similar version of the Hegelian dialectic at work in cultural evolution in his article, "The End of Meaning and the Birth of Man." Modernity spells the end of meaning, according to Giegerich. He claims that modernity has created an irreversible type or level of consciousness that no longer depends on or needs collective or personal myth. This new consciousness does not orient itself toward or by transcendent Being, but only by practical or instrumental notions derived from its own internal logic. In keeping with this historical development, psychology and the other social sciences have by now effectively interpreted and rationally understood all myth and theology, and thus they have emptied them of their symbolic value. They have "sublimated" them (i.e., transformed and replaced their contents with conscious knowledge). The Age of Meaning, in the sense that meaning traditionally grew out of myth and assumed a transcendent location from which human meaning was derived, is therefore now permanently and irrevocably behind us; logically driven, the Age of Man has now arrived. Naturally nostalgia for the good old days when meaning meant something remains, and one can find vestiges of this in even the most dedicated modern men and women from time to time, in a lapsed moment of emotional back-sliding or in efforts to resurrect such meaning through mythopoetic interpretation. Jung building his tower in Bollingen and retreating there to meditate on the immortal images of the collective unconscious is an example of this, in Giegerich's view. As a further consequence, because there is no longer a genuine need for myth or transcendent meaning, there is now also no legitimate cultural space for spiritual initiations. Initiation into the spiritual is nowadays anachronistic, even though it continues to take place in some culturally regressive ways. For those who have advanced to the state of modern consciousness, it is a mere relic of outmoded, pre-modern attitudes, or worse still, a lie, a fake, play-acting.

This is a powerful and sobering argument. Does this mean, then, that the archetypal psyche has also been sublimated into reason and that one is left only with the historical memory of what has been but is no more? This would seem to be Giegerich's point. Free of myth, the modern person is free to enjoy and play with the stories and images of antiquity, as told in what were once considered sacred texts. We are left with memory. I think it is also the point that produced Jung's personal crisis in 1913, which he surmounted by going modernity one better. I hope this will become evident in what follows. Not only Jung but also sociologists like Peter Berger and theologians like Harvey Cox have registered that in modernity both the question of transcendent meaning and various offers to answer it continue to appear, but these come from surprising sources (like the "secular city"), not from the traditional religions and symbol systems. These modern and postmodern sources do not announce themselves explicitly as symbolic. The archetypal returns, therefore, in new and hard to decipher symbols. Jung (1959) speculated, for instance, that the appearance of flying saucers in modern times was the signal of a new myth in the making and therefore as well of an emergent and modern expression of transcendence, albeit presented on a concrete material level.

Initiation into the spiritual continues, moreover, in earnest at the psychological level despite the inhibitions imposed by modernity. The difference is that this is not equated with the supernatural. It is taken up by the modern person and interpreted to mean something about psychological development, individuation, and a movement toward greater consciousness. In this shift, the supernatural has been sublimated by modern thought into the psychological. Gnosis becomes a psychological state of inner conviction and insight without depending upon the supernatural to offer warrants of authenticity.

The spontaneous arrival of Gnosis is not taken to be absolute knowledge about the nature of reality; it is self knowledge, a sense of conviction, a new identity. Nor is it necessarily coincident with an obvious state of need or discomfort that calls out desperately for an answer to the question of life's ultimate meaning. Without conscious need or provocation, the psyche may offer Gnosis spontaneously. In this instance, it answers a question that as psychological moderns we suspect may well have a place in the psyche but remains unconscious. Giegerich's account of modern persons may be correct when he claims that they do not experience the need to ask the meaning question, and whatever existential angst they might register in consciousness at the realization of being without a myth of meaning is easily and quickly dispelled by a dose of entertainment or pills. Even so, they may be taken by surprise and experience transcendence, as in Mark Strand's poem, receiving thereby a spontaneous initiation into the spiritual. *Vocatus atque non vocatus deus aderit* ("Invoked or not invoked, God will be present"),[4] as the Delphic oracle announced to the Lacedaemonians who were about to go to war against Athens. This motto, still relevant, should not be taken as a signal of pre-modern superstition or kow-towing to a supernatural presence. It means quite plainly that one is never out of reach of intervention by unconscious archetypal forces, for good or ill.[5]

One of the chief discoveries of depth psychology – itself a product of modernity[6] – was that there are archetypal processes (as well as archetypal images and ideas) in play in the psyche that manifest whenever and wherever they will, spontaneously, unwilled, and unsolicited by the ego. Jung (1938/1954: par. 153) writes with cautious scientific modesty:

> If I have any share in these discoveries, it consists in my having shown that archetypes are not disseminated only by tradition, language, and migration, but that they can rearise spontaneously, at any time, at any place, and without any outside influence.

In fact, he demonstrated at length and in detail the archetypal process that leads to "spiritual development" (Jung 1944: v) in the modern person. This he named the individuation process. In extensive commentaries on the dreams and visions of several notable people in analysis with himself and others,[7] he lays this development out in graphic detail, step by step. These case histories, moreover, contain numerous initiations into the territory covered by the term "spiritual," though without reference to anything supernatural. The point here is that these people were "modern" by any standard, and yet they received psychological Gnosis in great depth and abundance. In Jung's view, the "reality of the psyche" does not become subsumed under or sublimated by the attitudes and postures of collective consciousness, be they modern or otherwise conditioned. It remains free to offer its astonishing revelations even within this cultural context. For the people whose individuation processes were discussed by Jung, analysis provided the occasion for an initiation into the spiritual and became the setting in which they extended and deepened this initiation into a full spiritual development.

Whether interpreted psychologically or metaphysically, the process that unfolds in the individuation opus shows a progression of levels or stages, not necessarily linear but rather increasingly sharp and definite. The surprising and spontaneous initiation into a further stage of Gnosis and into an identity that matches it came to a "modern woman" who awoke one morning and found herself in possession of the following memory of a dream:

> I am walking along a long covered walkway that is very "architectural" with high ceilings, tall pillars on my left, and unmarked doors in the wall to my right. It is a monumental space and made entirely of gray stone. There is no one else in sight. The doors are shut and show no indication of what lies beyond. I am looking for the psychology Institute. This space has an otherworldly feeling to it.
>
> I see an open door and walk into a room. People of many nationalities are inside. Some are Chinese. A man dressed in white, who looks like someone I know, says in a matter-of-fact voice: "You are here to find out why you were born." He points to a bed that I am to lie down on and places a clear gel over the surface. I lie down on it and am covered with a blanket. He turns my head slightly to the right and a fluid flows out of my ear. I ask about this, and he says it is the cause of my arthritis.
>
> Later we go into a second room, and I sit in a chair.
>
> Later still, I am standing in yet another room and people, all of them dressed in white, form a line and stand before me, one by one. I am to look deeply into their eyes and determine where their consciousness lies and who they think they are, then to look deeper and deeper until I see their soul. My job is to connect people to their soul. There is only a brief eye contact, and then they go on. The job is done like this. Now I understand why I have been born – it has to do this work of connecting people to their soul.

Of this dream, which (as dreams typically do) simply arrived unsought and unasked for, one can observe that it follows the classic form of initiations.[8] There is first a sense of being removed from ordinary social life and entering into a *temenos*: the monumental architecture implies such a sacred and protected space. This sets the stage for a transformational ritual, including a healing ceremony,[9] followed by an extension of liminality while the subject sits and waits in an intermediate room. This middle stage is followed by a return to society with a new identity and consciousness of mission. At the time of the dream, this woman was living in retirement after a long career as a psychotherapist. It is therefore clear that this dream does not represent an initiation into a social/professional identity, a persona, but rather into the spiritual, which speaks about the deeper meaning of her life's work, a vocation that is not tied to a specific job or profession. At the time of the dream, she was not asking for meaning; meaning simply arrived. As a modern person, she has no affiliation with organized religion, does not believe in Creedal statements about the Divine or the supernatural, and was not in any sort of existential crisis requiring an "answer" of ultimate meaning. Existential anxiety, if such there was, in this case was entirely unconscious to her. She could have said she was done with meaning, but evidently, pace Giegerich, meaning was not done with her.

Initiation into the spiritual typically announces itself in the psyche of modern people spontaneously and without conscious request or intentional preparation for it. It comes because it has to happen, and it appears in a psychological form. Sometimes it is so shocking and anxiety provoking that it leads to a request for psychotherapeutic treatment. The all too familiar and by now cliché ridden midlife crisis in modern societies, which can and often does initiate a person into a period of profound psychological transformation, is an example.[10] This can nevertheless offer the opportunity for an initiation into the spiritual if taken up as such. One needs to recognize that this initiation into the spiritual is based on archetypal processes and runs from archetypal energies beyond the grasp of ego consciousness, and therefore it does not require social intent or engineering. It need not be explicit and public. In modernity, in fact, it is typically unofficial, undesired, and seemingly pathological. It often comes in the guise of private suffering, such as unaccountable or stubborn depressions, and the process following is played out in the analyst's office. Joseph Henderson (2005) documents several instances of this in his classic study, *Thresholds of Initiation*.

One should distinguish therefore between two types of initiation: the deliberate and the spontaneous. The deliberate type is undertaken intentionally and is organized along traditional lines by a recognized social or religious institution, and it shows an explicit purpose to transform identity and consciousness in a specific way. Examples of this type of initiation are found in the literature of anthropologists (Arnold van Gennep's (1960) *The Rites of Passage* being a familiar text of such a type, depicting adolescent initiation among the Australian aborigines) and in the history of religions (the works of Mircea Eliade are replete with such). Jung was fond of Franz Cumont's extensive studies of Mithraism, which describe a religion of the early centuries of the common era that seems to have worked with seven degrees of initiation: "The mystic (*sacratus*) successively assumed the names of Raven (*corax*), Occult (*cryphius*), Soldier (*miles*), Lion (*leo*), Persian (*Perses*), Runner of the Sun (*heliodromus*), and Father (*pater*)" (Cumont 1903/1956: 152). These grades were achieved through ritual initiations that may have involved ordeals severe enough to threaten the life of the initiant and perhaps involved, at the beginning and primitively, instances of human sacrifice carried out in the caves where the earliest initiations, carried out by the pirates of Cilicia

according to Plutarch (see Ulansey 1989: 40), were conducted. These initiation rituals were presided over by a special group of members who func-
tioned as priests and ritual elders, themselves most likely drawn from the
highest rank of initiates, the "Fathers." Cumont surmised that the animal
figures, like Raven and Lion, could be traced back to prehistoric times when
divinities appeared, or were represented, as animals (theriomorphic forms of
the Gods), and so by identifying with these animal images the Mithraists
took on the identity of the Gods. They thus became "deified" through the
initiation rituals. Masks would have been worn to strengthen this conviction
and identity. Through this deification process, the human individual was elevated, stage-by-stage, to a spiritual level of identity with a Deity. The human
and the divine become somehow intermingled in this type of religious initiation. In alchemy an operation with similar outcome was called *solificatio*, a
term much commented upon by Jung.

Jung's own initiation into the spiritual, while bearing a distinct relation to
the Mithraic mysteries,[11] was spontaneous, however, and it is instructive. As a
modern man, Jung did not seek out an explicit initiation into the spiritual.
While officially a Swiss Protestant and baptized and confirmed as such, this
affiliation held only cultural (i.e., persona-limited) significance for him. A
medical doctor trained in psychiatry and an early Freudian psychoanalyst, he
was a student of religious experience and sought to interpret and explain it
through the use of psychological and psychoanalytical concepts. He did not
join a religious cult, nor did he seek to found one. As a person holding
thoroughly modern attitudes and identified closely with his scientific career
as a psychological researcher, he did not believe in the teachings or the theo-
logical assertions of his own or any other religious tradition. He was not a
man of faith, clearly. He wanted instead, as he said many times, to know and
understand.

Jung confesses that at one point in his life, however, while in his late thirties
and just after finishing a massive study (titled *Symbole und Wandlungen der
Libido*) on the mythological background of the psychological images found
in the case of a young American woman, Miss Frank Miller, he felt acutely
and painfully the absence of myth in his personal life.[12] What does this mean?
Is it a lapse from the modern to a pre-modern sensibility? I would suggest
that it is simply human and can occur to anyone in any historical or cultural
context. This came, however, at a complex moment in Jung's young life, and a
critical one. He was just at midlife (thirty-seven years old), and a crisis was
brewing.

In *Symbole* (rendered into a rather questionable English translation by
Beatrice Hinkle as *Psychology of the Unconscious*), Jung had employed a
multitude of religious and mythological resources, including the use of
Cumont's books on Mithraism,[13] to interpret Miss Miller's fantasies and
visions. While working at a feverish pitch, Jung also realized with increasing
clarity that he was in the midst of a radical departure from the views and

teachings of his friend and mentor at the time, Sigmund Freud. With the publication of this work and Freud's dismissive misreading of it,[14] the tension between the two men rose to a climax, and they broke off relations in bitter acrimony. This took place in December 1912 and coincided with Jung's own questioning of himself about his personal myth and his entry into an extended midlife crisis. The conclusion of his work on *Symbole* and the decisive break with Freud as 1912 turned into 1913 catapulted Jung into a period of introspection and emotional upheaval, with dire threats, as he says, to his mental health and sanity. Reaching this extremity set the stage for his initiation into the spiritual. Powerful symbolic dreams ensued as well as a breakthrough into what he would later speak of as the practice of active imagination.

The key moment of his initiation into the spiritual occurred, in my opinion, through an active imagination carried out in December 1913. This is by no means to say that Jung did not have many significant experiences of the numinous before this, including some in his childhood,[15] but the process launched by this dramatic vision in 1913 resulted in a permanent and lifelong change in Jung's spiritual understanding and affected fundamentally, I believe, his sense of identity. It led directly into a transformational process, which created his mature consciousness of mission and meaning. It was nothing less than a dramatic initiation into the spiritual.

Jung calls this visionary experience a deification mystery.[16] It occurred in his second session of active imagination. The first session, which took place the day before, set the stage. In the initial one, he came upon a strange couple in a cave and was surprised when they named themselves Salome and Elijah. A black snake accompanied them. Salome was young and beautiful, but blind; Elijah was an old man, a wisdom figure. Elijah began teaching him about the objectivity of the psyche. In the second and, I think the critical, session, Jung decided to return to visit these figures again and learn more about them. Here he found himself in a different landscape – "the bottom of the world":

> Then a most disagreeable thing happened. Salome became very interested in me, and she assumed that I could cure her blindness. She began to worship me. I said, "Why do you worship me?" She replied, "You are Christ." In spite of my objections she maintained this. I said, "This is madness," and became filled with skeptical resistance. Then I saw the snake approach me. She came close and began to encircle me and press me in her coils. The coils reached up to my heart. I realized as I struggled, that I had assumed the attitude of the Crucifixion. In the agony and the struggle, I sweated so profusely that the water flowed down on all sides of me. Then Salome rose, and she could see. While the snake was pressing me, I felt that my face had taken on the face of an animal of prey, a lion or a tiger.

> (McGuire 1989: 96)

This imaged transformation was decisive. It was a deification mystery,[17] in which Jung, the Swiss psychiatrist and father of five children with a big house on the lake and a multitude of social and professional responsibilities that came with this persona and social position, was changed beyond recognition. In the image, he assumed the form and identity of Aion, an immortal being who ruled over time by holding control over the precession of the equinoxes.[18] Jung was familiar with this image of deity from his recent studies in Mithraism. Cumont's books contain several graphic pictures of precisely this image.[19] In his seminar account of this active imagination, Jung interprets it as follows: "In this deification mystery you make yourself into the vessel, and are a vessel of creation in which the opposites reconcile. The more these images are realized, the more you will be gripped by them" (McGuire 1989: 99). For him, this was clearly an initiation into an irrational process that would carry him ever more deeply into experiences of the archetypal psyche, a domain of experience where time and eternity phenomenologically are joined.

One of the prime dilemmas for the modern person who spontaneously undergoes initiatory experiences of this sort is their aura of weirdness. This is not exactly what one runs into at the shopping mall or in an airport. Since they are not contained and administered by a living tradition that oversees the initiation rites into these states of consciousness, these experiences appear bizarre and threatening. Without a traditional context overseen by ritual elders, Jung notes, one "is assailed by the fear that perhaps this is madness. This is how madness begins" (McGuire 1989: 97). Jung was a practicing psychiatrist with extensive exposure to people with severe mental disorders, and so he registered significant doubt and anxiety about what was happening to him: "You can be gripped by these ideas so that you really go mad, or nearly so. These images have so much reality that they recommend themselves, and such extraordinary meaning that one is caught." Immediately he also adds: "Awe surrounds the mysteries, particularly the mystery of deification. This was one of the most important of the mysteries; it gave the immortal value to the individual – it gave the certainty of immortality." But then following that testimonial, again we hear the caution of the clinical psychiatrist:

> Anybody could be caught by these things and lost in them – some throw the experience away saying it is all nonsense, and thereby losing their best value, for these are the creative images. Another may identify himself with the images and become a crank or a fool.
>
> (McGuire 1989: 99)

This accurately describes the modern person's anxiety about spiritual experience: it may be tantamount, or initiatory, to madness! And so it was for Jung, himself a modern man to the core. And yet he tipped in favor of letting the experience speak to him and, more courageously still, sharing it with the public in his seminar.

In a spontaneous address given some fourteen years later at the Eranos Tagung of 1939, and afterwards written up under the title "Concerning Rebirth," Jung (1968) once more took up the theme of initiation into the spiritual by interpreting Sutra 18 from the Koran ("The Cave"). This was a text he had used in conjunction with the Mithraic materials already some twenty-seven years earlier in *Wandlungen*. The Sutra opens with a reference to "the sleepers," a group of seven men who entered a cave and remained there for several hundred years, losing track of time (i.e., entering into a state of timelessness) and becoming thereby "immortals." About this Jung comments as follows:

> Anyone who gets into that cave, that is to say into the cave which every-one has in himself, or into the darkness that lies behind consciousness, will find himself involved in an – at first – unconscious process of trans-formation. By penetrating into the unconscious he makes a connection with his unconscious contents. This may result in a momentous change of personality in the positive or negative sense. The transformation is often interpreted as a prolongation of the natural span of life or as an earnest of immortality.
>
> (Jung 1968: par. 241)

This is resonant with Jung's experience following his first active imagina-tion, also an experience of entering a cave and finding himself among the "Immortals," Elijah and Salome.[20] Subsequent to the image of the sleepers in the cave, the Sutra presents the account of Moses' encounter and journey with an angel of God (recognized as Khidr, "the Verdant One," in Islamic mystical tradition), a figure who Jung says "symbolizes not only the higher wisdom but also a way of acting which is in accord with this wisdom and transcends reason" (Jung 1968: par. 247). This sequence of events is in line with Jung's own inner process following the dramatic initiation into the spir-itual that came about during his first active imaginations. Thereafter he began a long conversation (call it a symbolic journey) with the figure found in the cave, Elijah, who transformed later into the figure Philemon and eventually into yet another form named Ka.[21] That lasted for decades, and in the course of this encounter he discovered and explored the domain that he would refer to as the reality of the objective psyche. The Elijah-Philemon-Ka figure (Jung's Khidr) taught him, he says, psychic objectivity, and the process of active imagination introduced him to "the matrix of the mythopoetic imagination which has vanished from our rational age" (Jung 1989: 183 and 188).

In summary, it was ironically enough the transformation process that Jung studied with a skeptical analytic attitude and wrote about in *Wandlungen* that laid the foundations for his own experience of spontaneous initiation into the spiritual. In *Wandlungen*, he predicted that Frank Miller was about to undergo a schizophrenic crisis. His own crisis, which was triggered by the completion of his book and his break with Freud, picked up similar disquieting themes but resulted in a totally different, and ultimately meaningful, kind of initiation. This was due to his accepting the risk of allowing a frightening spontaneous initiation experience happen to him. Writing in German, of course, he advocated *"geschehen lassen,"* ("letting it happen") as the key to entering into this process. This is a telling instance within the context of modernity with its characteristic scientific, secular consciousness, where intellectual study and interpretation of traditional sacred texts at a specific and *kairic* moment in a person's life lead to an individual and spontaneous initiation into the spiritual, which in turn transformed identity and consciousness going forward entirely and irrevocably just as traditional initiations are meant to do. One should not conclude that the study of these texts caused the initiatory moment; rather, it provided some of the images and structures used by the autonomous unconscious to carry out its archetypal process of initiation into the spiritual.

Another example of a spontaneous initiation into the spiritual on the part of a "modern man," which also occurred during a period of intensive study of traditional texts and following the rupture of an important mentor relationship, can be adduced in the case of the Jewish philosopher Martin Buber.[22] The relevant period in Buber's life fell between 1903, when he retired from public life for a period of deep incubation and study after making a decisive break with the then leader of the Zionist movement, Theodor Herzl, and 1909, the year of his re-emergence when he came forward "with a stature and dignity that made men only ten years his junior look up to him as a leader and a sage" (Friedman 1991: 55). Buber was 25 years old in 1903 when he "retired," and he was 31 when he re-emerged and lectured in Vienna with such persuasive charisma on the topic, "Judaism and Mankind." What filled and occupied these six years was, importantly, an immersion in Hasidic texts, which culminated in the publication of a book that brought him his first fame as a writer, *Die Legende des Baalshem*, a retelling of Hasidic tales in contemporary language and style. Buber's authoritative biographer, Maurice Friedman, declares: "Buber's encounter with Hasidism can be described only as a breakthrough or a conversion" (Friedman 1991: 39). From this period of study and reflection, Buber's inner life and sense of identity was most significantly affected, however, by the discovery of meaning of the spiritual leader and guiding figure in Hasidic religiosity, the *zaddik*. For Buber, the *zaddik* became a living symbol and one that anchored his identity and provided the essential direction for his vocation as a teacher and writer.

Similar to Jung's break with Freud had been Buber's break with Herzl. Herzl was a charismatic father figure for the young Martin Buber, who until meeting him and being drawn into the inner circle of Zionists around him had been a typical, albeit gifted and promising university student of European philosophy. His early heroes were Kant and Nietzsche. As a student, Buber was blessed with a sharp intellect and a rare gift for languages, as well as a rhetorical flair that astonished many who heard him speak. Reading Herzl on Zionism and then meeting him, however, had the decisive effect of pulling Buber back toward his roots in Jewish culture. These had been firmly established through his close relationship to his paternal grandfather, the extraordinary Solomon Buber, who was a leading citizen and businessman in Lvov, Ukraine, and a great Talmudic scholar and the authoritative editor of the critical editions of the Midrash (Friedman 1991: 8ff.). Solomon also introduced his young grandson to the Hasidim of Belz and Zans, nearby villages that they would visit from time to time in order to observe this remarkable form of ardent Jewish religiosity. His later years of intensive philosophical study, and the cosmopolitan university life in Vienna and Leipzig, served to separate Martin from this traditional background, so that by the time he came into contact with Zionism and Herzl, its charismatic leader, he had gained considerable distance from religious Judaism. Zionism offered Buber a modern path back to his roots in Judaism. It also provided a brilliant opportunity for him to stretch his wings as a thinker and speaker, finding in this movement "a channel into which he could concentrate his energies, like his grandfather, and give himself to fruitful and unremitting work" (Friedman 1991: 25).

Buber soon began writing about Zionism as an aspect of a broader "Jewish Renaissance" that would free European Jewry from the fetters of "*ghetto* psychology" and unleash its latent potential for creativity. In time this became a carefully conceived program within the Zionist movement, and Buber took the lead in pressing a cultural and spiritual agenda forward in Zionist circles, publications, and conferences. Herzl's vision for Zionism, however, was radically and purely political and had nothing whatever to do with the values that were now central to Buber's vision. For Buber, Zion was a symbol; for Herzl, it was geography. The young Buber was a brilliant philosopher and religious thinker; the elder Herzl was an equally brilliant politician. Both were gifted orators and presented a charismatic figure on stage. On the difference between their versions of Zionism, however, hung their increasingly confrontational dispute. This began in 1901 and lasted until their decisive break in 1903, when Herzl accused Buber of having left the movement and suggested that he needed to find his way back. To this Buber took violent exception and refused to accept Herzl's judgment. The final parting of the ways, which took place during the Sixth Zionist Congress in 1903, was for Buber a trauma on the order of Jung's when he broke off relations with Freud. "The shattering that I experienced is perhaps the greatest of my life," he wrote to his wife, Paula (quoted by Friedman 1991: 35). To this Friedman adds, lifting Buber's own words from his autobiographical account, *Meetings*: "For the twenty-five-year-old Buber, this was one of the first times in which he set foot on the soil of tragedy, where all question of being in the right disappeared" (Friedman 1991: 35).

This shattering conclusion of his relationship with Herzl led shortly thereafter to Buber's withdrawal from public life, which lasted for six years. It was during this period that he discovered the texts of Hasidism and immersed himself in its stories and spirituality. In many ways this represented on one level a return to childhood. It brought him back to the Hebrew language, which he had studied with his grandfather, and to the images he remembered from their visits to the Hasidic communities around Lvov. Most importantly, he discovered a little book, *The Testament of Rabbi Israel Baal-Shem*, which introduced him to the figure Israel ben Eliezer, the great *zaddik* and founder of Hasidism. Buber writes of this discovery in a way that shows its profound impact:

> It was then that, overpowered in an instant, I experienced the Hasidic soul. The primally Jewish opened to me, flowering to newly conscious expression in the darkness of exile: man's being created in the image of God I grasped as deed, as becoming, as task. And this primally Jewish reality was a primal human reality, the content of human religiousness. . . . The image out of my childhood, the memory of the zaddik and his community, rose upward and illuminated me: I recognized the idea of the perfected man. At the same time I became aware of the summons to proclaim it to the world.
>
> (quoted by Friedman 1991: 39–40)

In his little book, *Meetings: Autobiographical Fragments*, Buber (2002) writes further of the *zaddik* as "the perfected man in whom the immortal finds its mortal fulfillment" (Buber 2002: 45). What he says in these passages about the *zaddik* corresponds with remarkable precision to Jung's description of the *anthropos*, the archetypal image of the completed human, the individuated personality. Buber's deep encounter with the sayings and stories by and about the Baal-Shem, and the struggles he (with the help of his literarily gifted wife, Paula) endured in order to transform the fragments of narrative into the book that brought him his first fame, *The Legend of the Baal-Shem*, led him to a fundamental realization about his own identity: "I bear in me the blood and the spirit of those who created it, and out of my blood and spirit it has become new" (quoted by Friedman 1991: 41). He wrote these words in the introduction to the first edition in 1907. Unlike Jung, Buber did not leave an account of his dreams and fantasies from this period, but from his words we can safely conclude that his meeting with the *zaddik* was a great deal more significant than a literary exercise. It was an encounter, and one that transformed his consciousness and gave him a new vision of his vocation. It constituted an initiation into the spiritual, which answered for him the question of his life's meaning and direction. He emerged from this initiation a new man with a new mission, grounded in an experience of the transcendent. The *zaddik* is an "Immortal," in the symbolic sense, which is how Buber grasped this reality.

Did Buber become identified with an archetypal image, the *zaddik*? No more than Jung became identified with Aion or with Philemon, the wisdom figure of his active imagination. For both of these modern men, the image of an "Immortal" and the experience of wholeness and meaning conferred by this intimate association remained an aspect of their identities, an available inner resource and guiding spirit, but at a clear distance from the ego. Buber writes of his relation to the image of the *zaddik* as follows:

> I who am truly no *zaddik*, no one assured in God, rather a man endangered before God, a man wrestling ever anew for God's light, ever anew engulfed in God's abysses, nonetheless, when asked a trivial question and replying with a trivial answer, then experienced from within for the first time the true *zaddik*, questioned about revelations and replying in revelations. I experienced him in the fundamental relation of his soul to the world: in his responsibility.
>
> (Buber 2002: 49)

At moments of encounter – or to use his later phrase, in I–Thou relationships – the *zaddik* would emerge in Buber and influence his consciousness, bending his identity in the direction of the teacher, the sage, the one who could speak "in revelations" and with full responsibility. This initiation into the spiritual, in which he met up with the symbol of the *zaddik*, became a resident fixture in Buber's consciousness, orienting him in his life's work and giving him a firm and abiding sense of meaning.

In summary, I should say that by using these two examples of famously modern men who experienced a spontaneous initiation into the spiritual, I do not intend to create the impression that this is limited to such exceptional individuals. On the contrary, I hope to convey the notion that this is a possibility for contemporary people, even if they are consciously modern and dedicated to science or post-Kantian philosophy and not left over benighted traditionalists. What a positive outcome of this initiation mainly depends on is an inner openness to the "call." This readiness to receive the transcendent Other creatively may well increase amidst painful experiences of rupture and loss of significant others – teachers, mentors, parents or parent figures – as we have seen in Jung and Buber. The crisis that ensues from such loss may open the way for the key transformation in a person's life, which sets the course for the years and decades to come.

Notes

1 See Kugel (2003) for a multitude of examples with extensive discussion of this phenomenon.
2 According to *The New Oxford Annotated Bible*: "Jacob's new name signified a new self: no longer was he the Supplanter but *Israel*, which probably means 'God

rules.' This name, which later designated the tribal confederacy, is interpreted to mean 'The one who strives with God' " (Metzger and Murphy 1991: 43).

3 Aristotle, *Nichomachean Ethics*, X.vii.8.

4 As is well known, Jung had this Delphic utterance, which he found quoted in a book by Erasmus (*Epitome*, 1563), carved in stone above the door of his home on the Seestrasse in Küsnacht. It has become a part of Jungian lore.

5 When asked in a BBC radio broadcast by Stephen Black what this motto above his door meant for him, Jung replied: "I wanted to express the fact that I always feel unsafe, as if I'm in the presence of superior possibilities" (Bennet 1962: 147).

6 See Homans (1995) for an incisive discussion of the relation between modernity and the rise of psychology, specifically psychoanalysis and analytical psychology.

7 I am referring specifically to Christiana Morgan, co-creator with Henry Murray of the Thematic Apperception Test (see Jung's psychological commentary on her active imagination published in Jung (1998) *Visions: Notes of the Seminar Given in 1930–1934*), Kristine Mann, an analyst and founding member of the Jung Institute in New York (see Jung's (1934) essay "A Study in the Process of Individuation") and Nobel Prize winner in physics, Wolfgang Pauli (see Part 2 of Jung's (1944) *Psychology and Alchemy*).

8 This was described and defined by Arnold van Gennep (1960) in his classic work, *The Rites of Passage*: the three stages of initiation involve rites of separation, transition, and incorporation or reintegration. They typically feature death and rebirth imagery.

9 I can add that the dreamer was in fact suffering from a mild form of arthritis in her hands at the time. Subsequent to the dream, the arthritis cleared up and disappeared.

10 I have discussed the midlife transition at length in two books: *In MidLife* (Stein 1983) and *Transformation: Emergence of the Self* (Stein 1998b).

11 See Noll (1999) for a rundown of these similarities. Noll, in this article, wants to make the point, however, that Jung was so deeply influenced by his studies of mystery religions, especially Mithraism, that his whole psychology was imbued with it to the point of constituting its major content. My view is that these early studies prepared the psychological ground for his initiation into the spiritual but were not causally related otherwise to this initiatory experience, and that their specific content – the *Leontocephalus* image, for instance – faded into the background as further experiences in active imagination unfolded. It was the process, not the specific content of the visionary experiences, which were important in Jung's spiritual development. In time, many traditions came together in his inner life, including importantly Taoism, Islam, the Upanishads, Buddhism, Christianity, Gnosticism, and alchemy. I think it is a mistake to privilege one of them – Mithraism – over the others. Jung's inner life was religiously eclectic, to say the least! His psychological theory, moreover, rests on a different level, which I have outlined in my book, *Jung's Map of the Soul* (Stein 1998a). There were many influences from numerous cultural sources on Jung and his theory-making (see, for instance, Stein 2005).

12 Jung gives a detailed report of this in *Memories, Dreams, Reflections* (Jung 1989: 171ff.).

13 The two works cited in *Symbole* are F.V.M. Cumont (1896–1899) *Textes et monuments figurés relatifs aux mystères de Mithra*, and Cumont (1903) *The Mysteries of Mithra*, trans. T.J. McCormack.

14 See Jung's letter to Freud of 3 December 1912, *The Freud/Jung Letters* (Freud and Jung 1974: 525), where he interprets Freud's underestimation of his work as a derivative of his anxiety neurosis, which on two occasions caused him to faint in Jung's presence.

15 Several of these are mentioned in the early chapters of Jung's (1989) *Memories, Dreams, Reflections*.
16 I am following here the account recorded in McGuire (1989) *Analytical Psychology: Notes of the Seminar Given in 1925*, pp. 95ff. This seminar, given in English, took place in the year of Jung's fiftieth birthday. A group of twenty-seven students of analytical psychology, mostly American and English, attended, and the notes from the seminar, privately taken, were later circulated in mimeographed form, though never checked and approved for publication by Jung. This same practice held true for the other seminars Jung gave, for which similarly mimeographed versions of his words were made available to students and later to the libraries of training institutes. Contrary to Richard Noll's (1999) sinister speculations, put forward in his "Jung the *Leontocephalus*" paper, about secretive cultic practices in Jungian circles with respect to the notes from these seminars, there was nothing especially hidden or secret about the mimeographed seminar notes. The fact was simply that sales were restricted because the notes had not been checked and approved by the author.
17 Jung's phrase. See McGuire (1989: 97ff.) for a detailed account of how Jung understood this.
18 See Ulansey (1989) for an extensive argument about the astrological features of Mithraism, about which Jung probably had some knowledge.
19 See, for instance, Cumont's (1903/1956) *The Mysteries of Mithra*, p. 105, where there is a picture of the Mithraic Kronos (Aeon or Zervan Akarana), about which Cumont says: "The statue here reproduced was found in the mithraeum of Ostia. . . . This leontocephalous figure is entirely nude, the body being entwined six times by a serpent, the head of which rests on the skull of the god."
20 Following Richard Noll's (1999) logic, this direct reference to the Koran in Jung's first active imagination would indicate that he became Islamic thereby!
21 The story of this extended dialogue is told in Jung (1989: Chapter 6), "Confrontation with the Unconscious".
22 Maurice Friedman has reconstructed Buber's life with great care and in meticulous detail in three volumes, *Martin Buber's Life and Work*, which he condensed masterfully in the single volume biography, *Encounter on the Narrow Ridge: A Life of Martin Buber* (1991). I am following Friedman's *Encounter* in this work.

References

Bennet, E.A. (1962) *C.G. Jung*, New York: E.A. Dutton.

Buber, Martin (2002) *Meetings: Autobiographical Fragments*, ed. Maurice Friedman, 3rd edition, London: Routledge.

Cumont, F.V.M. (1896–1899) *Textes et monuments figurés relatifs aux mystères de Mithra*, 2 volumes, Brussels.

Cumont, F.V.M. (1903) *The Mysteries of Mithra*, trans. T.J. McCormack, London: Kegan Paul, Trench, Trubner.

Cumont, F.V.M. (1903/1956) *The Mysteries of Mithra*, trans. T.J. McCormack, New York: Dover.

Erikson, Erik (1950) *Childhood and Society*, New York: W.W. Norton.

Freud, S. and Jung, C.G. (1974) *The Freud/Jung Letters*, ed. William McGuire, trans. Ralph Manheim and R.F.C. Hull, Princeton, NJ: Princeton University Press.

Friedman, Maurice (1991) *Encounter on the Narrow Ridge: A Life of Martin Buber*, New York: Paragon House.

Fukuyama, Francis (1992) *The End of History and the Last Man*, New York: Free Press.

Gennep, A. van (1960) *The Rites of Passage*, trans. M.B. Vizedom and G.L. Caffee, Chicago, IL: University of Chicago Press.

Giegerich, W. (2004) "The End of Meaning and the Birth of Man: An Essay about the State Reached in the History of Consciousness and an Analysis of C.G. Jung's Psychology Project," *Journal of Jungian Theory and Practice*, 6 (1): 1–65.

Henderson, Joseph L. (2005) *Thresholds of Initiation*, Wilmette, IL: Chiron.

Homans, P. (1995) *Jung in Context: Modernity and the Making of a Psychology*, 2nd edition, Chicago, IL: University of Chicago Press.

Jung, C.G. (1934/1950) "A Study in the Process of Individuation," *Collected Works*, vol. 9/i.

Jung, C.G. (1938/1954) "Psychological Aspects of the Mother Archetype," *Collected Works*, vol. 9/i.

Jung, C.G. (1944) *Psychology and Alchemy, Collected Works*, vol. 12.

Jung, C.G. (1959) "Flying Saucers: A Modern Myth of Things Seen in the Skies," *Collected Works*, vol. 10.

Jung, C.G. (1968) "Concerning Rebirth," *Collected Works*, vol. 9/i, 2nd edition, Princeton, NJ: Princeton University Press.

Jung, C.G. (1989) *Memories, Dreams, Reflections*, ed. Aniela Jaffé, trans. R Winston and C. Winston, New York: Vintage.

Jung, C.G. (1998) *Visions: Notes of the Seminar Given in 1930–1934*, ed. Claire Douglas, London: Routledge.

Kugel, J.L. (2003) *The God of Old: Inside the Lost World of the Bible*, New York: Free Press.

McGuire, William (ed.) (1989) *Analytical Psychology: Notes of the Seminar Given in 1925 by C.G. Jung*, Princeton, NJ: Princeton University Press.

Metzger, B. and Murphy, R. (eds) (1991) *The New Oxford Annotated Bible*, New York: Oxford University Press.

Noll, R. (1999) "Jung the *Leontocephalus*," in P. Bishop (ed.) *Jung in Contexts: A Reader*, London: Routledge.

Stein, M. (1983) *In MidLife: A Jungian Perspective*, Dallas, TX: Spring.

Stein, M. (1998a) *Jung's Map of the Soul*, Chicago, IL: Open Court.

Stein, M. (1998b) *Transformation: Emergence of the Self*, College Station, TX: A&M University Press.

Stein, M. (2005) "Some Reflections on the Influence of Chinese Thought on Jung and his Psychological Theory," *Journal of Analytical Psychology* 50 (2): 209–222.

Strand, Mark (2005) "My Name," *The New Yorker Magazine*, April 11.

Tillich, Paul (1963) *Systematic Theology*, vol. 3, *Life and the Spirit: History and the Kingdom of God*, Chicago, IL: University of Chicago Press.

Ulansey, D. (1989) *The Origins of the Mithraic Mysteries: Cosmology and Salvation in the Ancient World*, New York: Oxford University Press.

Chapter 6

The traditional Plains Indian vision quest

Initiation and individuation

Dyane N. Sherwood

I first read Joseph L. Henderson's book *Thresholds of Initiation* in 1971, while I was in a Freudian psychoanalysis and training setting. At that time, I felt at home when I read Jung, who wrote about inner life in a way I could immediately recognize from my own experience. However, as a professional-in-training, I valued rationally-framed developmental constructs and found security in a method which interpreted defenses, conflicts, and pathological transferences. At the same time, I felt that I was missing, or could not speak to, an essential aspect of my patients – just as my own analyst seemed to miss me and the meaning of my suffering when he made his transference interpretations of Oedipal conflicts. My dilemma was that I could not see how to bring Jung's more profound work into my clinical work.

During the year I spent in a clinical study group reading *Thresholds*, with its references to tribal forms of initiation and to clinical material with modern patients[1] I began to see how an archetype can manifest as both process and image. Knowing the territory seemed to affect what my patients brought into their work. I learned that symbols facilitate emergent processes that cannot be explained by developmental psychodynamic theories and began to get some glimpses into an entirely different meaning of the word "dynamic" as it is applied to the unconscious. Dr Henderson's psychological understanding of initiation, which he expanded into a model for male development, had added new dimensions, depth, and life to my way of being with patients.

Many years later, during a Jungian analysis and analytic training, I had the opportunity to study first-hand the vision quest as practiced by a hunter-gatherer culture with a tradition that has been unbroken for hundreds if not thousands of years, and here I take the opportunity to share my experience and observations of this profound cultural form of spiritual initiation.

The need for an initiatory experience can present itself at any time of life – if from within, as unbearable physical symptoms, visions, nightmares, or "big" dreams that do not seem to have a purely personal, everyday significance. Or the potential for initiation may be constellated by a close brush with death or the loss of a loved one. Death is always somewhere in the psychological field surrounding initiation. Initiation occurs at the crossroads of the personal, cultural, and the transpersonal. In order for an initiatory process to take place, some kind of "container" or ritual, as well as a human guide, are usually essential for the initiate to endure the ordeal, which may include feelings of dismemberment, disorientation, and altered states. This suffering must be borne as a choice of the larger personality, "something I need to face," despite the protestations of the ego. An unwillingness to submit to what the third century alchemist and Gnostic, Zosimos of Panopolis, called "an unendurable torment" (Jung 1938/1954: par. 86), is of course common and understandable: thus we too often resort to sleeping pills or tranquilizers, manic defenses of doing or aggression, or a passive identification as a victim. Initiation can be supported by an analytic relationship, as shown so beautifully by Joseph Henderson in 1967 and more recently by Mark Sullivan (1996), as well as by some of the other contributors to this volume.

Among the Plains Indians of North America, there is a form of spiritual initiation that occurs on an individual basis, which is known as the vision quest. When a person feels a need for guidance from the "spirit world," he or she approaches a spiritual elder to ask to be "put up on the hill." In families where there is a tradition of "medicine men," the vision quest is undertaken as a young person in order to find out if this will be the calling to be pursued as an adult.

I would like to describe the rituals connected with the vision quest, as practiced by the Oglala Sioux, or *Lakota* (as they call themselves), in some detail to show the importance of rituals of containment and spatial orientation, as well as the human guidance, care, and practical support provided by the spiritual elder and the initiate's supporters.

The Lakota way of life

The Lakota spiritual path is one of the few Native American traditions that have been preserved into modern times. The US Government banned Lakota sacred ceremonies, but the Lakota's fierce independence and the wild and desolate reservation to which they were confined allowed them to go out of view of the authorities and continue their tradition in secret. Nowadays, other Native American groups, who lost their own traditions and songs, have learned from the Lakota, and so I have heard a Cherokee medicine man sing in Lakota, and I have attended a sweat lodge near Mount Shasta in Northern California, where the songs were the same songs in the Lakota language that I had learned from the Lakota spiritual elder, Pansy Hawk Wing.

Before being nearly exterminated and moved onto hardly habitable reservations in the 1800s, the Lakota were true hunter-gatherers. These resourceful people had been driven west from Minnesota and Missouri in the 1700s by the Ojibwe (who pejoratively called them "Sioux"), from forest and meadows onto the Great Plains, where the necessities of life could be found only by traveling over a large territory each year. Their annual migration was guided by the stars, and they believed there was a correspondence between particular stars and particular places on the earth below. They were attuned to the wind, the calls of animals, the way plants grew and when they ripened. Moving through different habitats during different seasons, they gathered herbs, berries, wild turnips, roots, and red and white willow bark, and they hunted the buffalo. They observed animals, and for example saw that bears dug up a certain root (*osha*) when they were sick. In their world, everything had a spirit: the rocks, sky, earth, plants, animals, wind. They also had groups or cults depending upon what animal they dreamed about, for example, *mato ihanblapi*, meaning "they dream of bears" (Powers 1982: 96).

The Lakota attitude toward life and the natural world is perhaps best summed up in the phrase "*mitakuyé oyasin*," which can be translated, "All: My Relatives," or "We are all related."

Tatuye topa, the four directions

For the Lakota, orientation to the four directions, in the order of West, North, East, and South, plays a basic part in all of their ceremonies and rituals. This makes sense if you consider how sensitive people must be to direction when they are living a nomadic life. Colors and animals are associated with each direction. Among the Lakota, the colors are West: black, North: red, East: yellow, South: white. The animal associated with each direction varies among groups, although in many traditional songs the buffalo is in the West, elk in the North, deer in the East, and white eagle in the South.

In "Aion," Jung noted that,

> The quaternity is an organizing schema par excellence, something like the crossed threads in a telescope. It is a system of co-ordinates that is used almost instinctively for dividing up and arranging a chaotic multiplicity, as when we divide up the visible surface of the earth, the course of the year, or a collection of individuals into groups, the phases of the moon, the temperaments, elements, alchemical colours, and so on.
>
> (Jung 1951: par. 242)

For the Lakota, the four directions are more than a method of orientation to the outer world: the sacred Medicine Wheel (Figure 6.1, also in the color plate section) incorporates them into the simplest form of a *mandala*, a squared circle, creating a symbol which links the inner world (microcosm) and the outer world (macrocosm).[2] According to Jung's interpretation, *mandalas* suggest "a kind of central point within the psyche, *to which everything is related*, by which everything is arranged, and which is itself a source of energy" (Jung 1950: par. 634; italics added).

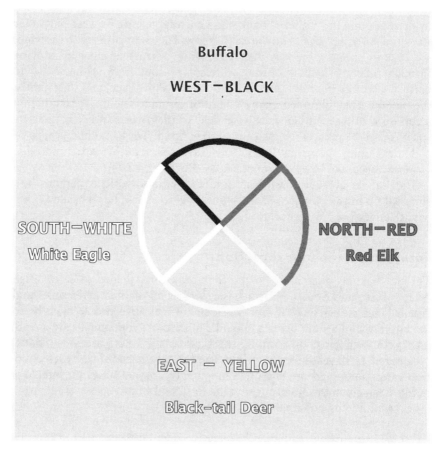

Figure 6.1 The Lakota medicine wheel, showing the four directions, their colors, and the animals associated with each direction, as taught by Pansy Hawk Wing. The animals associated with a direction vary among groups and holy people. Depending on their visions, the animals may change over the course of someone's life.

Dyane N. Sherwood, based on a figure by Pansy Hawk Wing. This figure is also in the color plate section.

Joseph Henderson has written about a dream of his own of four mountain ranges, with the symbol of a circle and an eagle's feather on the far side of each of them:

> The whole scene, with its symmetrical arrangement of the symbols, did not seem strange or in any way frightening. The image gave me the impression that the outer world of nature, the macrocosm, is not alien

but akin to our own unique inner vision. The symbol bridges the inner and the outer.

(Henderson 1990b: 156; also quoted in Henderson and Sherwood 2003: 92)

Four is a sacred number to the Lakota, and as one prays to the directions, one may feel something described beautifully by Lame Deer:

> *Four* is the number that is most *wakan*, most sacred. Four stands for *Tatuye Topa* – the four quarters of the earth. One of its chief symbols is *Umane*, which looks like this: [Figure 6.2]:

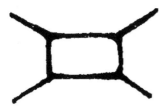

Figure 6.2 The Lakota symbol for *Umame*, the potential energy found in all things. Compare this to Jung's description of the *mandala* as symbolizing a source of energy, quoted in the text. Traditional symbol.

> It represents the unused earth force. By this I mean that the Great Spirit pours a great, unimaginable amount of force into all things – pebbles, ants, leaves, whirlwinds – whatever you will. Still there is so much force left over that's not used up, that is in his gift to bestow, that it has to be used wisely and in moderation if we are given some of it.
>
> This force is symbolized by the *Umane*.

(Lame Deer and Erdoes 1972/1999: 114)

To the four cardinal directions, the Lakota at times add the sky (blue, spotted Eagle) and earth (green, mole) as the fifth and sixth directions, so that one is oriented in three-dimensional space. This arrangement brings to mind the double pyramid with a shared square base, the *quaternio* of the alchemists (Jung 1951: par. 374).

The Lakota also have a seventh direction, symbolizing a person's spiritual center. Seven is the number associated across cultures and time with initiation (Henderson and Sherwood 2003: 46). According to Lame Deer, "Seven is a holy number too, representing the seven campfire circles of the Sioux Nation, the seven sacred rites, the seven bands of the Teton Sioux, but four is more *wakan*" (Lame Deer and Erdoes 1972/1999: 115). The seventh "direction," is paradoxically a point or mystical direction. The seventh direction is not located in the center of the medicine wheel and yet is felt to be in harmony with it.[3] I interpret this to suggest an awareness that one is part of everything but not merged with everything, a progression from the primal self toward a conscious relationship between what Henderson called "unique inner vision" and the wholeness within and without symbolized by the Medicine Wheel.

"Calling for a vision" (hanblechiya) according to three Lakota medicine men and one Lakota medicine woman

We really know very little about the visions of Lakota before Anglos began to make contact and record their accounts. There was no written language. The spiritual path was one of careful observation and experience, only partially oral, and its shamanic nature did not lend itself to recitation or text. There is also a strong feeling that one does not talk about sacred rituals except in a sacred setting. Therefore, many informants were reluctant to reveal what really went on. A few developed trusting relationships with Anglos and began to tell about the tradition, perhaps because they feared it would be lost altogether due to the disruptions of their way of life.

One of the most famous accounts of a Lakota "medicine" man, or *wakan wichasa*, is that of Black Elk (1863?–1950). He explained the vision quest as an inwardly motivated, individual process:

> There are many reasons for going to a lonely mountaintop. . . . Some young men receive a vision when they are very young and when they do not expect it, and then they go . . . that they might understand it better. . . . [P]erhaps the most important reason . . . is that it helps us to realize our oneness with all things, to know that all things are our relatives; and then in behalf of all things we pray [for] knowledge of [*Wakan Tanka*, the Great Mystery] that is the source of all things, yet greater than all things.
>
> (Black Elk 1988: 44)

Ptehe Woptuh^'a, or "[Buffalo] Horn Chips," (1836–1916) was the mentor of the famous warrior and healer, Crazy Horse. Horn Chips felt the call to go on his first vision quest on his way to commit suicide. On his vision quest, a snake came and gave him instructions, and he began a relationship with this snake, which guided him on his lifelong path as a healer and spiritual leader (Powers 1982).

John (Fire) Lame Deer (1903–1976) described his first vision quest at the age of 16 in unusual detail. The son and grandson of medicine men, he was put on the "hill" by his uncle, an old medicine man named Chest. It was the first time in his life he had been alone, and he was frightened as he entered, naked, into a pit in the earth, where he would spend four days without food or water. (The pit brings to mind both a grave and a womb.) Lame Deer wrapped himself in a beautiful star quilt made for him by his grandmother.

He kept it all his life, and as an old man said he wanted to be buried in it. Lame Deer also had a *canupa*, sacred pipe, which had belonged to his father and his grandfather, in which he smoked *canshasha*, tobacco made from red willow bark. His gourd rattle contained tiny fossil-stones, which were gathered by ants and placed in their mounds, as well as forty small pieces of flesh from his grandmother's arm, which she had offered in support of his vision quest. This kind of "flesh sacrifice" may seem barbaric, but in the way of the Lakota, it is one's flesh that is the greatest sacrifice as it cannot be bought or sold. In my observations, the attitude associated with this sacrifice has nothing to do with a pathological need for self-mutilation or with masochism – or it would not be *wakan*, sacred.

If we think of the archetypes, both the Great Mother and the Great Father were present in very real ways as Lame Deer lay alone in a pit on a mountain. He prayed to *Tunkashila*, Grandfather Sky and to *Unchi Maka*, Grandmother Earth. His loving human relatives were also present in primal and symbolic ways. Lame Deer had the warmth and tactile comfort of his grandmother's quilt next to his skin. His pipe's smooth, red stone bowl had been oiled by the hands of his father and grandfather, when they had used it to pray, holding its wooden stem up toward the heavens.

The fragrance of the willow bark (which is not inhaled) is soothing, and, after long association with its sacred function, brings one into a state associated with prayer. A gourd rattle, also used when calling to the spirit world for a vision, can be seen as symbolic of a womb, because of its shape, and with the potential for new life because of its many seeds. Lame Deer's rattle contained his grandmother's flesh offerings and the tiny, sacred fossil-stones, gathered by ants, a matriarchal society. A soothing scent, a soft quilt swaddling the skin-body, and a rattle, which allows one to create a sound not-from-oneself: all powerfully evocative of our most primal sensory and transitional (in Winnicott's (1951) sense) experiences as infants. In the vision quest, the experience of these sacred transitional objects supports the capacity to survive consciously our most primal human fear, one that is unbearable for a baby if not for most human beings: separation from all that feels safe and familiar, alone on a wild mountain without food and water – *without human contact*. Like a tiny infant, the initiate cannot move from the space in which he is placed but, unlike the infant, the separation has been chosen by the larger self. It is interesting, then, to note that the Lakota word for prayer, *wacekiye.*, means "to seek connection" (Lame Deer and Erdoes 1972/1994: xix).

As he lay in the dark in his pit, Lame Deer was full of anxiety and feared failure:

> What if I failed, if I had no vision? . . . [M]y Uncle Chest had told me. "If you are not given it, you won't lie about it, you won't pretend. That would kill you, or kill somebody close to you, somebody you love."
>
> (Lame Deer and Erdoes 1972/1994: 3–4)

He began to cry and could not stop. As he remained in the pit,

> Blackness was wrapped around me like a velvet cloth. It seemed to cut
> me off from the outside world, even from my own body. It made me listen
> to the voices within me. I thought of my forefathers who had crouched
> on this hill before me, because the medicine men in my family had chosen
> this spot for a place of meditation and vision-seeking ever since the day
> they had crossed the Missouri to hunt for buffalo in the White River
> country some two hundred years ago. I thought that I could sense their
> presence right through the earth I was leaning against. I could feel them
> entering my body, feel them stirring in my mind and heart.
>
> Sounds came to me through the darkness: the cries of the wind, the
> whisper of the trees, the voices of nature, animal sounds, the hooting of
> an owl. Suddenly I felt an overwhelming presence. Down there with me in
> my cramped hole was a big bird.
>
> (Lame Deer and Erdoes 1972/1994: 4)

Over the course of the vision quest, Lame Deer felt himself move up into the
sky, flying with the "winged ones," owls and eagles, and they "spoke" to him:

> We are a nation and you shall be our brother. You will never kill or harm
> any one of us. You are going to understand us whenever you come to
> seek a vision here on this hill. You will learn about herbs and roots and
> you will heal people. You will ask them for nothing in return. A man's life
> is short. Make yours a worthy one.
>
> (Lame Deer and Erdoes 1972/1994: 6)

Later Lame Deer saw a vision of his great-grandfather, chief of the Minne-
conjou, who had been shot in the chest by a soldier after making peace
with the US Cavalry. His grandfather's name was Lame Deer, and so the
young initiate understood that he was to take his grandfather's name. Thus
his new identity as a medicine man and future leader was signaled by the
change of his name. When Chest came to get him, at the end of four days,

> He told me that the vision pit had changed me in a way that I would not
> be able to understand at that time. He also told me I was no longer a boy,
> that I was a man now.
>
> (Lame Deer and Erdoes 1972/1994: 7)

Lame Deer's experience involved his whole being, much in the way we experience dreams, images, emotions, sounds, and body sensations that connect us
to inner experience. This is very different from visualizing a series of images
in a disembodied state, without suffering or soul-searching, that I have heard
touted as "visions" by individuals emulating Native Americans.

Pansy Hawk Wing is a contemporary Lakota spiritual leader, whose mentors were Dawson Has-No-Horses and Martin High Bear. She went on her first vision quest after a profound experience, where she saw that her life was at a fork in the road: one fork continued the destructive path of alcoholism and the other led to an unknown life. She felt terror and threw away a bottle of bourbon that she carried in her purse. She then went to Dawson Has-No-Horses and asked to be put on the hill. Her vision quest took place at Bear Butte in the Black Hills, which is one of the most sacred places to the Lakota. After making her preparations and undergoing a sweat lodge (*inipi*),

> We began the ascent of Bear Butte and were not to look back. We stopped four times on the climb and prayed at each stop to ask the spirit to relieve us of our bondage to material things: possessions, community, friends, immediate family, and other relatives ... I was afraid. At the summit they prepared my altar, and then I stepped inside while prayers were spoken and the sacred songs sung. Then the supporters left me in communication with the spirit world.
>
> (Hawk Wing 1997: 198)

Pansy describes an experience of heightened sensory awareness and fear. She drummed, rattled, and prayed throughout the night.

> Daylight came, and in front of me I saw there was a cedar tree that had no leaves but was rooted solidly into the ground. I began to realize that this was a symbol of my past. I was overcome with feeling and began to cry and give *wolpila* (thanks) for the lesson I learned.
>
> (Hawk Wing 1997: 198)

As she remained on the hill, she saw a strong man with long hair wearing a gray blanket, who came and danced in front of her: "This image later became my Internal Warrior, the one who steps forward during times of hardship and gives me courage to continue and to not give up." The image of an eagle (*wanbli*) also came to her, and she writes: "Later this represented my faith and trust that all things have a time and a place. This image of an eagle became my foundation" (Hawk Wing 1997: 198).

Henderson, who has written extensively about Native American culture and symbolism,[4] referred to the vision quest in a discussion of the "goal" of the alchemical *opus*. He quoted a passage from Erich Neumann:

> What in the primitive stage was realized as an unconscious bond, now returns on a higher level as the possibility of a symbolic realization of life's meaning when lived out to its fullest extent. ... Now neither the

extravert's outward vision of the world nor the introvert's inner vision remains in force but a third type of vision remains.

(Neumann 1948/1968: 408)

Henderson comments:

> This is true on an empirical level. The initiatory events seen in the normal psychological development of young people move from a primal source through experiences associated with the Great Mother, The Great Father, and the Group as the young person arrives at a first awareness of his or her own unique identity. This discovery may become manifest with the appearance of a Guardian Spirit, for example during what the American Indians call a "vision quest." . . . This introduces that third type of vision, of which Neumann speaks.
>
> (Henderson and Sherwood 2003: 149)

What is this third type of vision? Is it the experience of the Self in its largest, transpersonal sense? Perhaps Lame Deer encountered it as

> something within us that controls us, something like a second person almost. We call it *nagi*, what other people might call soul, spirit or essence. One can't see it, feel it or taste it, but that time on the hill – and only that once – I knew it was there inside of me. Then I felt the power surge through me like a flood. I cannot describe it, but it filled all of me. . . . Again I wept, this time with happiness.
>
> (Lame Deer and Erdoes 1972/1994: 6)

Learning through experience: a contemporary vision quest

The vision quest described in this section is based on my years of work with the Lakota Medicine Woman Pansy Hawk Wing (Figure 6.3). For a number of years Pansy took time off from her job as a counselor to Native American teenagers and flew to California to work with a group of women who met at my house.[5] We had many wonderful sweat lodges together, and we learned quickly that her way was not one of verbal instruction but rather of careful observation and making mistakes. We also noticed our tendency to make rules – someone would see Pansy do something and then tell someone else *that* was how you did it! This became very humorous, as the incidental or idiosyncratic was taken as essential while the essential was missed.

Pansy grew up on Pine Ridge, just between the Badlands (Figure 6.4) and Wounded Knee,[6] in a starkly beautiful place (Figure 6.5). Among the rocks and sand, in soil that is like a powder when dry and like gumbo when wet, there are the occasional yucca, soapweed, sagebrush, and cactus. Near the

Figure 6.3 Gathering Stones for a Sweat Lodge: Dyane N. Sherwood, Carol McRae, and Pansy Hawk Wing at Pescadero Beach, California, 1997.

Anonymous photographer.

far-too-few creeks, one finds western yellow pines, red cedars, junipers, cottonwoods, and willows. This place – eons ago it was at the bottom of an ocean – has an ancient, sacred feeling that seems to convey its connection to the origins of life itself. But its long service to life seems to have depleted it of all nourishment, like the dried-up body of a crone. This land cannot feed her human children: it is unsuited to farming or grazing, and winters are so extraordinarily cold that cattle freeze to death. During the intensely hot summers, wild grasses, sage, and some edible plants make a brief appearance. If one knows when and where to look, there are red plums, wild currants, coral berries, chokecherries, and wild roses. A special treat are the sweet turnips, *tinpsila*, which are delicious in a stew. But all these come and go quickly, and a great deal of land would be needed to support just a few people. Pansy's family can't afford a well, and long ago they abandoned the shack that sits on the land. They gather for the sacred rites, and then they leave for jobs off the reservation or return to a crowded, run-down apartment in the nearby housing project owned by the tribal government.

Figure 6.4A The Badlands of South Dakota: Rock formation.

Photograph by Dyane N. Sherwood.

Vision quest: preparation

For a number of years, my friend Carol McRae (also an analyst) and I spent our summer vacations on the Pine Ridge Reservation in South Dakota, the most impoverished place in the entire United States. We were honored to participate in the vision quest and Sun Dance on the sacred land belonging to Pansy's family, and we were moved at the generosity of the people we met on the reservation. The Lakota have a wonderful sense of humor, and when not in ceremony, we spent evenings around a campfire, where people told stories of their misadventures. This form of "teaching" is neither didactic nor shaming, and the children were "all ears."

A vision quest is not a common thing. It is undertaken under the guidance of a holy man or holy woman, sometimes translated into English as a medicine man or medicine woman. The person in need of a vision who approaches the holy person would most likely already be a "pipe-carrier," someone who has made a commitment to the spiritual path of living in harmony with all living things, following the "Red Road." This person would have used hand

Figure 6.4B The Badlands of South Dakota: Flowers blooming after a series of rains.

Photograph by Dyane N. Sherwood.

tools to make a pipe bowl out of red pipestone found in only one quarry in Minnesota. While the pipestone is soft, it is also very brittle, so this is a task requiring great patience and concentration. The pipe stem is carved from a hardwood, and the joining of the pipe and the stem, a sacred union of the opposites, is done only when the pipe is to be smoked, accompanied by special songs and ritual.

According to Lakota legend, White Buffalo Calf Woman brought the first pipe. She appeared as a beautiful maiden to two braves who were out hunting. One of them immediately thought of raping her, and he disappeared forever. The other treated her with great respect, and he was given the lesson of the pipe (Black Elk 1953: 3–9). According to Henderson:

> The theme of failure of initiation implies a tendency . . . to forget to honor . . . significant vestiges of the old feminine religion of the earth. . . . The Grail – like cauldrons, stones, [pipe bowls?] . . . – is a symbol for the ancient wisdom of the Earth Mother and her sibylline connection with the unknown powers. Where these are unknown to the initiate-as-questor, he is tempted to revert to the security of the hero myth and its

Figure 6.5 The Pine Ridge Reservation.

Photograph by Dyane N. Sherwood.

> consoling religion of the Father. Consequently the true initiate cannot remain a father's son only, any more than he remained a mother's son in the beginning.
>
> (Henderson 2005: 152)

The person who wants to undertake a vision quest brings the pipe to the holy person, signaling that the transaction is a spiritual one, not an ordinary conversation. He or she offers the pipe to the holy person, who refuses to accept it. This is repeated three more times: if the pipe is accepted the fourth time, then they will smoke it together and discuss the reason for the vision quest. While a vision quest can be made at almost any time, there are certain times of the year that are traditional, when a medicine man or woman might put a number of people up on the mountain.

Inner preparation is supported by the preparation of ritual objects used during the vision quest, such as offerings, tobacco ties, and the proper ceremonial clothing. This is done with special songs and prayers. A tobacco offering and prayer is made whenever something is taken from nature, such as sage or a tree branch.

While the specific instructions for preparations vary, generally the initiate makes strings of tobacco ties, which will eventually encircle the *hochoka*, the tiny plot of sacred space where she will remain during the vision quest. Tobacco ties are made by placing a pinch of tobacco in a small square of cotton fabric (traditionally buckskin) smudged with sage, one or two inches wide, and then rolling the fabric and doubling it over, finally tying a string midway so that it looks like a little ball containing tobacco with a skirt below. Pansy Hawk Wing instructed me to prepare strings of 101 tobacco ties in each of the colors for the six directions, black, red, white, yellow, green, blue. I made each of these 606 tobacco offerings while praying to the directions. Over the course of the 606, as instructed by Pansy, I reviewed my entire life up to that point. The ties eventually formed one long chain, which had to be saved in such a way that the string did not tangle when it was unrolled to create the *hochoka*. This attention to detail and containment within the *mandala* of the directions brought me into a sacred space.

The vision quest at Porcupine

As with all vision quests, those sponsored by Pansy at Porcupine on the Pine Ridge Reservation begin with purification in a sweat lodge or *inipi*, where the initiate receives further instruction and prayers of support, and specific songs are sung to the accompaniment of drums. From this time the initiate does not eat or drink; she is not touched, and she does not speak nor is spoken to, until undergoing another sweat lodge after the initiate comes down the hill. Once she begins her dignified walk up the hill, carrying her pipe and her staff, and wearing her humble ceremonial clothing (usually a calico dress and a shawl, without any jewelry), she does not look back. These aspects of the ritual have been likened to having died, and one can feel a tremendous sense of isolation from the moment of leaving the sweat lodge.

A vision quest is most often taken in a high place, to which the holy person leads the initiate and her supporters, who carry her ceremonial objects, as well as chokecherry branches and wild sage. When the place is chosen, the *hochoka* is created by the supporters. At each of its four corners, a chokecherry branch five to six feet tall is placed in the ground, and on it a prayer flag (in the color of that direction), and a tobacco offering is tied to the branch. Then the tobacco ties connected by string or sinew are tied to the branches and wound around the perimeter, delineating the space. If the thread becomes tangled, the supporters must untangle it. The area is covered with fresh sage. An altar is made to hold the pipe and other ceremonial objects, such as a medicine pouch, drum, and rattle. Two blankets, one old and one new to be given away, are also placed in the *hochoka*. A spirit-offering bowl containing berries or kidneys is placed outside the *hochoka*. When the supporters have completed these tasks, the initiate steps barefoot into the *hochoka* through the "door" created by making a moveable portion of the perimeter. She places her staff in the northwest quarter of the *hochoka*. At this time the holy person says prayers and may sing a song.

The initiate is left alone, and she faces each direction in order, beginning with the West – praying silently or with drumming and singing. The initiate prays not to a personified deity but to *Wakan Tanka*, the Great Mystery, *Tunkashila*, Grandfather Sky, and *Inchi Maka*, Grandmother Earth. One of the special songs for this occasion can be translated roughly as, "I stand in the Center of the Earth and pray. I call to the Sacred as I stand in the Center of the Earth."

At the end of the quest, which lasts from one to four days, the initiate walks with her staff to the camp, where her supporters have been doing sweat lodges and praying for her. Someone is always awake should she come down the hill during the night. Still, no one speaks to her or touches her. She waits in a dignified way while a sweat lodge is readied, and it is within the lodge that she recounts what has come to her on the quest. Songs are sung, and at an appropriate time, the medicine woman offers her some water to drink. The initiate recounts her vision, and the holy person may comment on it, with others also speaking but in a very conscious, ceremonial way.

From beginning to end, the vision quest is not about having a dissociative experience but about entering an altered state while remaining conscious with one's entire being. The extremes of weather in South Dakota insure that the person must be mindful about physical care. In addition, great self-discipline is required to remain awake at night to pray and to struggle with all the anxieties that present themselves when one is alone and vulnerable. While it is not difficult to go without food, going without water is another matter, especially in an unsheltered site in the long, scorching summer days of South Dakota (120° F on my first vision quest), which can be followed by cold, wet, and windy nights, and perhaps a thunderstorm which lights up the sky and swirls around, moving at remarkable speed across the plains. (I was very envious when I read about medicine men who were able to go into a pit!) It is humbling to realize how fragile a human life is and how much we depend on the elements, the earth, and other living things. We have so many technological supports built into our modern way of life that we may forget this.

The Lakota way and analytical psychology: the opposites, the shadow, initiation, and individuation

Over the years we have known each other, Pansy and I have had many conversations about some of the similarities between the Lakota way and Jungian psychology. For example, the Lakota tradition includes the opposites and the shadow. The pipe has both masculine and feminine parts, the stem and the bowl, and its parts are joined only within a special ritual of song and prayer, so that, we might say, the *coniunctio* is sacred. A pipe is not kept filled but rather filled only when it is intended to be smoked, so that there is a very respectful and conscious attitude toward its mystery. The smoking of the pipe sends prayers to the spirit world and has a purifying and healing effect on those who smoke it, leaving behind the scent of the roots and bark that are used to make the tobacco.

Among the Lakota, there are people who identify themselves as *heyoka* or "contrary." These people do just about everything backwards: they say the directions prayers turning toward the left rather than the right. In the Sun Dance, they may turn their backs to the tree while others face it; they pray to the sky when others pray to the earth, and so on. They wear black and white clothing, and they can be clowns. For example, on the third day of the Sun Dance, when the dancers are so dehydrated that they no longer sweat, a *heyoka* clown (sometimes a beautiful maiden to tempt the men's lust) comes into the Sun Dance with a big bucket of water and a ladle, splashing and tempting the dancers. Some of the great medicine men (including Black Elk) have been contraries, and Pansy says that every medicine person has a good dose of *heyoka*. A ceremony such as a sweat lodge may "spontaneously" become contrary if that is the energy that is needed for a kind of balance. This is sensed by the holy person who is running the lodge, who will sing *heyoka* songs or instruct people to do things in an opposite way. These lodges and songs can have great healing in them. One of my favorite songs, for example, is the spider healing song, the spider being a big trickster, *heyoka*, in the Lakota world.

Pansy has also told me that many medicine men have what Jungians might call a shadow personality, whom they call "Scottie." She does not know where this name came from, but Scottie is a greedy person who wants all the material things that can come from the Euro-American world. Scottie is tempted to leave the Red Road, the way of the Pipe, and get people to pay for doing ceremonies or have sex with all the young white women or men who have crushes (or we might say transferences) on Indian medicine men or women. The temptations are great, especially as life on the reservation is extremely difficult. Pansy says the men who have a (consciously-held) Scottie tend not to fall into those traps, while many others have. Pansy has a shadow personality named Gladys, who likes long, painted fingernails, fancy shopping malls, and just about anything shiny and glitzy. Gladys becomes quite humorous and adds a wonderful balance to the intensely spiritual life that Pansy leads.

For those who remain on a Lakota spiritual path, development continues throughout life. While people begin praying with the animals and colors generic to the tribe or the medicine person who is guiding them, over time the person may have the experience of an animal appearing in a certain direction. I mean this in terms of a felt experience, although it could be an actual animal if that is experienced in a synchronistic way. This signifies the need for a relationship to the nature of that animal, in a sense taking this animal as a teacher. The image of this animal may remain in the same direction for years, until that process has found a natural completion and a different animal appears. The colors of the six directions remain the same, but the seventh color may undergo a change at a point in the person's development when he or she is becoming more independent of the holy person and may be ready to lead sweat lodges or other ceremonies.

The Lakota way is shamanic in nature. As such, it is constantly changing and adapting, based on the visions of the people. Thus Black Elk had a vision of the horse dance (Neihardt, 1932/2004: 124–135) at a time after horses had been introduced to the Great Plains, and the medicine man to whom he told his vision felt it should be brought into the community and actually danced. In this environment, the initiatory process in the vision quest does not involve the subordination of an individual's spiritual or cultural life to a rigid doctrine or dogma. Rather, it is an initiation into a deeper relationship to the mystery of life, and I wonder if we might acknowledge that it is a path that supports a process that Jung called *individuation*.

Vision quests are undertaken throughout life by people who have the calling to be healers as well as others who have made a commitment to the way of the pipe. Here we see the importance of initiation for individuation, but only when that initiation is not regressive and dogmatic but based upon a shamanic model.[7]

In the final chapter of *Thresholds of Initiation*, Henderson posits that there are three conditions necessary for an individuation process to become an *actuality* (as opposed to being *anticipated*, for example in dreams):

> (1) separation from the original family or clan; (2) commitment to a meaningful group over a long period of time, and (3) *liberation from too close an identity with the group* [italics added]. Only when all these stages have been adequately realized, together with a partial resolution of the conflict necessarily felt to exist between the claims of the group and the needs of the individual, can one speak of individuation. As Jung explained, "on the one hand individuation is an internal subjective process of integration, and on the other hand an equally indispensable objective process of relationship."
>
> (Henderson 2005: 202)

According to Henderson, the stages of initiation are "a rite of *submission* followed by a period of *containment* and then a further rite of *liberation*" (italics in original). However, he continues,

> Where it is a question of individuation, these latter two may be combined in a single rite in which the opposite tendencies for containment or release are transformed, with the conflict generated between them serving as a medium of their transformation. . . .
>
> . . . [T]his combined transformation, through the experience of death and rebirth, seems to lead to an as yet undefined final stage in which the individual may truly experience himself alone. At the same time he must, in accordance with Jung's definition, find his essential position in that form of reality which relates him to the people with whom he is most intimately involved. We must therefore look for an image of initiation

which no longer needs to borrow its symbolism from the tribal rites of passage, no matter how differentiated or abridged they may become.

This final stage . . . is a unique state of being in a place which cannot even be symbolized except very tentatively and which, in ancient iconography, is most frequently represented by an empty circle or round object. . . .

. . . [I]ndividuation forces a man to obey the immanent law of his own nature in order to know himself as an individual.

(Henderson 2005: 205)

In this way, one is unique and yet not separate from all that is.

Notes

1 Betty De Shong Meador and Virginia Beane Rutter, who have contributed chapters to this volume, have written about the initiation process in the female psyche.
2 For an example of this symbolic linkage in an alchemical painting, see Henderson and Sherwood (2003: 89–91).
3 Personal communication, Pansy Hawk Wing, 1993.
4 Several of his articles on Native Americans are reprinted in Henderson (1990a).
5 I met Pansy Hawk Wing at a small conference organized by the late analyst Don Sandner, when she led a sweat lodge and spoke about some aspects of Lakota spiritual tradition. Pansy is one of a few Lakota who are willing to work with non-Indians, and she does this with integrity and for no personal financial gain. The issue of non-Native Americans participating in Lakota rituals is highly charged: there is a great fear that non-Natives, the *Wasichu*, or "those who take the fat," will corrupt and exploit their tradition, as indeed has happened.

When I asked Pansy why she was willing to work with "Anglos," she said that her spiritual path was not for one group only but for all people, that the medicine wheel has black, red, yellow, and white as the colors of the four directions, and that one way she understands this is that the teaching is for all races of people, black, red, yellow, white. However, it took me many years before I overcame my discomfort at participating in what I saw as a "tribal" religion, until the teachings had become part of who I am. The Lakota way is a spiritual path rooted in the Great Plains of North America but in my view no more tribal and local in the depths of its wisdom than Christianity is to Palestine or Buddhism to India.
6 For more information about the history of the Lakota, see Brown (1970); Matthiessen (1983/1991); Peltier (1999); Walker (1980/1991).
7 Adolf Guggenbühl-Craig has written about the shamanic aspects of analytical psychology, although to my knowledge, his remarks have never been published. See also Sandner (1997) and Te Paske (1997).

References

Black Elk (1953) *The Sacred Pipe: Black Elk's Account of the Seven Rites of the Oglala Sioux*, recorded and edited by Joseph Epes Brown, Harmondsworth, UK: Penguin.
Black Elk (1988) *The Sacred Pipe: Black Elk's Account of the Seven Rites of the Oglala*

Sioux, recorded and edited by Joseph Epes Brown, Norman, OK: University of Oklahoma Press.

Brown, Dee (1970) *Bury My Heart at Wounded Knee*, New York: Henry Holt.

Hawk Wing, Pansy (1997) "Lakota Teachings: Inipi, Humbleciya, and Yuwipi Ceremonies," in Donald F. Sandner and Steven H. Wong (eds) *The Sacred Heritage: The Influence of Shamanism on Analytical Psychology*, New York: Routledge.

Henderson, Joseph L. (1990a) *Shadow and Self*, Wilmette, IL: Chiron.

Henderson, Joseph L. (1990b) "The Four Eagle Feathers," in Joseph L. Henderson, *Shadow and Self*, Wilmette, IL: Chiron.

Henderson, Joseph L. (2005) *Thresholds of Initiation*, Wilmette, IL: Chiron.

Henderson, Joseph L. and Sherwood, Dyane N. (2003) *Transformation of the Psyche: The Symbolic Alchemy of the Splendor Solis*, New York: Routledge.

Jung, C.G. (1938/1954) "The Visions of Zosimos," *Collected Works*, vol. 13.

Jung, C.G. (1950) "Concerning Mandala Symbolism," *Collected Works*, vol. 9/i.

Jung, C.G. (1951) "Aion," *Collected Works*, vol. 9/ii.

Lame Deer, John (Fire) and Erdoes, Richard (1972/1994) *Lame Deer, Seeker of Visions*, New York: Pocket Books.

Matthiessen, Peter (1983/1991) *In the Spirit of Crazy Horse*, New York: Penguin.

Neihardt, John G. (1932/2004) *Black Elk Speaks*, Lincoln and London, NE: University of Nebraska Press.

Neumann, Erich (1948/1968) "Mystical Man," in Joseph Campbell (ed.) *The Mystic Vision*, Princeton, NJ: Princeton University Press.

Peltier, Leonard (1999) *Prison Writings: My Life is My Sun Dance*, New York: St Martin's Press.

Powers, William K. (1982) *Yuwipi: Vision and Experience in Oglala Ritual*, Lincoln, NE: University of Nebraska Press.

Sandner, Donald (1997) "Introduction: Analytical Psychology and Shamanism," in Donald F. Sandner and Steven H. Wong (eds) *The Sacred Heritage: The Influence of Shamanism on Analytical Psychology*, New York: Routledge.

Sullivan, Mark (1996) "The Analytic Initiation: The Effect of the Archetype of Initiation on the Personal Unconscious," *Journal of Analytical Psychology*, 41: 509–527.

Te Paske, Bradley (1997) "Eliade, Jung, and Shamanism," in Donald F. Sandner and Steven H. Wong (eds) *The Sacred Heritage: The Influence of Shamanism on Analytical Psychology*, New York: Routledge.

Walker, James R. (1980/1991) *Lakota Belief and Ritual*, ed. Raymond J. DeMallie and Elaine A. Jahner, Lincoln, NE: University of Nebraska Press.

Winnicott, D.W. (1951/1975) "Transitional Objects and Transitional Phenomena," in D.W. Winnicott, *Through Paediatrics to Psychoanalysis*, New York: Basic Books.

Chapter 7

Hitchcock's rite of passage

A Jungian reading of North by Northwest

John Beebe

Thanks to the high quality of the critical literature that has grown up during the past half century around Hitchcock's sixtieth birthday film *North by Northwest* (1959), it is possible to recognize this perennially popular movie as a film text whose multiple meanings are paradoxical and contradictory.[1] The mountain of analysis, for a contemporary commentator, is now as daunting as Mount Rushmore was for Cary Grant's Roger Thornhill in 1959 when he complained that he did not like the way Theodore Roosevelt was looking at him. (This was just before Roger would have to scale the monument himself.) Ever since the English Canadian critic Robin Wood made serious Hitchcock analysis fashionable with his 1965 book, *Hitchcock's Films* (now in its third edition: Wood 2002), it has been customary to assume that though a comedy, *North by Northwest*, along with other films from the same period, like *Vertigo* (1958), invites a developmental reading in which the insights and values of psychoanalysis would not be out of place. Although Wood himself soft-pedaled the theme (and was ahead of his time in questioning the ethical appropriateness of the head of the Central Intelligence Agency (CIA) as its ultimate father-figure) the movie's highly sequential scenario (see Appendix) does lend itself to a Freudian understanding of the middle-aged hero's passing through a series of developmental stages to confront an unconscious mother complex that can finally only be resolved by encountering and submitting to patriarchal imperatives. (The most exhaustive reading of the film's strategy along Oedipal lines has been that of Raymond Bellour (1975), whose 116-page Lacanian exegesis leaves no image untested for evidence of Roger's need to undergo symbolic castration in order to be accepted as a legitimate male by other Americans also operating under the Law of the Father.)

Against such depth psychological certainty, there has been a deconstructive counter-movement which takes its cues from the many centrifugal elements that anyone who has seen the film cannot fail to have experienced and puzzled about: Ernest Lehman's parodic scenario, with its manic energy carrying its central characters across America in a series of zigs and zags and hops;[2] Cary Grant's extraordinary comedic capacity, the equal of Hitchcock's own, which enables the star to talk back to and at the same time physically burlesque any seriousness that might gather around the events of the story, however threatening to his own interests they may be; and the mad fandango of Bernard Herrmann's score, which underlines the propulsive, zany energy of the director's carefully choreographed filmmaking. Those following these hints at the level of style of a counter-narrative have seen *North by Northwest* as much more subversive than a comedy about castration anxiety: they find it to be an assault on meaning itself, at least at the level of cultural signs supporting established values. They regard the film as a send-up of the grand heroic story in which the consolidation of Roger O. Thornhill's character is ostensibly "inscribed." Postmodern critics like Geoffrey Hartman (1985), Frederic Jameson (1992), and Christopher D. Morris (2002) point out that Roger himself confesses that his initials stand for ROT, suggesting a decomposing identity that is hollow at the center. (Roger tells Eve Kendall, the woman he meets on the "Twentieth-Century Limited" train he takes to Chicago, that the "O" stands for "nothing.": Lehman 1999: 78.)[3] From the standpoint of these skeptics, the narrative, though filled with symbolic hints, finally dangles over an empty ground, signifying an existential void even more daunting than the castration anxiety that psychoanalysts have tried (in the style of therapeutic interpretation) to diagnose.

My task in what follows will be to develop an interpretation of *North by Northwest* broad enough to comprehend, first, the Oedipal structure of the narrative (so carefully plotted by the screenplay), second, the irony with which the emergence of that structure is approached within the film (again through the skill of the scenarist, but even more emphatically by that of the star and the director and the latter's cinematographer and editor), and third, the sense of suspense over emptiness that is constructed as the story proceeds (an effect that is underlined by the dangling rhythms of the musical score).

I believe these requirements can be met by an analysis of the film that is guided by an understanding of the archetype of initiation as extrapolated within a decade of *North by Northwest*'s release by the Jungian analyst Joseph Henderson from the dreams and fantasies of Americans whom he thought showed clear signs of being engaged by such an archetype (Henderson 1967/ 2005). To adapt Henderson's Jungian insights to the study of *North by Northwest* is not merely to apply a not often-enough considered depth psychology to the study of that particular film. It is also to allow the film to help Jungian psychology decide how to regard its "archetype of initiation," a question that I feel my discipline has not often enough put to itself. Such interdisciplinary cross-referencing can be invaluable. What draws Alfred Hitchcock's cinema and Jungian psychology into the same frame,[4] is the question of how a person develops. This problem engaged both Hitchcock and Henderson from the beginning of their professional careers, which for both men involved formative experiences in England, German-speaking Europe, and America. Despite vast differences in the size of their respective audiences, the nature of their achievements, and the degree of fame they garnered by doing what they did, it is instructive to compare their trajectories.

Born in 1899, Alfred Hitchcock, an Englishman of Irish stock, started as an art student who created film titles and developed his craft through a silent-film apprenticeship in Germany, where he observed silent film directors like Fritz Lang and F.W. Murnau first-hand. This was followed by a period of maturation in England, where after several silent successes he was allowed to direct the first British sound film, *Blackmail* (1929), and then, after the mid-1930s, with *The 39 Steps* (1935), became internationally known for his spy pictures. In 1940, he moved to Hollywood, where his style matured and flowered: by the end of his life, he was probably the most famous film director ever.

Born in 1903, Henderson, an American from Nevada, had gone to German-speaking Switzerland at the very end of the 1920s to analyze with Jung, took his medical training in the 1930s in England, and returned to America in 1939 to practice as a Jungian analyst, arriving in Northern California in 1940, where he established the C.G. Jung Institute of San Francisco and developed an international reputation as a teacher of Jungian psychology, a field he helped to prosper.

These men both rose to the very top of their respective fields, where they are very well known, but their fame, given their different careers, has been of vastly different proportions, and the nature of their talents was also different. Yet each has succeeded in sharing with others a gift for understanding the meanings of imagery, and though both have been able to demonstrate a sophisticated psychological consciousness of the symbolic overtones of images, neither has been content to let an image be the dogmatic sign of just one thing. This openness to the polysemic nature of symbolic images is as basic to Hitchcock's pure cinema as to Henderson's Jungian psychiatry. One wonders how they learned it. We do know that both men were significantly buttressed by contacts with Thornton Wilder, who was Henderson's mentor in secondary school and Hitchcock's screenwriter on what for years he described as his favorite American film, *Shadow of a Doubt* (1942), which he dedicated to Wilder, the only person to whom the great director ever extended that honor. Wilder, though a canonical American playwright and novelist, is in many ways an elusive figure, but his first novel, *The Bridge of San Luis Rey* (1927), which treats the collapse of a span in Latin America as a synchronistic event in the lives of the people who happened to be on the bridge at that time, reveals him to have been keenly attuned to the patterns that emerge as lives coincide. He had a psychological imagination, primed to recognize the archetype governing a human situation.

The capacity to spot the overarching pattern is something that one finds in many artists and psychologists, and it is certainly there in both Hitchcock and Henderson, but there is also something more. It is difficult to formulate, but perhaps Thornton Wilder taught them how to *contemplate* an archetype once they had recognized it – to evaluate it with a nose for its ethical implications. Wilder had the cool, hermetic conscience of the person who does not think collectively when contemplating collective materials. This is what so many people who engage themselves with archetypes lack. And, although numbers of journeymen directors have filmed heroic initiation scenarios that suggest (with a sort of moralizing that borders on cynicism) that the only way for a man or woman to have her or his effectiveness recognized is to accept and submit to an ordeal, through Hitchcock's lens, there is more critical distance. Initiation, for him, is not just another "grand narrative" of the ego's progress, not merely a test of strength or capacity. Instead, he notes that the archetype comes into its own when it is resisted, and its heroic potentialities discounted.

Similarly, Henderson often stood apart from other Jungians, in both his practice and his writing, by positioning himself outside the heroic perspective. I recall him saying at a lecture, replying to a question that invited him to suggest the "best way" to solve some common human problem, which he absolutely refused to do, "Do you see how hard it is to get past the hero?" He refused to use the archetype simply as a prescription, and this stance governed his understanding of initiation. He realized that initiation, like other archetypal patterns that Jung had taught him to recognize, needed to be looked at with a grain of salt, because it was always a bit uncharted, and would likely somewhere fail the person who sought in it a fully transforming experience. Henderson did not yet have all the words for his own vision when he was writing his classic papers on initiation, but according to the psychological attitude that he was developing, initiation needed to be understood less as an explanatory paradigm for maturation than as an archetype with its own specific dynamism,[5] an emergent phenomenon (Cambray 2006) that makes its appearance in the life of an individual not simply to reiterate a collective pattern of personal development, but much more mysteriously, to address a problem that is implicit to the time and place in which that individual must live.[6] Therefore, an initiation is an experiment that cannot be repeated by anyone else, living under another set of time conditions. Something like this is the vision that informs the hermetic comedy of *North by Northwest*.

The contemporary analytical psychologist's concerns about the danger of accepting collective guidelines as to what initiation should be are anticipated in the film. The character known as "The Professor," the CIA Chief who orchestrates Roger Thornhill's initiation, sounds (and looks) not unlike Joseph Henderson a decade later, at the time he wrote *Thresholds of Initiation* (1967), arguing for the need to accept an ordeal if one wants to be truly ready for mature marriage and citizenship. But it is the genius of Hitchcock the artist to pick up also on the *tone* of a practicing analyst such as Henderson, who would ever complicate his own maturational paradigm with a note of irony. (An analysand once dreamed that Henderson had appeared in front of him in a Boy Scout uniform, holding a trumpet and playing reveille, as if to awaken him up from undisciplined slumbers. Henderson and the reluctant initiate who had the dream proceeded to laugh together for the next fifteen minutes.) For Hitchcock, the logic of *North by Northwest*'s narrative *demands* that Roger Thornhill be a reluctant initiate. (And why should this particular protagonist feel the need for initiation? He is already – as everyone can see – Cary Grant.)

Had analysis been an option for the character, a practitioner like Henderson, in the way he conducted therapy with his analysand-initiates (and there were not many like him in the 1950s), would have understood Roger Thornhill's need for a sense of humor throughout the procedure, and he would have let Cary Grant remain Cary Grant. Hitchcock's humor, however, went well beyond a compensation for excessive *gravitas* about the potential for personal transformation via strenuous, heroic means. Roger Thornhill's survival, and that of his beloved, depends not so much on his submitting to an initiatory scenario as to Roger's motivation to subvert the spy film genre that Hitchcock had helped to inscribe in the modern mind made emblematic of modern initiation. When *North by Northwest* was first released, several critics disparaged Hitchcock's reprise of themes from *The 39 Steps* and *Notorious* (1946) as unconscious self-parody. Perhaps they were responding to the tricksterism of the narrative, since its manic energy seems to be shaped as much by an archetype as by a screenwriter or director and to achieve a form and a tone that would seem to be beyond anyone's ability to plan for and control. The story of a mother-dominated advertising man pursued by secrets-brokers, including the young Martin Landau as a coded 1950s "homosexual," may have tended to inspire a psychoanalytic reading, but the theme that engaged Hitchcock, Lehman, and Grant, and that also informs the surprised tone of Bernard Herrmann's score, was not the threat of psychosexual impotence or smoldering perversity as a consequence of maternal domination, but rather the fascinated astonishment that a modern person encounters when confronted by the unfamiliar demands of the archetype of initiation.

This was the theme of Henderson's landmark clinical treatise, *Thresholds of Initiation* (1967), which put psychoanalytic notions of maturation into a broader Jungian frame, in which it was possible to understand the purposiveness of the broken identifications and hazings of the developmental process as what it takes to enable an individual to mature and move beyond the confines of an identity fixated at a level of arrested development that has enormous collective cultural sanction. Henderson at that time had only begun to develop his notion of a cultural unconscious, but it was clear that he saw initiation as not just a harrowing inculcation of collective values, but as a realization of the self that most collective versions of identity-consolidation, including the psychoanalytic, had left incomplete. This raised a question that Hitchcock had already raised (and just as obliquely) in *North by Northwest*, the degree to which the filmic initiation of its New York advertising man hero, who begins the film as a typical "Man in the Gray Flannel Suit," is politically subversive to this character's identity as a mid–1950s standard-issue American man (Cohan 1997).

Democracies tend to reject initiation as an elitist notion, one that insinuates a dangerous element of grade or rank into the populace. As Henderson recognized, the individual's need to mark the passage from one stage of psychological development to another has been largely bypassed in favor of the view that all adults are citizens of identical status. Hitchcock visualizes the consequence in the opening sequence of *North by Northwest*, which begins with the reflections of traffic on the glass facade of a building in New York City and then shows people busily moving into subways and into Grand Central Station. In the midst of this mass of humanity in transit, Hitchcock himself appears. The bus he tries to board will not open its door to him, and the vehicle pulls away. Like many of us, Hitchcock seems to be having a problem finding his individual way through the collective situation that characterizes modernity. For some people in analysis, the bus comes up as a symbol of initiation, which is precisely about submitting to a collective path and yet being able to wind up at one's own individual destination. Yet who could have initiated Hitchcock, a pioneer of modern cinema, the creator of a style and a genre and an approach to filmmaking? The idea is as absurd as trying to "initiate" the already fully formed star-actor, Grant. Yet Hitchcock, also a true original one would not want to have any other way, turns to the topic as he approaches his sixtieth birthday, wondering what this archetype could still offer him – or any modern man.

Such a question would have been entirely unconscious for Roger Thornhill at the start of the movie, when he emerges, shamelessly uninitiated, from a sleek Manhattan office building. Although he is a successful Madison Avenue advertising executive, he has managed, in high midlife, to have developed little for himself beyond the formidable sophistication with which he deploys his stylish persona. Twice divorced, he still pushes his way through his world mostly indifferent to the feelings of people around him. He is terrified, however, of displeasing his mother, who scorns his self-indulgences. He drinks too much, and ought, perhaps, to diet. He is modern man in the grip of a mother complex.

Meeting clients at the Oak Room bar of the Plaza Hotel (also, though the film did not directly say so, a pick-up spot for discreet 1950s homosexual men: Cohan 1997: 7), Thornhill's initiation begins, and immediately it has the feel of a ritual. Ernest Lehman wrote *North by Northwest* to be the ultimate Hitchcock film, and it is easy while watching it to feel you are following a rite you already know by heart. Calling a bellman to send a telegram to his mother, who does not know where to meet him before their theater date later that evening, Thornhill manages to advertise himself to the couriers for a spy ring, who think he is answering their page for George Kaplan, an undercover

CIA agent whom they believe is staying at the same hotel. The couriers, pointing guns at his heart, abduct Thornhill and take him away to an estate (named "Townsend" – suggesting the end of town, the space just outside of civilization in which initiations typically occur),[7] in a Nassau County hamlet where (like any initiate, separated from his mother and tested to see if he can survive) he is addressed by an unfamiliar name, "Mr Kaplan." After a brief interrogation by "Mr Townsend" himself, toward whom he is totally uncooperative, he is made to ingest an intoxicating substance (bourbon, poured down his throat, according to the spies' assassination protocol) and then forced to steer an unfamiliar car, while drunk, down a dangerous cliff-edge road.

Thornhill's initial foray thus fits the classic initiation scenario – separation from the mother, being given a new name, ritual intoxication, an ordeal that carries the risk of death – but Lehman and Hitchcock have also problematized the archetype by making it a bit farcical. By placing self-assured Cary Grant in the role of the mother's son who is forced to undergo initiation, the movie leads us to ask, "Is all of this really necessary? Is there not something absurd about the heroic expectation?" Grant never fundamentally changes in this film; he is merely marvelous throughout at being himself, his persona surviving every attack and ridicule. There's a funny bit in a train station restroom, where a burly "masculine" man shaving with a straight razor looks askance at Grant, who is using a borrowed lady's razor, but nonetheless achieving a perfect shave. Through all, Grant positions himself as outside the heroic initiation being laid on him. (In this, he resembles J.K. Rowling's young magus-in-training, Harry Potter, who likewise is forced to undergo a heroic initiation not of his own devising, and in the course of it becomes more stubbornly himself.)[8]

Henderson distinguishes the ambition of the hero, who imagines he can transcend the limitations of the Self, from the aim of the true initiate, who submits the heroic aspirations of his ego to conditions set by the Self. In *North by Northwest*, it is James Mason, playing Grant's pursuer Vandamm, who most represents the heroic self-expectation. Vandamm's old Dutch family name suggests "of the female parent" and thus implies a mother's son, carrying her ideas of what her son should be. He is a representative of the mother's animus, in the scenario a spy who has insinuated himself into the patriarchal order. The fact that it's Vandamm who oversees Thornhill's initiation at the "Townsend" estate suggests that as part of the separation from the mother, there has also been (as Henderson 1967/2005: 33–61 postulates) a return to the mother, to face her animus down and to rescue what can be found of her authentic femininity. Because of his capacity to lock down his feelings, Vandamm appears to be much more sinister than what we have seen so far of Thornhill's mother, who is merely sarcastic, but because he has the unruffled poise that Thornhill's mother would perhaps like to see in her son and is even more withering in his disapproval of Thornhill's haplessness,

Vandamm comes across as an image of her expectations. He is therefore the signifier of the destructive aspect of her skeptical animus, which is forever mocking her son's own approach to masculine adaptation. Vandamm, in fact, replaces her in that critical role once Thornhill has left New York and his mother behind to try to get to the bottom of the mystery of why he has been mistaken for Kaplan. In their first confrontation, when Thornhill finally tracks Vandamm down in an auction-house in Chicago, Vandamm taunts him mercilessly, summarizing the plot so far:

> Has anyone every told you that you overplay your various roles rather severely, Mr. Kaplan? First you're the outraged Madison Avenue man who claims he has been mistaken for someone else. Then you play a fugitive from justice, supposedly trying to clear his name of a crime he knows he didn't commit. And now, you play the peevish lover, stung by jealousy and betrayal. . . . Seems to me you fellows could stand a little less training from the FBI and a little more from the Actors' Studio.
>
> (Lehman 1999: 124–125)

Yet it is just this ironizing that the heroic expectation (signified by "Kaplan") needs. The hero belongs to a trio of archetypes, including also the puer aeternus and the trickster, which Henderson (1967/2005) recognizes as ever-present threats to the progress of a true initiation. We encounter the puer aeternus in the famous crop-duster sequence, set near a prairie bus stop, beside a cornfield in the middle of nowhere, to which Thornhill has been lured through a message Eve reluctantly relays from Vandamm. A low flying plane (strikingly unrelated to all the other forms of transportation that figure in the film: Bellour 1975/2000: 181) circles the cornfield and sprays him with bullets and insecticide: it is clearly trying to dust him off. The little biplane, one of Hitchcock's greatest visual achievements, is an unexpected image of the puer. In its ruthless hostility toward everyone on the lonely road below, the anonymously piloted plane suggests the contemptuous attitude of this transcending archetype toward anything that might want to develop close to the ground. This is perhaps the one attitude that would be fatal to initiation, which requires that one submit to others. Bellour reads the crop-duster sequence psychoanalytically as an attempted castration of Grant. And, since the ever-circling plane is like Poe's pendulum and the cornfield in which Grant's character Thornhill tries to hide is like an open pit, the sequence has been read also as a filmic recreation of Poe's famous story (Perry 2003: 67–84), which does end in the release of the prisoner. The threatening plane has been sent by the relentless inquisitor of Thornhill, Vandamm, and so through a Jungian lens we can see that the mother's animus is behind this expectation that Thornhill must come clean about his bad behavior or, like the son-lover in a matriarchal corn ritual, be harvested once and for all to purge him of his boyishness. And the effect of the incursion of the mother's animus (as is so often the case when the "negative" mother problem is engaged in analysis) is to empower Thornhill by forcing him to develop his trickster side. From the standpoint of the model of initiation that Henderson lays out in his book, we have been witness to a true ordeal (Henderson 1967/ 2005: 89–97), and it has moved Thornhill's initiation forward. Although the crop-dusting scene is anticipated with cruciate imagery in the shots of the Indiana highway, which taken together with the implications of Roger's last name, rather blatantly attempts to inscribe him onto the path to Golgotha, it is clear that Grant's character is not willing to stay there and become a human sacrifice. He emerges from his ordeal a man determined to survive and willing to become a trickster to do so. (He gets away by flagging down one truck and hijacking another to hightail it out of there.)

The trickster archetype has up to now manifested itself in the movie in the way people use feeling to manipulate each other. Hitchcock punctuates *North by Northwest* with minor characters that display different kinds of theatrical insincerity. "What a performance!" Grant exclaims at the Townsend estate, while Vandamm's sister is pretending to be Mrs Townsend, filled with concern for him. I take the film's many references to performing to refer to the ritual aspect of any initiation, and to theater as pointing to the need to maintain an as-if distance from taking the play of initiation too literally. Like a fairy-tale protagonist, Grant is able to hold fast to his own identity in the face of the performances around him, but he can do so only by integrating more of the trickster than he had before and moving beyond the victim role that is always the masochistic shadow of the hero.

Another way the film complicates the usual heroic scenario that governs most Hollywood stories of initiation is the fact that although some female players in the smaller roles exaggerate their femininity, there is no true anima figure in the film. Eve Kendall, as uneasily played by Eva Marie Saint, comes into the scenario just after Roger Thornhill's mother drops out of the story. She is in a way a new mother to him, but she is not a confident one. Because she is (working undercover for the CIA) Vandamm's mistress, she comes across mainly as an image of frightened assailability trying to maintain a cool facade. She is never convincing as someone who would really be able to hold her own confidently with Grant, but her anxiety makes her a nice complement to the overconfidence with which Grant began the film before his initiation got underway. In the language of analytical psychology, Eva Marie Saint's Eve, though a coolly attractive Hitchcock blonde, is in this film not an image of the anima, but of the auxiliary function of the ego, a secondary but important ego capacity which in this film is rendered not as an additional patriarchal competence, but as a consciously vulnerable femininity learning to cope with the dangerousness of the world. I think a subtle feature of post-heroic initiation is being rendered by the emergence of her character as companion to the initiatory development of Grant's character, Roger Thornhill. Henderson says in *Thresholds of Initiation*,

> Over and over again, when a young man who is still too much a boy asks,
> "How shall I become a man?" or when a little-girlish woman asks, "How
> shall I become a woman?" I find in their dreams the firmly paradoxical
> answer: by becoming both man and woman.
>
> (Henderson 1967/2005: 97)

In achieving this subversive position under the very noses of the Fathers of
the American Republic on Mount Rushmore, Grant seems less concerned
with rescuing his young co-star than with sharing with her what he has
learned about the perilousness of both their positions.

The culminating chase across Mount Rushmore scales the limitations of
heroic filmmaking, for the task of rescuing the characters within the mindset
framed by the preposterous expectations of the patriarchal animus is impossible. Visualized in the figures of Washington, Jefferson, Theodore Roosevelt,
and Lincoln, carved out of proportion and perched inhumanly high, is the
inflated patriarchal ideal that Henderson's true initiate is able to get beyond.
That Hitchcock shrugs it off by simply cutting away from the climax enables
Roger to get Eve over the absurdity of being put in such a position. We are
led to ask, did he square himself against the world of the fathers, having left
the world of the mother, or are these imposing presences a final aspect of the
mother's overweening animus, to which he can never live up? A woman's
animus is often a multiple figure, composed of "an assembly of fathers or
dignitaries" (Jung 1966: 207, par. 332), so that we may be looking finally at
the patriarchal expectations of her animus, which demand that a man be a
hero. Here, the Professor, as a real father figure, orders the shooting of the
last "son" of Vandamm, Leonard, which finally allows Roger to pull Eve up
out of this impossible scenario. Roger simply refuses to be inscribed in the
traditional patriarchal order, and the director lets him escape the monument
in a magical match cut that continues Roger's gesture in a train going home.
Yet even this omnipotence is an initiatory achievement for Roger in legitim-
izing his own identity, with the approval of his ultimate master of initiation,
the film director. When the now postmodern Grant pulls her confidently up
at the end (fulfilling and at the same time refuting the requirements of
Henderson's "trial of strength": Henderson 1967/2205: 99–133), he is suggesting not only the beginning of an empowerment of women beyond the
collective pattern that had obtained until the end of the 1950s, but also the
achievement of a new, comfortably androgynous consciousness in place of
the erotized power-struggle that Vandamm (a signifier of the mother's
animus) and his stiff, somewhat corpselike secretary Leonard (the signifier
of the son whose anima has been pre-empted by the mother) had been
locked into.

There remains a final motif for Hitchcock to supply to propitiate (and
escape) the symbolic demands of traditional initiation: the rite of vision
(Henderson 1967/2005: 133–174). In one sense, this has been the movie itself:

a roll of film is the secret that spills out of the movie's "Maltese Falcon" of a Hitchcock Macguffin (a pre-Columbian statue of a Tarascan warrior, whose heroic image shatters against the Mount Rushmore Monument as Leonard falls), and the moviemaking calls explicit attention to itself in the film's parting shot, which again is one of transport and passage, this time in the train back to New York. As the now legally paired Roger and Eve prepare to make love in the upper berth of their compartment (a space actually of *re*birth like the one into which Roger, his actual identity in hiding, once had to be confined), the train goes into a tunnel. This "Freudian symbol" is from a Jungian standpoint the signifier of a satisfactory final intercourse between masculine and feminine sides of newly constructed ego identity, as well as the indication of a prosperous sacred marriage with power to revitalize the entire country (Cavell 1981/2005). It is a happy image, which inevitably makes an audience chuckle because of the pleasure it takes in flaunting its obvious bodily meaning. But Hitchcock is not done with what he wants us to understand. The laughter also contains the anticipation of release from tunnel visions, like the Freudian one, in which the hero myth is always embedded. In many cultures, for all the reasons one can imagine, passing through a round passage of some kind is the signifier of a completed initiation. Here, a mass audience is made to witness this summarizing initiatory motif. Hitchcock's suggestion of impending release carries a promise that Henderson was able to envision for psychology as well, the intuition of a development beyond the confines of the hero myth.

Appendix: a summary of the scenario of *North by Northwest*

Using the three-act formula routinely employed for the construction of a Hollywood script, Ernest Lehman's (1999) screenplay can be summarized as follows.

Act One: Roger Thornhill, a busy Madison Avenue advertising executive, is kidnapped from a hotel while trying to send a message to his mother about where he will meet her for a theater date later that evening. His abductors take him to a Long Island estate marked Townsend, where Thornhill is questioned by the leader of a spy ring, Philip Vandamm, who pretends to be "Mr Lester Townsend." "Townsend" asserts that Thornhill is really "Mr George Kaplan," an undercover agent for the US Government who has been trying to undermine Vandamm's spy ring. When Roger Thornhill insists he is certainly not George Kaplan, he is forced by Vandamm's henchmen to drink a great deal of bourbon and then placed behind the wheel of a car going rapidly down a dangerous Long Island cliff road. Arrested by the local police for driving over the speed limit under the influence of alcohol, Thornhill is taken into custody. From jail, Roger places a call to his mother, who posts bail, and the next day accompanies him with the police to the house where the forced intoxication was said to have taken place. Now Thornhill's party is met by Vandamm's sister, posing as "Mrs Townsend," who convinces the police that Roger is a friend of hers who simply had too much to drink at her party the night before and then borrowed a convertible from one of the other guests in order to drive home. When she explains that her husband is unavailable for questioning because he will be addressing the United Nations General Assembly that afternoon, the police abandon pursuit of the investigation, and Roger's mother insists he simply pay the fine. Nevertheless, she is willing to accompany her son to the hotel where he said he was abducted, and there they do find that a George Kaplan has registered. Roger goes on to the United Nations, where he meets the real Lester Townsend, who tells him at once that he is a widower and that his Long Island home is unoccupied. Before he can say more, one of Vandamm's henchmen directs a knife into Townsend's back. While Townsend is falling over dead, Roger pulls out the knife, which makes it look to the many witnesses in the General Assembly lobby as if he is the killer. He flees the scene.

Act Two: Without a ticket, Roger manages to stow away on the "Twentieth-Century Limited" train to Chicago, which Vandamm had mentioned would be Kaplan's next scheduled destination after New York. On board the train, he meets a beautiful young woman, Eve Kendall, who hides him in the upper berth of her sleeping compartment. She allows that she knows who he is, but indicates that since he has a nice face, she is open to a romantic interlude. In reality, she is under orders from Vandamm to keep Roger away from the police who are chasing him. Roger learns that she will be staying in the same hotel in Chicago as Kaplan, and he enlists her help in contacting him. Pretending to have done so, she gives Roger instructions as to when and where to meet the elusive Mr Kaplan – at a bus stop in rural Indiana. Roger takes a bus to that stop, where he finds little beside a desolate stretch of flat highway next to a field of ripe corn. Kaplan never shows up, but a plane dusting crops with insecticide starts to fly menacingly over Roger in a series of ever closer turns, eventually spraying him with bullets. Roger hides as best he can in the cornfield until the crop spray released by the plane is too much for him. Finally he runs out to the highway and flags down a huge passing truck. When the truck stops suddenly, the crop duster, flying too low, crashes into it; a fire breaks out, and in the confusion that results, a little crowd gathers and Roger is able to steal a bystander's vehicle. He drives it back to Chicago and tracks Eve Kendall down to an auction house, where he can see that she is accompanying Vandamm (the spymaster's correct name is called out by an auctioneer). After confronting them both with their deceptions, Roger makes a scene in the auction house so that he will be arrested by the police. He assumes he will be taken to jail, but instead the police receive orders to drive him to the airport, where he is met by a mastermind of US Government intelligence operations, "The Professor," who explains to him that Eve Kendall is really an American agent and that "George Kaplan" is only a fictitious decoy, a series of hotel reservations designed to keep Vandamm from realizing that his mistress Eve is the actual agent. So that Vandamm will not suspect her, Thornhill accepts the assignment of pretending to be Kaplan a little longer.

Act Three: The Professor arranges for Roger to fly to Mount Rushmore where he will be able to confront Eve again, this time allowing her to shoot him (with a gun that fires blanks) so that it will look to Vandamm as if she has killed him and thus cannot be associated with him in any way. Roger plays his part perfectly, but when he learns that the Professor is going to allow Eve to go on with Vandamm to Moscow, he sets about to rescue her on his own. He finds his way to Vandamm's house and private landing field near Mount Rushmore. Slipping inside unnoticed, he eavesdrops on a conversation between Vandamm and one of his henchmen, the discreet homosexual Leonard, who has figured out that Eve is a double agent. Thornhill gets a warning message to Eve, whose life is now in danger, and the two are able to escape together by running away from Vandamm's hideaway onto the top of Mount Rushmore, carrying with them the secrets Vandamm was trying to take to Russia. They start to climb down the monument beside faces of great American presidents, in a dazzling, cliff-hanging finale. Predictably, the spies chasing them are finally killed or caught, and the two somehow make it to the security of another compartment bedroom on the "Twentieth-Century Limited" train, as Mr and Mrs Thornhill, this time going back to New York. Hitchcock's final shot – the train going through a tunnel – suggests the happy conclusion of the adventure in the consummation of the couple's marriage.

Notes

1 The film was released by MGM in 1959 and is easily available in both VHS and DVD formats for home viewing. The most accurate rendering of the scenario is the continuity script, which can be found in the Rutgers Films in Print volume edited by Naremore (1993), which also contains a sampling of critical commentary. A summary of Ernest Lehman's screenplay is provided as an appendix to this chapter.

2 The entire film is structured like a manic episode suffered by Thornhill, as Ayako Saito (1999) has demonstrated in her essay on the trilogy of Hitchcock films characterized by pathological affect to which *North by Northwest*, in her view, belongs: it is in the middle between the melancholic *Vertigo* and the paranoid/schizoid *Psycho* (1960). It is my view that the manic energy of *North by Northwest* is a commentary on the way the American character is pushed by the insistence of the collective patriarchal animus on the hero archetype as the signifier of successful adaptation, a situation which the inclusion of women in the expectations of that archetype has only made worse. If initiation is to mean anything under such conditions, it will have to be initiation out of that expectation, which is I think is affirmed by Thornhill's determination to get him and Eve over it in *North by Northwest*.

3 It was more common in mid-twentieth-century America, when presenting a dignified persona was more important than it has become in our more casual and confessional day, for a man to adopt a middle initial that was (as President Harry S. Truman had said of his own meaningless middle initial) "an alphabetical garnish."

4 Hitchcock did not explicitly bring them together himself until the mid-1960s, with his film *Marnie*, in which Sean Connery, playing a character that is in many ways Hitchcock's stand-in (Beebe 2001), suggests that the disturbed title character (Marnie, played by Tippi Hedren) read Jung's (1957) *The Undiscovered Self*.

5 The term "archetype," conveying a life-shaping phenomenon that, like the self and the notion of transcendence, arises from the unconscious, is in Jung's Kantian view of it, a "borderline concept," that is, something that is only partly knowable, even though we can recognize its pattern in particular images and behaviors. It is at best the name Jung uses for the evidence that there does exist something "beyond the borderline, the frontiers of knowledge" (Jung 1978: 104–105). The theory of archetypes is therefore only a "working hypothesis toward a psychology of the future" (Henderson 1967/2005: 8) that would account for the ways in which even the most unusual vicissitudes of human behavior involve patterns recognizable in earlier forms of recorded expression, now given purpose and meaning in a new historical and personal context.

6 In *Answer to Job*, Jung (2002) tells us that archetypes make their appearance when they are needed. He argues that even Christ, whether a numinous human figure identified with an archetype or the actual incarnation of God, had to appear on the human scene to solve an historical problem that had developed in God's relation to man. Once the *Book of Job*, "written somewhere between 600 and 300 BC" (Jung 2002: 58) had manifestly recorded its evidence that God not only is good but also can more or less arbitrarily cause man to suffer, and Job's complaint about that, God then, in Jung's view, had to become man Himself in order to give an adequate "answer to Job."

7 In *The Ritual Process*, Victor Turner (1969) called such spaces in which initiatory transformation of identity can occur "liminal," a word derived from "limen," which means threshold and is related etymologically to "limit" in the sense of "boundary," thus referring to a psychosocial locus at the border of civilization, an idea well conveyed by the name "Townsend."

8 The film director Mike Newell (2005) told an interviewer that he used *North by Northwest* to guide the actor Daniel Radcliffe in how to react in the movie version of *Harry Potter and the Goblet of Fire*:

> I was explaining my idea of the story to Dan, and he said, "What have you been watching?" I told him, paranoid thrillers: *Three Days of the Condor*, *The Parallax View*, *North by Northwest*. They're all about people who don't know what's happening to them ... I told him specifically to watch *North by Northwest*, because there you are, it's a sunny afternoon, you're happy with your life, but suddenly stuff starts happening, and then you're up against the bad guy, who had plans for you all along. That's exactly what happens to Harry Potter in this book.

Further reading

Cohen, Tom (2005) *Hitchcock's Cryptonymies*, 2 volumes: vol. 1, *Secret Agents*; vol. 2, *War Machines*, Minneapolis, MN: University of Minneapolis Press.

Conrad, Peter (2000) *The Hitchcock Murders*, London: Faber & Faber.

Corber, Robert J. (1993) *In the Name of National Security: Hitchcock, Homophobia, and the Political Construction of Gender in Postwar America*, Durham, NC: Duke University Press.

Henderson, Joseph L. (1963) "Ancient Myths and Modern Man," in Carl Gustav Jung, *Man and His Symbols*, New York: Doubleday, pp. 104–157.

Henderson, Joseph L. (1991) "An Ancient Modern Man" (Review of Rivkah Kluger's *The Archetypal Significance of Gilgamesh: A Modern Ancient Hero*), *San Francisco Jung Institute Library Journal*, 10 (3): 5–11.

Leitch, Thomas (1991) *Find the Director and Other Hitchcock Games*, Athens, GA: University of Georgia Press.

Millington, Richard H. (1999) Hitchcock and America Character: The Comedy of Self-construction in *North by Northwest*, in *Hitchcock's America*, Jonathan Freedman and Richard Millington (eds.) New York: Oxford University Press, pp. 135–154.

Naremore, James (1988) *Acting in the Cinema*, Berkeley, CA: University of California Press.

Perrottet, Tony (2006) "Mount Rushmore," *Smithsonian*, 37 (2): 78–83.

Pomerance, Murray (2004) *An Eye for Hitchcock*, New Brunswick, NJ: Rutgers University Press.

Walker, Michael (2005) *Hitchcock's Motifs*, Amsterdam: Amsterdam University Press.

References

Beebe, John (2001) "The Interpretation of Film as a Psychological Art," in Mary Ann Mattoon (ed.) *Cambridge 2001: Proceedings of the Fifteenth International Congress for Analytical Psychology*, Einsiedeln, Switzerland: Daimon, pp. 513–522.

Bellour, Raymond (1975/2000) "Symbolic Blockage: On *North by Northwest*," trans. Mary Quaintance, in Raymond Bellour, *The Analysis of Film*, Bloomington, IN: Indiana University Press, pp. 77–192.

Cambray, Joe (2006) "Towards the Feeling of Emergence," *Journal of Analytical Psychology*, 51 (1): 1–20.

Cavell, Stanley (1981/2005) "*North by Northwest*," in William Rothman (ed.) *Cavell on Film*, Albany, NY: State University of New York Press, pp. 41–58.

Cohan, Steven (1997) *Masked Men: Masculinity and the Movies in the Fifties*, Bloomington, IN: Indiana University Press.

Hartman, Geoffrey (1985) "Plenty of Nothing: Hitchcock's *North by Northwest*," in Geoffrey Hartman, *Easy Pieces*, New York: Columbia University Press, pp. 93–107.

Henderson, Joseph L. (1967/2005) *Thresholds of Initiation*, Wilmette, IL: Chiron.

Jameson, Frederic (1992) "Spatial Systems in *North by Northwest*," in Slavoj Žižek (ed.) *Everything You Have Always Wanted to Know about Hitchcock (but were afraid to ask Lacan)*, London: Verso, pp. 47–72.

Jung, C.G. (1957) *The Undiscovered Self, Collected Works*, vol. 10.

Jung, C.G. (1966) *Two Essays on Analytical Psychology, Collected Works*, vol. 7, 2nd edition, Princeton, NJ: Princeton University Press.

Jung, C.G. (1978) *Flying Saucers: A Modern Myth of Things Seen in the Skies*, Princeton, NJ: Princeton University Press.

Jung, C.G. (2002) *Answer to Job*, Princeton, NJ: Princeton University Press.

Lehman, Ernest (1999) *Alfred Hitchcock's* North by Northwest *(Screenplay)*, London: Faber & Faber.

Morris, Christopher D. (2002) *The Hanging Figure: On Suspense and the Films of Alfred Hitchcock*, Westport, CT: Praeger.

Naremore, James (1993) *North by Northwest: Alfred Hitchcock, Director*, New Brunswick, NJ: Rutgers University Press.

Newell, Mike (2005) "I was so fearful of breaking the spell" (Interview with David Gritten, filed October 28, 2005 with *Film.Telegraph*). Online: http://www.telegraph.co.uk/arts/main.jhtml?xml=/arts/2005/10/28/bfpotter28.xml

Perry, Dennis R. (2003) *Hitchcock and Poe: The Legacy of Delight and Terror*, Lanham, MD: Scarecrow.

Saito, Ayako (1999) "Hitchcock's Trilogy: A Logic of Mise en scène," in Janet Bergstrom (ed.) *Endless Night: Cinema and Psychoanalysis, Parallel Histories*, Berkeley, CA: University of California Press, pp. 200–248.

Turner, Victor (1969) *The Ritual Process*, London: Routledge & Kegan Paul.

Wood, Robin (2002) *Hitchcock's Films Revisited*, revised edition, New York: Columbia University Press.

Part IV

The archetype of initiation in aging and death

Chapter 8

Separation, sorrow, and initiation

Betty De Shong Meador

I begin with words about sorrow from Jung. In his commentary on *The Secret of the Golden Flower* he says, "All religions are therapies for the sorrows and disorders of the soul" (Wilhelm 1975: 126). His comment comes in response to a letter from a former patient. The woman writes:

> By keeping quiet, repressing nothing, remaining attentive, and hand in hand with that, by accepting reality – taking things as they are, and not as I want them to be – by doing all this, rare knowledge has come to me, and rare powers as well, such as I could never have imagined before.
>
> (Wilhelm 1975: 126)

Jung says of her letter, "This attitude is religious in the truest sense, and therefore therapeutic" (Wilhelm 1975: 126).

With a Jungian perspective, we pay close attention to the unconscious. Jung implies here, and Joseph Henderson (2005) states very clearly, that initiation in its "undefined final stage" occurs in a person, who, like Jung's patient, has accepted individuation as a way of life, a life lived in connection with inner processes. When one can do this, Henderson tells us, "The individual may truly experience himself alone" (Henderson 2005: 205).

Taking individuation as a way of life involves trusting the outpouring of imagery from the silent interior, the unconscious. These images, dreams, fantasies, even feelings, thoughts, and emotions, fuel a process with which we – as awake, conscious persons – actively interact. This relationship gives meaning and substance to our own living experience. The interactive process is the core of a commitment to individuation.

Wise sorrow

I speak from the threshold of old age, where I confront the pleasures and perils of retirement, endless opportunity for solitude, aches and pains, disease, and of course the reality of death. In this place I am surprised – why should I be – by the frequent visitation of sorrow. I do not mean remorse or regret – that grinning, "gotcha" harpie who endlessly recites her list of past indiscretions, failures, embarrassments, and down-right bad acts. She accompanies us to the grave. Sorrow's assignment is of another sort, of the moment, a signal for purposeful attention. Her smile is filled with compassion and poignancy. Her hand is soft on my shoulder when she says, "Now you must let go." She helps me sink completely into the experience of being utterly alone. The ones I love the most – my children, my husband – she says I must let go. She comes at unexpected moments, for example, while I am reading in the morning paper: "In Darfur, husbands murdered, women and children desperate." I sink into deep sorrow over these events, and sorrow says, "There is nothing you can do. This is reality. Thoughtlessness, self-serving power-mongers, real evil will always have a place." She is not cynical and not complacent. She merely insists that I see reality as it is, and hold that view with her deep poignancy and compassion.

Sorrow over horrifying tragedies is not an unusual response for a civilized, sensitive human being. I began to realize that the intense sorrow that overcomes me has a dual origin. Its global or external trigger is ignited by catastrophes, some natural, others the self-serving horrors human beings inflict on each other. Sorrow over these events precipitates in me a meditative state where I find myself in the dark, sweet loam of sadness and compassion. If I sit still and hold the tragedy in consciousness, I find that the sorrow expands in its intensity. I have come to believe that holding this sadness is my job – all I can do in the face of tragedy. Oh, I could send money or write my senator, but immersion in the sorrow of it begins to alter my worldview. I have to accept that this tragedy, this disaster, occurred and will continue to occur in other forms, because this is the way the world is made. The realization is painfully poignant. I can hardly bear the sadness of it. At the same time, I feel a sweet relief, like an old, old woman who has peeked through a crack in the mystery and has seen the hand of deity both forming the world as it is and weeping over its suffering. The revelation in this experience is a full-bodied recognition that tragedy and suffering are intrinsic in the fabric of life on this planet.

Personal sorrow

The second type of sorrow is much more personal. Its origin is in my body, my history. There I carry the imprint of the ancestors, the circumstance of my upbringing, the bends and twists we call wounds or complexes, all of which form the scaffolding of myself. Its shape is a hard given, impossible to escape. Jung, who calls this "our narrow confinement in the self," follows with a paradox: "Only consciousness of our narrow confinement in the self forms the link to the limitlessness of the unconscious" (Jung 1963: 325).

I wonder how this can be? Waves of remorse still overcome me and sting most often with the pain of regret. Why did I not do this or that? Why *did* I do this or that? Most intense are the memories of actions or circumstance that hurt the ones I love.

Jung seems to respond. His narrowly confined self is just that – a narrow, limited given. This is what happened. This is who you are. These are the threads of your life. Your job is to carry the threads as best you can toward an evolving consciousness. When I can hold this perspective, sorrow accompanies the full recognition of who I am, of the threads I have always carried. My job is to be a digesting factory, assimilating the raw incompleteness at the beginning, gradually taking in the facts of the past, and developing an awareness of the narrow confines of the self. With whatever mix of emotions we look back over our lives, sorrow plays a natural and necessary role. How can we not weep for *this* child, born into the confines of *this* family, *this* circumstance, who grows up in her own limitation to be so specifically and narrowly herself.

Sorrow forms the bridge between dreadful remorse and a full awareness of our life's path. Sorrow is a signal for purposeful attention. It comes with the deeply human recognition that my life could not have been otherwise. That glimpse the old woman caught through the crack in the mystery offers a silent affirmation that each human life has its job which, when taken up intentionally, carries forward the evolution of those particular threads. Done well, the change that the individual enacts heals as it takes out of circulation certain pieces of the distorted, restricted, undeveloped aspects given each individual at birth.

Sorrow as a signal for purposeful attention pulls me back from wandering lethargy or envy-driven pursuits, to my main given role, to take up my assigned tasks within the narrow confines of the self. My job, once accepted, alters my perception of past, present, and future. These threads of mine are attached to those of my original family. To view my family as they struggled to make their lives meaningful fills my heart with compassion and a poignant recognition. What happened could not have been otherwise.

Yet, my own destiny may have little to do with the cultural and personal realities in my original situation. The process of accepting and allowing the true and limited self to be, can lead to the recognition of a passionate sense of purpose I can only articulate in metaphor and symbol.

Two worlds

> The best thing is, as I say, to assume that we are standing in between two worlds, a visible tangible world, and the other invisible world, which somehow has a peculiar quality of substantiality, but very subtle, a sort of matter that is not obvious and is not visible, that penetrates bodies and apparently exists outside of time and space.
>
> (Jung 1997: 206)

The "rare knowledge" and "rare powers" that Jung's patient acquired came to her after she began to repress nothing and to accept reality as it is. In what Henderson calls "the undefined final stage of initiation," the individual has come to depend on the interaction between the two worlds that Jung describes, the everyday world seen through "the narrow confines of the self," and "the invisible world" of images, dreams, thoughts, and emotions.

My hope is that I can hold the two worlds, one in each hand, and observe their interaction, and in the process discover who I am at the core, my "true self." No easy task, this interaction seems to be ongoing for the rest of my life. Once, however, long ago, a goddess accomplished such a transformation in one fateful encounter with the Queen of the Underworld. The ancient Sumerians, in what is now Iraq, left us a story that is a telling metaphor of death of the old self and birth of the new. We know the story as "Inanna's Descent to the Netherworld."

Inanna was the patron goddess of the city of Uruk, a city in the fourth millennium BCE that was the center of a culture that reached from its location on the Euphrates in southern Iraq, north into modern Syria, Turkey, and west to Iran. No other culture in antiquity saw its influence spread over such an expanse of geography. Only Rome, several millennia later, grew to be a larger city than Uruk.

In the city, Inanna's temple complex called the Eanna, House of Heaven, is the oldest, continuously inhabited section of Uruk, its earliest occupation dating to around 5300 BCE. We cannot be sure that a goddess named Inanna occupied the Eanna from its beginning, but she was there during the height of Uruk's expansion in the fourth millennium. Scholars call her the most important deity in the ancient Near East. We should not be surprised that the people of this highly civilized and creative culture have given us a profound myth of initiation.

In the myth, Inanna, now a great goddess of heaven and earth, queen of heaven and earth, decides on her own to go to the Underworld, the realm of her older sister Erishkigal. The myth says, "She in great heaven / turned her ear to great earth."[1] She heard something. Something stirred inside her. As the myth progresses, it becomes clear that Inanna – the principal goddess in a highly civilized culture, a culture replete with creations and inventions in art, science, literature, religion, and civil institutions – the prized queen of this remarkable achievement followed the urges from its opposite, the primal reality of the dark world below.

She left not only her temple in Uruk, but also all her temples in the important cities throughout Sumer: Badtibira, Zabalam, Nippur, Kish. She dressed in her finest robes, her crown, her gold ring and jewels, her emblems of authority and power. Inanna went down below.

Aware of the terrible danger of her journey, she called Ninshubur, her special minister, and told her the plan. She instructed Ninshubur to wait three days. If she did not return, she would be in peril. Ninshubur, wearing for her goddess the rags of mourning and lamentation, was to go for help. First, go to Enlil, most powerful of the gods, god of wind, god of the air that separates heaven and earth. Then, to Nanna, the moon god and Inanna's father. If neither would help, go to Enki in Eridu, god of the sweet waters under the earth, god of cunning, wisdom, and magic. Surely he could devise a plan to save her mistress. Inanna went down below.

At the ominous gate to the Netherworld, Inanna pushes, shoves, and cries out, "Open up, Doorman, open up the House." Neti, the great doorman, answers, "You! Who are you?" Inanna identifies herself as the bright morning and evening star: "I am Inanna, star of evening, traveling toward the dawn." "Why are you here where no traveler turns back?" Inanna replies: she has come for her sister Ereshkigal whose lord, the great bull of heaven, has died. No more is ever said about him. Perhaps Inanna uses this explanation as a ruse.

"Stand there Inanna. I must speak to my queen," says Neti. Breathless, he runs to Ereshkigal, tells her what happened. Great Ereshkigal "slaps her thighs / bites her lips," has a plan. "Bolt the seven gates of the netherworld; then one by one, open each door of the Palace Ganzir. Let her come in! Capture her! Strip off her clothes! Carry them away! Bring her to me!"

As he was ordered, Neti bolts the seven gates, says, "Come, Inanna, enter." At each gate Inanna is stripped of one article of her royal attire. "What Is This?!" she cries. At the seventh gate, someone takes her royal robe. She is naked and bowed low. Approaching Ereshkigal's throne, she ruthlessly shoves her sister aside and sits on her throne. Ereshkigal, Queen of the Great Below, rises to her full power, has Inanna beaten into a piece of meat, "hangs her rotting flesh on a peg."

For three days and three nights Ninshubur wails for Inanna, "cries in lamentation by the ruins," ruins of Inanna's deserted temples. She "plays a drum song, drums for her in the throne court, wanders for her, wanders through the houses of the gods." She "tears at her eyes, tears at her mouth, tears at the place she shows no one, wears rags for her, only rags." Remembering what Inanna said, Ninshubur goes to the great temples of the gods, Enlil, and then Nanna. Both refuse to help saying, "Inanna wants great heaven, wants great earth below; forbidden are those desires, desires for netherworld powers. Who seizes them must stay there down below. Who would ever want to come back from that place anyway!"

Now at the temple of Enki in Eridu, Ninshubur tells her tale. Enki replies, "My daughter, Inanna, mistress of all the lands, what has she done? I am deeply troubled." He devises a plan. From the dirt under his fingernails he creates two creatures, the *galatura* and the *kurgara*, and sends them off to rescue Inanna. They succeed in tricking Ereshkigal, now great with child. The little creatures sprinkle the piece of rotting meat with the plant of life and the water of life. Inanna is revived.

The underworld judges, the seven Annunaki, free Inanna from the place where "no traveler turns back." She may return above, they say, only on the condition that she send someone in her place. She leaves accompanied by ruthless underworld demons, escorts for her chosen replacement. First, the demons try to take Ninshubur. Inanna refuses to give them her minister who mourned, lamented, rolled in the dust, helped to free her. She refuses them Shara, her hairdresser and manicurist, who trembles in his rags of mourning. She refuses them Lulal, her honeyman, still wearing his rags of mourning. They go then to Kullab, to the great apple tree. There sits Dumuzi, her husband, on a splendid throne, wearing a magnificent robe. Inanna stares at him the eye of death, speaks words of wrath, cries out, "Sacrilege!" Says, "Carry him away!" The demons take Dumuzi in her place.

Can this profound myth give us clues to what Henderson calls intriguingly "the undefined final stage of initiation?" (Henderson 2005: 205). For us poor mortals, as we struggle in our commitment to individuation, the myth offers important instructions. The first instruction is to listen. Inanna is pulled to the Underworld because she hears something. From her place of supreme outer world achievement, Queen of Heaven and Earth, she hears the promptings of the dark interior. Henderson describes this experience as "an awakening of . . . earth-bound nature," the call of "the existence of spirit in nature," the existence of "an ancient wisdom of the Earth Mother, the Primal God image" (Henderson 2005: 152, 165, 167). Inanna hears a call, in her case a response to her failing connection to the Queen of the Underworld. Something was missing in her all too successful accomplishments as Queen of Heaven and Earth. For us, the lack we feel, the dis-ease, is an avoidance of the world below. Messages from the dark Queen of the Underworld insist that we stand knee deep in primal nature and acknowledge our animal kinship. She is the divine source of life coursing through matter in the natural world. Inanna's intuition and ultimate ordeal throw her before her sister Ereshkigal, Queen of the Great Below, whose being infuses all matter with her holiness, down to the lowliest of creatures.

A second instruction from the myth is to mourn. For Ninshubur, terrible sorrow envelops her over the loss of her mistress and goddess. For us, sorrow comes with the struggle, disappointment, and loss we inevitably encounter in life. Sorrow engulfs us with the despair of emptiness. As with Ninshubur the gods abandon us. We lose our connection to the unconscious psyche and the meaningful experience of self that connection can bring. We are forsaken. Life has no shred of meaning. The appropriate reaction, Inanna implies, is to wear rags, roll in the dust, wail in the courtyard of the temple, wander through the houses of the gods, tear at your eyes, tear at your mouth, tear at the place you show no one.

Inanna's final instruction is to go for help. "Then set your feet to Enlil's house," she says. Mourning down to the dregs has its release. Now, though you carry the stark reality of your loss, do something. Inanna anticipates the final humiliating experience of rotting on that peg. Hers is the extreme loss. She can be saved only by cunning and trickery. The trickster god Enki knows his way around impossible conundrums. He has a plan. The plan works. The next thing we learn is that she is on her way back and strangely transformed. Demons surround her, cling to her side. The demons are said to "know no food, know no drink, are never held in the sweet legs of a spouse, never kiss a sweet child, will snatch the child from the nurse and the bride from her wedding bed." Inanna's pleasure-drenched husband is the first recipient of her new-found eye of death. She has left behind the eye-clouding effects of over-done reliance on human feeling. She has gained impersonal judgment. Like the other-worldly demons, Inanna now uses a clear-headed, unsentimental perception of "things precisely as they are" (Wright 2004: 85). Dumuzi will be her substitute in the Great Below.

Ereshkigal strips Inanna of all external forms of her identity, leaving her naked and bowed low. Descent into the Underworld does that to us. Transformation at this level gives that old, old woman an experience of rock-bottom reality, stripped of illusions of self-importance, permanence, and control. Is this wrenching away of the meaningful structures of life useful? Naked in this pit of despair – is this the transformation I longed for? Jung's patient received rare knowledge there, and rare powers. Can I count on Ereshkigal to grant these gifts?

This myth, which I suspect is as old as time, implies that such an experience bestows on the recipient clear eyes, a new way of looking at life, a fresh and expanded perception. For me, seeing the world from that rock-bottom place brings a sort of peace, a sense of relief. Everyday anxieties, pressures, fall away. I am only who I am, no praise, no blame. I have my job – it is mostly mundane – and yes there is sorrow. Intense love and compassion fills me, for those I know and for sufferers I only hear of. The experience is simple but profound. Jung describes the attitude a person may take toward his or her given job:

> There is an old Eastern saying that every human being should play the role that is assigned to him, the king should play the king, the beggar the beggar, and the criminal the criminal – but always remembering the gods. That would mean that one should take one's role in life as a sort of mask, not identifying with it, yet recognizing it as one's task, and always reminding oneself of the divine being that cannot possibly be identical with the more or less incidental roles.
>
> (Jung 1997: 127)

For some, this stripping brings revelation. Poets and other visionaries give us insights that can occur in the midst of intense sorrow.

Poets and other visionaries

The remarkable experiences poets and visionaries describe in their writing are frequently associated with intense pain and despair. Here is an example in this poem by Franz Wright:

Prescience

We speak of Heaven who have not yet accomplished
even this, the holiness of things
precisely as they are, and never will!

Before death was I saw the shining wind.
To disappear, today's as good a time as any.
To surrender at last

to the vast current –
And look, even now there's still time.
Time for the glacial, cloud-paced

soundless music to unfold once more.
Time, inexhaustible wound, for
your unwitnessed and destitute coronation.
           (Wright 2004: 85; reprinted in Wright (2006)
       God's Silence, New York: Alfred A. Knopf, p. 75)

The visionary in this poem suffers an "inexhaustible wound." His vision grasps "the holiness of things / precisely as they are." Ready to face death, "today's as good a time as any," he sees "the shining wind" and hears "the glacial, cloud-paced / soundless music." He believes he will see and hear them again: "there's still time."

I read the poem when it was first published in a magazine, cut it out, and pinned it above my desk. Some weeks later, Wright, whose poetry I had not known before, won the 2005 Pulitzer Prize. He said in an interview, "It's nothing short of a miracle I'm still alive" (Stimpson 2006). The interview described how Wright struggled with alcohol and drug addiction, and finally, mental illness, twice hospitalized with psychotic depression. Shortly after his recovery and subsequent marriage, the interviewer reports, "He had a sudden and profound experience that he can only characterize as 'an experience of literal belief in God' " (Stimpson 2006: 37). The imagery in *Prescience* describes an intense vision of the divine in matter, a visual as well as auditory experience: he "saw the shining wind" and heard the "soundless music." Wright calls his "narrow confinement in the self" an "inexhaustible wound," a designation his history makes palpable. His vision of holiness includes the "coronation" of the wound that is himself, a coronation that is "unwitnessed and destitute." The poet is alone in his own confined self in the midst of a hierophany.

Rilke's *Duino Elegies* are among the best known verses that elucidate with his "heart work" the encounter between suffering, sorrow, and "some ultimate vision of human life and destiny" (Rilke 1939: 9). Here is the first verse of *The Tenth Elegy*:

> Someday, emerging at last from the violent insight,
> let me sing out jubilation and praise to assenting angels.
> Let not even one of the clearly-struck hammers of my heart
> fail to sound because of a slack, a doubtful
> or a broken string. Let my joyfully streaming face
> make me more radiant; let my hidden weeping arise
> and blossom. How dear you will be to me then, you nights
> of anguish. Why didn't I kneel more deeply to accept you,
> inconsolable sisters, and, surrendering, lose myself
> in your loosened hair. How we squander our hours of pain.
> How we gaze beyond them into the bitter duration
> to see if they have an end. Though they are really
> our winter-enduring foliage, our dark evergreen,
> one season in our inner year –, not only a season
> in time –, but are place and settlement, foundation and soil
> and home.
>
> (Mitchell 1995: 389)

"Hours of pain" are not merely to be endured "into the bitter duration." Life viewed from the dark loam of sorrow, the "winter-enduring foliage," "dark evergreen," settles the poet into a true orientation where his being belongs, from which he can "sing out jubilation and praise to assenting angels."

From childhood on, medieval nun Hildegard of Bingen (1098–1179) experienced visions of intense light, "much brighter than the cloud which bears the sun" (Wilhelm 1975: 104). She comments, "While I am enjoying the spectacle of this light, all sadness and sorrow disappear from my memory." Her experience, which Jung calls one of "symbolic unity," is comparable to that of Franz Wright who "saw the shining wind" (Wilhelm 1975: 104, 105). Rilke's description of discovering a true orientation, grounded in a unitary "foundation" is an element of a similar experience.

Finally, I go back in time, 2300 BCE, to verses of the first known poet, the Sumerian high priestess Enheduanna, who for forty years served the moon god and goddess, Nanna and Ningal, in their temple at Ur (from which city Abraham was to depart some 500 years after Enheduanna's death). In a long devotional poem to her personal goddess Inanna, Enheduanna describes the experience of a group of women, consecrated to Inanna:

> those warrior women
> like a single thread

come forth from beyond the river
do common work in devotion to you
whose hands sear them with purifying fire

your many devoted
who will be burnt
like sun-scorched fire bricks
pass before your eyes

(Meador 2000: 133)

Later in the same poem, Enheduanna writes these verses:

Your storm-shot torrents
drench the bare earth
moisten to life
moisture bearing light
floods the dark

(Meador 2000: 134)

The warrior women live a life of devotion to Inanna. Jung reminds us of the necessity of our devotion to individuation. He says the union of consciousness and life "if lived in complete devotion brings on an intuition of the self, the individual being." This kind of devotion, he continues, involves an active conscious return of "attention and interest ... to an inner sacred domain, which is the source and goal of the soul" (Wilhelm 1975: 99, 100).

Each of the examples I have given mentions not only suffering and sorrow, but also light. In his commentary on *The Secret of the Golden Flower*, Jung explains the necessity of fire and light in the process of producing Tao, citing the initial verse of the *Hui Ming Ching*:

If thou wouldst complete the diamond body without emanations,
Diligently heat the roots of consciousness and life.
Kindle Light in the blessed country ever close at hand,
And, there hidden, let thy true self eternally dwell.

(Wilhelm 1975: 95)

Heat emanates from the sorrow and suffering of loosening our intense attachments to the outer world. Heat, Jung explains, increases the "heightening of consciousness in order that the dwelling place of the spirit can be 'illumined' " (Wilhelm 1975: 95). Thus life in all its splendor is intensified as well, so that life and consciousness come together in a union illuminated by the intuition of the self and the experience of the presence of the totally Other, the objective psyche. This experience happens over and over again, and in a life "lived so exhaustively, and with such devotion," eventually "no more unfulfilled life-duties exist, and . . . there are no more desires which cannot be sacrificed without hesitation" (Wilhelm 1975: 112).

These beautiful words inspire me as I trudge up and down over life's difficulties. I keep them in mind (and heart) as a preparation for death. I doubt that my experience will ever be so clear and pure as that of Hildegard or the poets. I do trust them, however. I continue to slog along, finding it easier to root myself in the earth than to wait for a vision, consoled by Jung's assurance, as in this statement:

> God wants to be born in the flame of man's consciousness, leaping ever higher. And what if this has no roots in the earth? If it is not a house of stone where the fire of God can dwell, but a wretched straw hut that flares up and vanishes? Could God then be born? One must be able to suffer God. That is the supreme task. [The carrier of God] must be the advocate of the earth. God will take care of himself. . . . Let us therefore be for him limitation in time and space, an earthly tabernacle.
>
> (Adler 1975: 65)

Note

1 All quotations from the myth are from my translation (Meador 1992).

Acknowledgement

"Tenth Elegy", translated by Stephen Mitchell, from The Selected Poetry of Rainer Maria Rilke by Rainer Maria Rilke, translated by Stephen Mitchell, copyright © 1982 by Stephen Mitchell. Used by permission of Random House, Inc.

References

Adler, Gerhard (ed.) (1975) C.G. Jung Letters – Volume I, Princeton, NJ: Princeton University Press.

Henderson, Joseph L. (2005) Thresholds of Initiation, 2nd edition, Wilmette, IL: Chiron.

Jung, C.G. (1963) Memories, Dreams, Reflections, New York: Pantheon.

Jung, C.G. (1997) Visions: Notes of the Seminar Given in 1930–1934, ed. Claire Douglas, Princeton, NJ: Princeton University Press.

Meador, B. (1992) Uncursing the Dark, Wilmette, IL: Chiron.

Meador, B. (2000) Inanna: Lady of the Largest Heart, Austin, TX: University of Texas Press.

Mitchell, S. (ed. and trans.) (1995) Ahead of All Parting: The Selected Poetry and Prose of Rainer Maria Rilke, New York: Modern Library.

Rilke, R.M. (1939) Duino Elegies: The German Text, with an English Translation, Introduction, and Commentary by J.B. Leishman and Stephen Spender, New York: W.W. Norton.

Stimpson, H. (2006) "The Son Also Rises," in Mary Gannon (ed.) Poets and Writers, March/April: 34–39.

Wilhelm, R. (trans.) (1975) The Secret of the Golden Flower: With a Commentary by C.G. Jung, New York: Causeway.

Wright, F. (2004) "Prescience," The New Yorker, February 2, p. 85.

Wright, F. (2006) God's Silence, New York: Alfred A. Knopf.

Chapter 9

A meditation on death
"Cast a cold eye"

David Tresan

This chapter treats the last stage of human development. It is about death, potentially the most human of all experiences. It is also about the period directly prior to death that follows the turn from the last generative years to a final stage of depletion immediately preceding the end of life as we know it. This period is to death what the perinatal is to birth.

That the experience of death resists all objectification, all factual glosses, and all hard science restores faith in the fathomlessness of the human condition and the uniqueness of individuals. The inscrutability of death's secrets lends itself best and only to heartfelt human sensibilities, the arts, and the artistry of depth psychology. The progressivism that has prevailed in science since at least the seventeenth century and in psychology for a century has changed nothing of death the experience, has told us nothing of it. No doubt in time science will discover ways to extend life, but death will only have been pushed back. As the arch-defining constituent of the human condition, it will always come, and we will always have to contend with it as an unremitting mystery, death by death, individually. That is the most incontestable truth that a human may know.

Strictly defined and taking liberty with the title subject of this book, dying is not an initiation. Initiation in its classic form, as spelled out by Joseph Henderson after van Gennep and Victor Turner, entails three phases: a "before," a liminal state (free of all roles and social identity),[1] and an "after" (Henderson 1967). With death, as with individuation,[2] the "after" cannot be known as humans generally know things. Instead, both death and individuation remain liminal states in perpetuity and never emerge into a stage beyond. As such, they shall never be adequately predicated, never circumscribed by the mind from any Archimedean still point. Only in traditional religious systems is an "after" promised and rituals promulgated for how to enter death. This kind of certainty is not what I am writing about nor am I writing for those who are blessed enough to have such certainty. I write for the benighted regarding their knowledge of death but not for all benighted, for we are all truly that. I write only for whosoever values and knows how to value the examined life and also hopes to participate in the ending of it with as much consciousness as he or she has endeavored to participate in the other sacramental events of personal life.

There is a mythic account that says in the time of Kronos people were allowed both to know the time of their death and also to wear their clothes when they pass over, the latter meaning that deeds in life accompanied people into death. Prepared by foreknowledge, people clothed themselves in their most meretricious garments, and as a result heaven soon became overfull, bursting with the worthy dead. And so, with the passing of Kronos and the accession of Zeus, the latter decreed that the time of death was henceforth to be unknown and all clothes left behind. One went to death nude, not knowing the fate of one's soul (Plato 1961: para. 523, p. 303). And so it continues with us who come nude to death without an appointment.

It releases me to write about death as a categorical unknown, without having to fend off scientistic attempts to explain things away or respond to the contention among some that dreams are ineluctable proof of afterlife. To my mind, the only science that pertains to the thinking about individual death is the science of the humanities, the systematic advances we have made into the soft truths of the human soul. The hope of outcome lies not in the staving off of death but in finding a tolerable entente in the end that makes for some kind of personal and perhaps even objective meaning, *mirabile dictu*, a death that might be called "just" in the judgment of the dying person.

And so the first and last indulgence of a mortal is to test this thesis, whether a certain kind of work in life on the very essence of our humanity can alter our experience of death. I would like to think so.

Late styles

At the end of the seventh decade of his life, my age also as I write this chapter, Edward Said, the critic, teacher, and musician, died of leukemia. His last project, no wonder, was an inquiry into what he called "late style," the subject of a posthumous book gathered from papers and talks from the last decade of his life in which he contends that the effortful accrual of aesthetic craft and wisdom over years culminates in an ultimate style that characterizes the latter works of great artists such as Beethoven and Shakespeare. After noting the breach between the aesthetic realm and the physical body, by which he intimates his intention to pit in some way the exquisitely evolved non-creaturely mind against decay and death, Said states his premise:

> my intention is as follows: all of us, by virtue of the simple fact of being conscious, are involved in constantly thinking about and making something of our lives, self-making being one of the bases of history.
>
> (Said 2006: 3)

Elaborating further, a reviewer of Said's book comments:

What artist does not yearn, some day, to possess a "late style"? A late style would reflect a life of learning, the wisdom that comes from experience, the sadness that comes from wisdom and a mastery of craft that has nothing left to prove. It might recapitulate a life's themes, reflect on questions answered and allude to others beyond understanding. . . .

We want to be reassured that there really is something progressive about human understanding. We want to feel that in a final confrontation with mortality, something profound takes place. When the end is near, we want there to be a sign of this in the work itself, some proof of accumulated insight.

(Rothstein 2006)

Said limits his particular inquiry to those whose development can be vouchsafed in terms of their art, yet his thesis generalizes to whosoever has strived over a lifetime to understand and contend with the human condition and one's personal life such that last years may bring another kind of late style to be measured in terms other than formal art. The contention applies tacitly to the obverse: that those who have not so strived will have another kind of ending, perhaps equally or even more happy in some ways but perhaps less personally consequential in their own eyes, if truth be known.

In the instance of the non-artist, what Joseph Henderson has called the psychological attitude[3] becomes the ground against and through which the singular human life can shape itself as its own *chef d'oeuvre*, its own work of art. The late style of which Said speaks translates into a living art form, an artistic product synonymous with the very warp and woof of a person's unique and ongoing life and state of mind.

Such a dynamic life tapestry well woven may be seen as one symbol of what Jung called individuation.[4] My interest does not presently lie in exploring individuation, which state I would characterize roughly as tantamount to hard won maturity. It is more exactly late individuation that I wish to address, what comes of an individuation that perdures over time and goes finally to death. As Said (2006) points out, following Adorno, late style is also last style and coincides with last years. For Henderson it bespeaks a "late-stage or ultimate Self" (Henderson 1984: 97). The question has to do with the characteristics of psyche and also style, by which we might recognize a finely evolved and terminal individuation as we might recognize the late string quartets of Beethoven however weakly played. It is not a matter in this inquiry of the attainment to a station called individuation but rather what comes of the mature formed individual in time even unto death, an account preferably told as best possible from inside the experience.

History of discovery

I presumed that Said's taking up the subject of late style was determined at least in part by his terminal illness ("no wonder"), and in the same vein I have sought the sources that have drawn me to the same subject over equivalent years. I feel more than I know that one clear impetus was the fatal diagnosis I received eight years ago, which, after two interesting months, revealed itself as a misdiagnosis. Those two months granted me a proleptic visitation by things to come,[5] the thoughts and feelings around imminent death. I was surprised and grateful that – from beyond my will and without my consent – I found myself during that time ensconced in a peace and an easeful acceptance that I had not anticipated. The memory stays, so too the gratitude to have felt that death can be a bearable and even acceptable event, one both humanly very complex and certainly riveting.

The second impetus has to do with my relationship with Joseph Henderson, my former analyst and now longtime friend and mentor, a wonder, it seemed, who in 2003 was still practicing analysis at age 100. Around the occasion of his centennial birthday I was taken with the question of what more he had learned of his own very late development since age 64, at which time he had written an authoritative and rather complete clinical exposition of individuation (Henderson 1967: 196–221).[6] My question sought what had changed in him in the intervening almost forty years. This inquiry became the article "Thinking Individuation Forward" (Tresan 2007), but even this article had had its antecedents in the form of prior inquiries into developments I had begun to discern in patients with whom I had worked for up to and over thirty years and who were growing old in the traces of analysis with a vitality, creativity, and capacity to learn that was increasing, not diminishing. As a result, I began to think in terms of a latter life growth spurt that began in the early sixties, thoughts which coincided with entering my own seventh decade. These ideas led to an article in two parts on the phylogenetic and personal development of consciousness and transcendence (Tresan 2004). And so, I was led to the subject of late development by a groundswell of awareness regarding my own and others' aging and my equal wonder at the enduring powers of psyche.

Now at the end of my sixties, I have been led naturally and logically to the enantiodromia, the awareness that all this shall end. I am led there as I experience my own limits and those of the people I love and work for, who, so recently vital, now show signs of decline not evident a short time ago. I ask myself if our work of so many years brought to bear on the procession of our lives – theirs and mine – will count for naught at death? Will all this searching and finding mean nothing when the end is in sight except for the company we will keep each other as sentient creatures? How will it end for each of us, what the denouement, what the individual states of mind, what the styles of departure?

Refining the quest

As this chapter treats a narrow period of life, so, too, does it address a limited population.[7] I am not writing about those who die early or those who die unexpectedly and suddenly, nor about those who have almost died and did not, coming back with visions of a life after death. Nor am I writing for those who die with no reflection, be the cause physical, such as sudden stroke, heart attack, or overwhelming pain, or be it psychological, as in aversion to reflection in general or more specifically to the contemplation of death. I am writing rather to those who have lived an examined life over years and who have finally worn out, either from the timely unraveling of the genome in the most natural of ways or from any illness, such as cancer or even Alzheimer's, which lingers and allows some conscious hiatus between life and death.

Still more precisely, though, I am addressing those whose lives have actually been constructed around an epistemic hunger and questing supported by profession and/or propelled by personal *daimon*. These are, in my thinking, those who may be called, for lack of any formal appellation, people of the mind for whom life is consistently shaped by deep thought and considered imperatives, although such a committed orientation may not have been constellated or recognized until later years. The people I include in this population are not locked away in their minds or private towers, but occupy and have occupied many salt-of-the-earth roles in the world. They have acquitted themselves responsibly of the exigencies of life, have known love, and have been householders, parents, caretakers, partners, and such, but have also, over many of their years, found a way to perform their quotidian duties on, one might say, the top burners of their stoves, while simultaneously slowly baking in the oven below the abiding, perennial, existential questions of life itself.

Perhaps one may find such people more readily among writers and artists, scholars, clergy, and self-defined philosophers, but it is not to be presumed. A certain intelligence may be necessary and a certain education beneficial, but of themselves these are not sufficient. Unlike some accomplished symphony musicians who, when they retire, put their instruments away forever, the people of whom I speak never put their instruments away and never stop making music qua meaning with passion. Of all the professions, I know most particularly and personally of one that tends to be constitutionally defined by such lifelong activity. It is that of the psychoanalyst, who, while tending to the real cares and concerns of his or her patients' everyday lives and psyches, must in integrity constantly nurture and refine attitudes and philosophies that will support and inform the influences he or she brings inexorably to bear on the vital life situations of so many people. This is not to say that all or even many analysts aspire or even agree to this view of the profession nor that any live up to its demands, and I am certain that none do at all times. With regard to death and analysis, for that is what this essay is partly about, if an analyst works with a long-term patient until the death of either approaches, a certain distinction of roles becomes blurred, for the common fate that both analyst and analysand will share in time overcomes any illusion of superiority or privilege of position. At such a time, the conduct of life and analysis are finally no longer separate categories, as, I think, they have never truly been for the analyst who works and waits often for many years for his or her patients to come to full self-enfranchisement and stature. Death is the final leveler, the ultimate enforcer of mutuality.

In no way do I intend to make value judgments or give guidelines as to what makes for proper dying.[8] I hold every death unique and sacrosanct for each person who, in its throes, is not bound to any standard other than his or her own, a freedom conceivably more extensive than at any other time in life. At the instant of death all observation attests to the fact that one dies alone, no matter how many people are standing about one's bed, and the only constraints regarding what one thinks, feels, and says are those that are imposed by choice or frailty. One's experience of imminent death is totally one's own if one has the fortune, desire, and temerity to recognize it as such, to own it and resist distraction. In our western culture, it seems that anyone who turns a felicitous or stoic face towards his or her own death is in danger of being accorded hero status. People in their nineties, for instance, are often treated to gratuitous comments about their strong spirit with little reference to the substance and quality of their thinking and the conduct of their lives. Apotheosis for simply surviving into advanced age, I think, alienates a person from intimacy and from him or herself, although accolades for bearing up are certainly understandable, indicated, and unavoidable. It is my hope that for the conscious person (more about that below) in terminal straits, the heroic and its implications will have been considered over some time and not allowed in the final hour to dominate the experience of giving over. My contention is that in dying, not heroism but a certain level of consciousness which does not shrink from the event is what serves instead to shape the experience of death in a salutary way.

Consciousness and the examined life

For the psychoanalyst, consciousness is the stock in trade and the essential stuff to be worked on, although no one knows what it is or how to talk about it. A friend and scholar suggests that it is the modern and politically correct word for soul (Hughes 1996), which formulation, I think, has great merit but still offers no real clarity. To say a good soul makes for a good death is no doubt true but not useful. To try to resolve the problem of consciousness with scientific exactness is madness, but it is necessary to try to say something from experience about consciousness and its dynamics, something systematic that has the ring of truth so that the notion of a "just death" is supported by reason and stands as more than just a facile juxtaposition of words. The problem is made more difficult by our need to differentiate a less developed consciousness from one more evolved and hence more effectual as a buffer against meaningless death.

In the pursuit of consciousness – consciousness seeking consciousness – we are beset by a dilemma in that we cannot find a point of view outside the very field that we are trying to see. It is like an eye trying to look at itself. In such matters the ancient time-honored solution, the only solution, is to create a virtual viewpoint from which to look objectively, and it is from such imaginal perspectives that we tell tales about the origins of world and awareness, stories whose claims to truth lie only in their explanatory powers and sense of fit with regard to our experience. Plato's cave allegory is one such tale,[9] perhaps the prototypical example of what has been called the philosopher's myth, a way of speaking truths that otherwise are difficult or impossible to tell, hence true tales. In modernity, as we shall see, even the created viewpoint is folded into the story and ceases to remain even imaginally objective.

Let us now turn to a present-day tale that aspires to truth about individual consciousness. Consider that in young and not so young years we find ourselves in the throes of competing demands in the form of the exigencies, responsibilities, and appetites that vie with one another for attention and energy. The story unfolds if we now imagine each and every interest situated in one place on the rim of a single circle with its competing opposite on the same rim exactly 180 degrees across and if then we imagine an individual traversing this circle innumerable times, back and forth, as he or she tries to make right choices. First it's this interest, then that interest; this friend, that friend; this school, that school: this lover, that: this profession, another; save, spend; this house, no house; this car, no car; marriage, no marriage; children, no children; one child, two; this nanny, that; this vacation, that; *ad infinitum.* The multitude of crossings through the years pass through one and only one common point at the very center of the circle which, over time, becomes more known than any other place in the entire mindscape. The center point is devoid of bias; it is equidistant from all issues on the rim. As such, it is only a felt entity with no qualitative coloration derived from external sources; it does not belong to anyone or any thing on the rim, neither spouse, children, nor profession. It belongs only to the person whose circle it is and who crosses. When the prominence of the center becomes a point of repose of such significance and interest that it competes with aspects of the rim, then one's consciousness has been altered in a certain way. Energy is no longer solely heroic in that it is not all goal-directed, not materialistic in that it doesn't seek only worldly boons. There is now a center in its own right to consider, purely subjective, entirely self-justifying, and absolutely ineffable. The rearrangement is not necessarily dramatic nor radically life altering, but it may be.

For a few (a perennially "thin and ineffective" stratum of humankind, says one thinker: Voegelin 1974: 217), the advent of discovering oneself is tantamount to a nuclear explosion in two different senses. The first is that it is a revolutionary experience at one's essential core and may set off a chain reaction of realizations whose energies once released may continue for the remainder of one's life. The second sense is that as an explosion, it qualifies as a catastrophe in the sense that Bion uses the word, a globally upending experience that radically alters life as it has been known. It is, by and large, the experience of Parmenides (fl. 500 BCE), when, along with other pre-Socratic philosophers in pursuit of the one element common to all things, he discovered the answer in the ubiquity of Being and experienced it as divine. He realized that it was not only the common ground of all that existed but also imperishable and eternal. So, too, can any person be similarly impacted who encounters in awareness for the first time the center that introduces the notion of pure being, namely, his or her own.

The vehicle that such energies fuel may be any kind of work in the world that people usually pursue. Many kinds of *prima materia* basic to the arts, to hard sciences, to economics, etc., are potential windows into the deepest mysteries of the world. But often the energy seeks its métier in a profession whose raison d'être is the continuation of the exploration of itself, the exploration of consciousness seeking consciousness, a tautology experienced by the seeker to be of intrinsically consummate value. The search set in motion becomes yet another chapter, no matter how modest, in that infinite regress that has been spoken of in history as the *anthropologische Wendung*,[10] traditionally translated in English as the turning to the subject. The ever inward turning of observing consciousness, the preoccupation with epistemology, began in earnest in modernity with Descartes and moved a quantum leap ahead with Kant. It continues through the present in such people who are still drawn to turn their minds into the core of their own subjectivity, seeking ever more comprehensive understanding of their human condition, and, over the years, like peeling layers from an onion, finding various degrees of success while being changed by the search.

As a dog chases his tail or the eye strains to see itself or like the boy who turns into butter as he runs around the tree fleeing the tiger, this reflexive activity, the "I" looking for "I," finds focused awareness and directed consciousness of limited use. Instead, the search without a beginning and without an end finds itself part of an ambient field of sentient and intelligent activity, and the idea of looking for a simple object as answer becomes incomprehensible. Consciousness is no longer consciousness of anything but itself, and Cartesian subject-object syntax no longer pertains. Participant in the search, the seeker is no longer at a remove looking on; he or she is part and parcel of the search. As such, what is called consciousness stands as a perpetual reflexive process, a function, a methodology with discrimination but without an author, and the contribution of the seeker, in addition to the energy, is the sensorium in which all takes place, one that is forever container to the perpetual turn down and in of mind, a process betrayed only if foreclosed by a fixed system or other reification such as archetypes can erroneously be taken to be.[11] The logic of the ambient state is bi-logical (Rayner 1995); opposites exist without canceling one another out. The sentient field abounds with unresolved antinomy and paradox, fed by the power of its own preoccupation. The view from the ambient field of consciousness is the psychological attitude that Henderson speaks of as overarching and comprehending all other worldly attitudes.

A language for consciousness

Jung knew that consciousness as an ambient field necessitated what he called "antinomian" language (Jung 1963/1970: 534, 538). He said such a field (the *Unus Mundus*) was only theoretically possible and the matter of language therefore moot (p. 538), but, regarding language, he accomplished similar ends nonetheless by the use of symbols and myth to capture paradox and antinomy. Nothing in the pursuit of depth is more important than language. We must have language. Having none is like having an expressive aphasia that entails not only a loss of the language to express oneself but also the loss of the very ideas that cannot be expressed. The perennial continuation of the *anthropologische Wendung* always demands a dialectic with oneself and others including the ineffable other. On this depends our penetration of reality and our deepening. The matter of language is made particularly difficult because the inner dialogue is a field and a process, and there are no direct referents or representations for it in the world of the senses. This is why there is a reversion to symbol, myth, and the philosopher's tale, all of which use sensory language and images to limn out what cannot be known directly. How otherwise, for instance, can one speak of emergence or transformation, initiation or even understanding without referencing at some point some thing in the world? How does one depict spirit or soul or even psyche?[12]

The appearance of an enduring extrasensory consciousness declared itself for the first time in the history of the western world in Mesopotamia with Abraham and in Greece with the pre-Socratic philosophers. In the latter, the need to express the experience in terms other than revealed writ or history gave rise to the invention of philosophy and the coining of the concept *daimonios aner*, spiritual man, he who could traffic in such intangibles. We are still negotiating that époque that began in Greece with the implications of Being, that most diaphanous of qualities and the least often noted or heeded (Zubiri 1969/1970/1994: 19–20). Bion, perhaps unique in psychology, postulated a virtual "language of achievement" fashioned after Keats' negative capability which allows for antinomy and stands as an alternative to the language of the senses.[13] All art forms also qualify as language of soul; so too, it has been noted, do symbols and myths properly used and adequately grasped.[14] Such language is also the imageless logos, after Hegel, of which Giegerich speaks as the soul's logical life (Giegerich 2001). In the same vein, the piece you are now reading may be understood as simply one more attempt to express something of the most-difficult-to-express.

It is common wisdom to assume that people often do not care to speak about death, even when it is reasonably imminent, because they are afraid. Although I think that observation bears out this assumption to a large extent, I also think that another reason for the silence, perhaps the more significant, is that no one knows quite how to talk about it. Very few seem to have the language. It is my experience after reading portions of this piece to some mature people who have qualified as recalcitrant-speakers-about-death that when language is made available, much changes. When I read portions of this piece to an older patient, not only was his interest mobilized but also a kind of fascination and an impetus to update themes of a long life. Shortly after, he dreamed that he should not let me talk to him about death because his task remained still one of seeking out the bountifulness of life. Our animated discussion continued with a softening of the polar positions of talking versus not talking about death. Fear did not seem to play a part in the matter. Before this discussion, as it had been for years, the two of us had been as if alone on the brink of an abyss, looking down into the dark and bottomless void. There had not been much we were able to say about it.

Life, not schematics

The circle above is, of course, only a tale with its ramifications. As such, it is only a schematic about life and begs a better fleshing out in terms of human experience. For instance, the center of which I speak is always present throughout life, early and late. It is often experienced through intimations and in occasional states that are often evanescent but which may haunt one's memories. Sometimes, the environment suppresses it so that its presence remains an unknown even to itself (Winnicott 1958/1975: 212). For many people the center dwells in the wings of a person's life tacitly attendant on what is transpiring on stage, letting its presence be known only if ecstatic or in love or in reaction to serious transgression. Its establishment as a stable and paramount entity in awareness – Jung's reality of the psyche – is not to be taken for granted as a given in any one human or as a necessary feature of the human condition. Its presence in some constancy is not a ubiquitous attribute. Moreover, in Jung and others it is left unclear whether the process that leads to a strong instantiation of self is a natural one, mediated automatically by nature, in which a transformation takes place of its own accord if one simply engages authentically in life or whether something unnatural is needed. I think the latter is the case, although it is indisputable that in many lives, even at very young ages, an epiphany is granted that in some form announces one's sense of self to oneself. The effect of the revelation may persist for a lifetime, or it may not. The saints of the twelfth and thirteenth centuries were all young men and women who came to ineffable experiences at young ages, whereas we tend to think of such stations of maturity as manifesting in the second half of life and after much worldly travail.

In my experience, the move to a more radical state of Self recognition is a quantum event that, although it comes in a piece and often at the advent of a crisis of some sort, is afterwards seen to have been in the making for a long time. Although the galvanizing experience for each person is unique, experience suggests that there are three essential conditions that pertain, no one sufficient in itself to effect transformation. The first is that life be lived not only authentically but effortfully as well; that is to say that one live at the edge of oneself as much as reasonably possible, awake to one's sense of potential and opportunity and attuned and morally responsive to one's inner urges and categorical imperatives when discerned. The second is that one be able to love something or some living sentient being, without which occurrence it is impossible to satisfy the third condition, which is to know loss and suffering. The last in particular, loss and suffering, often ushers in the shift in consciousness of which I speak and also predisposes to knowing death and the difference between a just death and one that is unjust.

Unjust death

The two experiences that I cited above as motivating my writing on the subject of death (i.e., my misdiagnosis and Joseph Henderson) were a deliberate incomplete accounting. I have withheld a third until now because it introduces the present topic, that of unjust death which is legion. Not keeping with common understanding, when I speak of a just or unjust death, I speak of a judgment made only by the dying person or by one who has truly taken in the poignancy of that person's experience. No one else, neither institution, society, nor science, can make that kind of judgment. As such, a death may be just or unjust in the eyes of the collective, and only the dying may know which it is. Examples of such are to be found in the accounts of Christ and Socrates and also in the person of Sydney Carton, the belated hero of *A Tale of Two Cities* (Dickens 1859) who, at the end, says to himself that his dying is a far better thing than he has ever done before. As examples show, the collective may change its mind in time as it comes to appreciate the subjective state of the dead and the true nature of his or her death.

Ernest Becker, following Kierkegaard, writes that no one has the temerity to face death consciously and undefended with perhaps the rare exception of a very few, and those few have been drafted into the select by having "tasted of death," a quotation he takes from Martin Luther (Becker 1973: 88). I think Luther is emphatically right about such necessity as a requisite for a salutary consciousness in the face of death. Confrontation with one's own imminent death or the death of a truly loved other is an all or none affair that qualifies, if any does, as an unmitigated catastrophe that deeply rearranges consciousness, but the special effect of what one feels to be an egregiously unjust death is experienced as beyond catastrophe, if such be possible, and stands to churn consciousness to an even greater pitch if collapse does not come first. In an unjust death, the specific circumstances leading to death are an important consideration as is the time in life and how someone dies.

My personal experience with death did not begin early in my life. I think that many people who write of death have been deeply impacted by an experience of it, often an untimely experience and often in childhood by the loss of a close relative or friend. But this was not the case for me. I remember as a child wondering for years why no one in my family died. I had a morbid curiosity born of the absence of experience in the face of the palpable awe and hush of adults, emotions which accompanied the deaths of others in the community, especially the deaths of children. It was the time of World War II and although uncles were fighting and soldiers dying, no one that we knew died, or at least I was not told of it. No one spoke to me of soldiers' deaths. Vague lamentations extended to the distant unknown family in Poland, long anonymous after some decades except for glimpses from old black and white photographs. Death was more an ambiance than a fact. It seemed to me from all this that, first, nothing in the world was more important than death, second, no one actually knew the least thing about it, third, the subject was obligatorily hidden, especially from children, and was treated with great delicacy by adults, lest, it seemed, one do harm through insensitivity or simply by stirring unwelcome feelings, and fourth, death was the worst thing one could have happen. To have access to the arcanum of death and to the recently dead seemed to me to be the privilege of special people who had the need and right to know either through role (clergy or doctor) or kinship (family). Such connections are what allowed one into the most tender inner sanctum of those closest to death and to the taboo-like knowledge that lay there. It seemed to me that in such places were to be found, if ever it could, the very secret of life.

As a child, I was never privy to such venues, could never hope to be, and yet, unknown to all but myself, I was beset by wonderment about how the deceased died, exactly how, what the passing looked like, what was said, and, finally, how the family could tolerate irrevocable loss. I longed to know and knew I never would as long as I was a child. I imagined that were I present at a death and were I truly attentive beyond what others could conceive of being, perhaps I could see something that had not been seen before, unlikely as that seemed even to me. I see in retrospect that the rationale lay in what I saw as the capitulation of adults to the inevitability of death in contrast to my faith that I, although full of doubt, might see something that they had given up even looking for. I kept these fantasies to myself, quietly and patiently aware that there might come a time when they could be tested. The opportunity came for the first time in my psychiatric residency.

In medical school and internship I had encountered death on a number of occasions but, in a strange sense, not one of them belonged to me. Each person who died was basically being treated by the institution of which I was a part, and although a member of a team, I was by and large a bystander. I had occasion to speak personally to the dying, but I found myself strapped by the same constraints that the adults of my childhood had seemed to experience. I had no explicit permission to intrude and was loath to upset the calm of the dying process by asking questions that might be offensive or at best awkward. Moreover, my neophyte status as student or intern seemed to me to lack an authority that could otherwise have been experienced by a dying patient as reassuring and consoling.

The first death that I truly experienced as my own, so to speak, was that of a young man in the hospital freshly diagnosed with leukemia, whose wife, overwhelmed by her reaction to the sudden devastation of her life and young marriage, asked for psychiatric consultation. On repeated requests to the nurses, she was told that no psychiatrist was willing to consult with her but that one could be found if it were a matter of imminent suicide. I was not aware of these negotiations. It was shortly after I saw her that the husband, a frightened and very bright graduate student who seemed somehow ill disposed to psychiatry,[15] allowed me to try to help him with his extreme restlessness and agitation during his first isolating stint of reverse isolation while receiving chemotherapy. On my suggestion, his strong will enabled him to remain motionless in bed while he put every sensation into words. Our engagement was successful. His body and mind came back under some control.

In a short while he had the hoped-for remission, and we continued to meet regularly over the next year until he died. That I call this "my first death" had to do with the degree of identification I brought to his life and overall condition and his allowing it. I found myself inside his situation, so to speak, and also deeply empathic with the wife's experience. His death came in the hospital after two or so days of coma, and, running from a meeting not fast enough, I missed his actual demise by minutes. His wife did not. She was present until he drew his last breath, which was what she had hoped to be able to do and had feared in the beginning she could not. That she was present both psychically and physically at the end was her pyrrhic victory. Frightened and truly brave, though seeming sometimes disaffected and defended against softness and sentimentality, which I think might have been his wont, the patient allowed me a proximity to the intimacy of death that I had never before had. His devoted wife also.

Nonetheless, all the while I had struggled with a sense of incomplete engagement. I wondered later whether it was his fear and natural reserve or my fear and inadequacy of depth that was responsible for what I felt in the aftermath. In retrospect and with the writing of this account, I have come to understand a dream of his whose significance I had missed at the time, and I now better realize that in spite of his seeming reserve, he had indeed allowed me to coach him in his final ordeal. In the dream, the revered Vince Lombardi places a reassuring hand on the patient's shoulder as the patient works the flippers of a pinball machine to prevent the white balls from overwhelming the red.[16]

Immediately after his death I felt a sense of deep failure, which I kept secret. The wife, a writer, subsequently wrote a book about his death in which I was accorded accolades, but what I felt was shame. No one knew. I hardly let myself know except for the feelings that made me want to hide my face and made it impossible for me to read the book for several years. It was as if my first real encounter with death had defeated my lifelong expectation that I would see something of consequence that, even if the vision did not heal, would bring something new, something consoling, something comprehensible to death.

Looking back with sadness, I realize that I had also been unwittingly looking for some flaw in my patient's life, something I could recognize as wrong, if not in his character or relationships, then perhaps in his alignment with the order of the cosmos (whatever that kind of stoic notion meant to me at the time) or perhaps some familial history of deep anger maybe, something. There was nothing convincing that I could find. If I could have discerned something, anything, so the tale would go, I might have been able to impede his impending death. Of course, none of this was more than a naive fantasy. The patient's only flaw was being human and hence mortal, mine in unwittingly acting as if premature death bespoke personal imperfection and retribution for something; that is, a punishment.

Later

Twenty years passed. My professional life was a consistent tending to difficulties, pain, and suffering of various sorts. My children became older and more independent, and upon receiving an invitation to present a paper at a large conference, I felt that I had at last arrived at a clear and settled enough plateau in my life with enough discretionary time and energy to write something substantial purely of my own choosing and from my own interests. I chose a topic that had over the years been the most enigmatic to me in its refusal to be circumscribed but also carried the aura of joy and celebration. The subject was Jung's concept of the anima, what he called, among other things, the archetype of life itself.

It was a fool's errand. I intended to write the definitive explication of the idea and instead found myself at the computer for months becoming more and more distraught, my thoughts more and more fragmented. What I did not realize was that I was dealing in problems of category. I intended to bring focused awareness and directed thinking to an analogical and transcendent issue whose essence was its very irreducibility and its other-dimensional nature.[17] It was an issue of thinking in antinomies which, to retain their identity, need to remain dissolved in the matrix of an ambient field of consciousness, for which at that time I had neither language nor experience of nor even recognized as such. The effect was that my mind was rent asunder, and only at deadline and in desperation did I come to a very incomplete statement that relied upon personal anecdotal material and my first foray into a "language of achievement" before the letter (Tresan 1992: 73–110). As I approached completion, I felt delivered of an enormous burden, and to celebrate what had been months of agonizing inadequacy and essentially monk-like asceticism, I arranged a brunch at home for several old friends whom I had not seen for that period of time.

What happened next is important for this account in two matters only. The first is that something dear to me died. The second is the effect it had on me and its subsequent implications for consciousness in the face of death. What I will present may be seen by others in other ways. That is their right. I have no interest in insisting on my view as the exclusive consensual truth, only on the veracity of my experience as I alone know it. I mean no deliberate harm to anyone in the telling of this, although I must admit to holding the principals in no esteem but also in indifference. I considered making up another story entirely to make the same point, but the actual events were uncannier and more symbolically trenchant than anything my imagination can conjure even after these many years.

In short, it was in the fullness of spring, and the grounds around our house in the woods were like a Garden of Eden. Coming up the front flights of stairs, a then dear and trusted friend bent over and picked up a passing garter snake and threw it onto the shoulder of his wife, who was several steps above and in front of him as she approached the house. I don't think he intended for it to happen, but the snake seemed to help out and sprung from his hand as he threw. Surprised and absolutely alarmed, she shrieked, tried to beat her shoulder with papers she held in the same hand, pumped her legs, and ran suddenly forward towards the house. Between her and the house was my dog, who had been leading our procession up the stairs. He too was completely surprised and alarmed, and with his mouth seized the forearm of the hand with the papers, one strong holding bite that he released at once on command. I was about five feet from all that happened. So much for the Garden of Eden. So much for the quest for knowledge.

My animal was a well-bred, papered, trained show dog, an American Staffordshire Terrier whose breed fell within the category of pit bull look-alikes, a group under constant attack at that time for its behavior, properly in some instances it would seem, certainly not in all. For this bite, he was peremptorily and automatically classified as a dangerous dog, the draconian constraints entailing a regimen appropriate for a jungle animal. For us, it meant we were sued for two and a half million dollars. It was averred that he had had previous dangerous incidents that we had not disclosed. I think and still insist that this was not a properly informed, accurate, or fair contention. In my opinion it was a self-serving misrepresentation. No matter. I frantically appealed to the common sense of the local humane society, to veterinarians, to the city manager who headed the animal control committee for all the county's cities, and to the county counsel as well. I could not believe that for such an understandable event, my dog would be so mercilessly treated. Moreover, other guests had witnessed the entire happening at close quarters, and that their accounts were being completely discounted left me incredulous and my sense of reality and decency outraged.

The immediate situation, though, was that my household did not know what to do with a forcibly closeted and now very unhappy dog who before had been joyous. Fear had been struck into us by the threats alone that any further untoward behavior on his part would seal his doom. We feared to leave him even in his outside pen, and we irrationally feared that the next person who came to our house might somehow find reason to lodge some kind of complaint and force his death by decree. We were all living each day in dread, sadness, and an air of darkness. I pondered long and hard and came finally to imagine, against reason and inclination, that the right thing for all, including my dog, was to kill him, which I did, or rather had done. This I did in an agony mixed of deep despair and toothless rage. He was five years old, the apple of my eye, my bonded companion. If you don't know what this is about, I am sure I cannot tell you. My guy was without expression when the injection was administered. I had never killed anything I loved before. I thought I would be able to rise to a seemingly ordained sacrifice, but I found it was not to rise but to stoop and lower than imagination can fathom.

The next day I sought out my wife at her work. "What have I done, what have we done?" I said. The light had gone out in my life and stayed out for the next three years. Longer.

Another life

At the age of 58, Tolstoy published *The Death of Ivan Ilyich* (Tolstoy 1886/1981). It portrayed the death of a man of some position who died as lonely as he had lived and who was without awareness of his plight until he knew he was dying. One might say that it is a story of an unconscious death or, at best, a death where the waking came too late either to mourn his life or to rectify what had been so wrong. That Ilyich might have experienced his as an unjust death would have to do with its having come too prematurely for repentance and too early for having learned what faith is about. It's a cautionary tale, this death, and the interest it holds for me lies not with Ivan Ilyich but with the man whose life enabled and motivated him to write it, Tolstoy himself.

Around the age of 48, Tolstoy experienced a sea change within himself and later wrote a stark account of it in his book *A Confession* (1879–82). Of the change, he says:

> Then occurred what happens to everyone sickening with a mortal internal disease. [He was not physically ill.] At first trivial signs of indisposition

appear to which the sick man pays no attention; then these signs reappear more and more often and merge into one uninterrupted period of suffering. The suffering increases, and before the sick man can look round, what he took for a mere indisposition has already become more important to him than anything else in the world – it is death!

That is what happened to me. . . .

I felt that what I had been standing on had collapsed and that I had nothing left under my feet. What I had lived on no longer existed, and there was nothing left.

(Tolstoy 2001: Chapter III)

Successful in all worldly ways, renowned, wealthy, connected in high places, gifted, robust, he had no reason to despair and yet he did. For three years, according to *A Confession*, Tolstoy grappled every day with the desire to kill himself. His psychic situation is best portrayed, I think, by the following dream with his own introduction:

a few days ago, when revising it [his written account of his ordeal] and returning to the line of thought and to the feelings I had when I was living through it all, I had a dream. This dream expressed in condensed form all that I had experienced and described, and I think therefore that, for those who have understood me, a description of this dream will refresh and elucidate and unify what has been set forth at such length in the foregoing pages [of *A Confession*]. The dream was this:

I saw that I was lying on a bed. I was neither comfortable nor uncomfortable: I was lying on my back. But I began to consider how, and on what, I was lying – a question which had not till then occurred to me. And observing my bed, I saw I was lying on plaited string supports attached to its sides: my feet were resting on one such support, my calves on another, and my legs felt uncomfortable. I seemed to know that those supports were moveable, and with a movement of my foot I pushed away the furthest of them at my feet – it seemed to me that it would be more comfortable so. But I pushed it away too far and wished to reach it again with my foot, and that movement caused the next support under my calves to slip away also, so that my legs hung in the air. I made a movement with my whole body to adjust myself, fully convinced that I could do so at once; but the movement caused the other supports under me to slip and to become entangled, and I saw that matters were going quite wrong: the whole of the lower part of my body slipped and hung down, though my feet did not reach the ground. I was holding on only by the upper part of my back, and not only did it become uncomfortable but I was even frightened. And then only did I ask myself about something that had not before occurred to me. I asked myself: Where am I and what am I lying on? And I began to look around and first of all to look down in the direction which my body was hanging and whither I felt I must soon fall. I looked down and did not believe my eyes. I was not only at a height comparable to the height of the highest towers or mountains, but at a height such as I could never have imagined.

I could not even make out whether I saw anything there below, in that bottomless abyss over which I was hanging and whither I was being drawn. My heart contracted, and I experienced horror. To look thither was terrible. If I looked thither I felt that I should at once slip from the last support and perish. And I did not look. But not to look was still worse, for I thought of what would happen to me directly I fell from the last support. And I felt that from fear I was losing my last supports, and that my back was slowly slipping lower and lower. Another moment and I should drop off. And then it occurred to me that this cannot be real. It is a dream. Wake up! I try to arouse myself but cannot do so. What am I to do? What am I to do? I ask myself, and look upwards. Above, there is also an infinite space. I look into the immensity of sky and try to forget about the immensity below, and I really do forget it. The immensity below repels and frightens me; the immensity above attracts and strengthens me. I am still supported above the abyss by the last supports that have not yet slipped from under me; I know that I am hanging, but I look only upwards and my fear passes. As happens in dreams, a voice says: "Notice this, this is it!" And I look more and more into the infinite above me and feel that I am becoming calm.

I remember all that has happened, and remember how it all happened; how I moved my legs, how I hung down, how frightened I was, and how I was saved from fear by looking upwards. And I ask myself: Well, and now am I not hanging just the same? And I do not so much look round as experience with my whole body the point of support on which I am held. I see that I no longer hang as if about to fall, but am firmly held. I ask myself how I am held: I feel about, look round, and see that under me, under the middle of my body, there is one support, and that when I look upwards I lie on it in the position of securest balance, and that it alone gave me support before. And then, as happens in dreams, I imagined the mechanism by means of which I was held; a very natural intelligible, and sure means, though to one awake that mechanism has no sense. I was even surprised in my dream that I had not understood it sooner. It appeared that at my head there was a pillar, and the security of that slender pillar was undoubted though there was nothing to support it. From the pillar a loop hung very ingeniously and yet simply, and if one lay with the middle of one's body in that loop and looked up, there could be no question of falling. This was all clear to me, and I was glad and tranquil. And it seemed as if someone said to me: "See that you remember."

And I awoke.

(Tolstoy 2001: Chapter XVI)

Coming about

Ernest Becker died in 1974 at the age of 49.[18] Two months later, his classic work *Denial of Death* won the Pulitzer Prize for general non-fiction (Becker 1973). Becker had written it the year before at about the same age as Tolstoy was at the onset of his ordeal depicted in *A Confession* quoted above.

Unlike Tolstoy, Becker never had the opportunity to experience a later life development. In his book he brilliantly articulates the basic foundational dilemma of the human condition and his ideas about how it is solved by humanity in general. We are beings conscious of ourselves and our lives, but we still must die. In response to this paradox, our terror of death gives rise to a ubiquity of denial through heroics, which is, according to Becker, the natural reaction to the ubiquity of dread. The indisputable strength of Becker's book is the posing of the problem, but he did not live long enough, nor die protractedly enough, to know the truth of the answers he suggests. He offers nothing convincing (to me) of how death may end in a denouement that may be neither tragic nor denied. His answers for humankind are, without argument, a brilliant, speculative, and intellectual tour de force, but they do not correspond with experience, at least not my own nor that of others I have known.

Becker is of historical interest with regard to the attitudes toward death in the 1970s and to the short distance I think we have come with regard not to compassion and openness around death but to understanding. Becker began his work as the spiritual, the existential, and the psychedelic were just beginning to impact the culture in a major way, albeit with great initial resistance. The subjective was coming into prominence in psychology as an ultimate source of truth and what psychoanalysis had previously pathologized in human behavior was being championed as variants of the normative. Kohut had entered the scene from within orthodoxy, and self psychology had been launched. Humanism in its commonsense goodness was mixing with the notion of the transcendent as the east came to the west in the form of Tibetan and Zen Buddhism, Jungian psychology, cults, and communes. Becker was one of a group of potent academics who were bringing a non-medical paradigm to traditional psychoanalysis and psychotherapy. Among them were Thomas Szasz, Erwin Goffman, Phillip Rieff, *inter alia*, the influential Szasz being the only one in the medical academy.

Becker champions the inevitability of a psychology that includes religion and metaphysics so that we can put aside the defensiveness and heroic behavior of a limited human consciousness and, surrendering to larger powers, feel reasonably secure even in the face of death. Immediately, though, he betrays himself conceptually. The human, he says, beneficially trades the lesser cultural and worldly heroism for "cosmic heroism." What he does not factor in is that a religious attitude in whatever realm is the antithesis of the heroic, notwithstanding the fundamentalist agendas that abound today. The hero is characterized by the overcoming of obstacles, the attainment of goals, and the celebration of strength and prowess, attributes fit for worldly pursuits. It stands in contrast to the quintessential religious attitude of surrender. One begins to think that it is the hero in Becker who is paradoxically writing about not being heroic but, all the while, not embodying the spirit of surrender. In his writings, he shows himself a vigorous dialectician, a powerful polemicist, and an even more impressive advocate. He is a hero, I think, actually a very appropriate way to be at age 50.

Towards the end of *Denial of Death*, Becker proposes a psychology mixed with religion and metaphysics such that it becomes an "adequate belief system" (Becker 1973: 272). The first way towards this end is to be a creative genius as a psychologist, like Freud, and "use psychology as the immortality vehicle [*sic*] for oneself." The second is "to use the language and concepts of psychotherapy in much of one's waking life, so that it becomes a lived belief system." The third way is

> to take psychology and deepen it with religious and metaphysical associations so that it becomes actually a religious belief system with some breadth and depth. At the same time, the psychotherapist himself beams out the steady and quiet power of transference and becomes the guru-figure of the religion [!]
>
> (Becker 1973: 273)

I think the above is enough to demonstrate that having tasted of the transcendent, Becker is rather lost regarding its laws and nature and how to conceptualize or facilitate it heuristically and realistically in the practice of therapy or psychoanalysis or life. To me, it has always been a potential fallacy of humanism that the human will unwittingly dominate and then absorb the transcendent and fail to maintain a salutary balance. The fallacy seemed to show itself in the sometimes almost swaggering potency of guru-like figures during the heyday of humanism who, it seemed to me, had incorporated the mana of the divine without indigestion. They were like self-appointed cultural heroes with followers. In effect, though, with regard to the transcendent, Becker cannot get off the ground, transcendent language notwithstanding. And, as he fails to effect a resolution born of experience, it is with a certain impotency that he ends. Here is the last sentence of the last chapter of *Denial of Death*. It is not even despairing:

> The most that any one of us can seem to do is to fashion something – an object or ourselves – and drop it into the confusion, make an offering of it, so to speak, to the life force.
>
> (Becker 1973: 285)

What Becker did not have the chance to experience was the instruction that

Luther had given him and that I referred to above: "As Luther urged us: 'I say die, i.e., taste death as though it were present' " (Becker 1973: 88).

And:

> The self must be destroyed, brought down to nothing in order for self-transcendence to begin. Then the self can begin to relate itself to powers beyond itself.
>
> (Becker 1973: 89)[19]

It is a sad commentary, an unjust death, I think. Had Becker had the time or had he perhaps miraculously recovered from his cancer, maybe with the help of dubious fortune he could have followed out the psychology that begins when a person finally loses everything, "absolutely everything, in a way that no one has lost it in reality," adds Kierkegaard (Becker 1973: 91).

Continuing

In Tolstoy's later years, his committed religious life and his movement to disabuse himself thoroughly of worldly goods in the service of the peasants who worked his lands bespoke an enduring metanoia, a thoroughgoing change of heart and mind. His munificence was contested by his wife, and like the biblical Jacob, his last years were by no means tranquil (Zornberg 1995: 243), but all that is in keeping with the lack of ideal resolutions that Said (2006) says pertains to late style.[20]

In the dream from *A Confession*, Tolstoy's precarious suspension over the void speaks most directly to my experience after the death of my dog. The upshot of killing my dog was that I felt I had essentially lost my life. I was certainly lost and in acute pain, and the stark finality of death impressed itself on me as a new and uncanny realization. My situation felt utterly hopeless, for it was irreversible. I was deeply impacted on the very first day by the overwhelming silence that I felt everywhere. It surprised me and haunted me. In the house, I realized that I kept listening for the tinkle of his dog tags. In several days, the experience was of a silent scream, like in the painting by Munch. I cried all the time and my head often just hung from my neck. It was clear that I had to take time off from work for everyone's sake. During that interim, with very few exceptions, patients did not leave my practice. Already dealing with a recent serious illness of a child, a relatively new patient had dreamed of sitting across from me in my office gently stroking a boiled and hairless dog in his lap. We both felt it appropriate for him to find help elsewhere. Two other patients seemed disturbed beyond consolation, angry that I could not simply put my grief aside to be as I had been. Others, among them people who had lost a parent in childhood, seemed to benefit from being privy to what was happening with me that I could not hide, and they were moved to revisit with awareness their own childhood alienation in the course of the death in their respective families. When I returned to work, I found that it was impossible for me not to associate to what had happened and what was happening (the law suit and the grief), but it surprised and interested me that whatever specific aspect of my problem was being ineluctably conjured up in any one hour seemed relevant to the patient I was with. With one person I would find myself fearing that testimony in the legal case would be falsified, with another I would be taken again with the terrible sadness of loss, with another it was anger or alienation, and with yet another the guilt and shame at having killed my dog. These different reactions I took to be specific countertransference reactions, hence meaningful information about the issues in the room over and above my ubiquitous preoccupation. I was relieved to find these discriminations helpful and think they allowed work to move forward with integrity, at that time a matter of concern for me as a freshly and unquestionably wounded analyst.

I continued to have no appetite and lost weight. I did not sleep. I exercised regularly and felt I was a different person from the one who had worked out when I had my dog. Familiarity with myself seemed curiously unavailable without my companion. I wondered if it would ever be different. Colleagues judged me and did not realize that, bereft of my skin, I was involuntarily judging them also at the same time, taking them in. I felt I could see who knew what I knew, who had known deep pain, who had no clue, who was kind and who insensitive, who peremptory in their judgment, and who interested in knowing what had really happened. I found that few were kind beyond amenities, and few cared about knowing the facts of the matter, which now seems all right. I think that many judged me harshly simply for the intensity of my feelings. I felt like a pariah, but there were a few people who were truly compassionate and wanting to understand. I have never forgotten these people. In time and without recrimination, though, I have altered my expectations of people. I have reset my default position for what passes for normal relatedness in groups I know. It was very surprising that in groups where one might anticipate compassion, it was lacking, while in others more seemingly superficial, a spontaneous instinctive understanding was readily forthcoming.

I felt hate, and I placed blame. I was grateful for the hate. I think it helped keep me alive. Killing myself, I thought, would have been taken as some kind of admission of guilt for what had happened and an additional betrayal of my dog, who had already been betrayed once. The blame was replete with outrage. It was the absolute incredulity that this could have been allowed to happen when it so easily did not have to be. I imputed it then and now to the moral and intellectual laziness of people, their easy viciousness when affronted, and the danger to the individual even in intelligent communities from the impersonality of bureaucracies. I came to feel that no one is so small that he or she cannot cause the most egregious harm. I felt alienated from my neighbors (one of whom I felt had opportunistically exploited my situation for personal ends), from my colleagues, the official dog worlds, my local governments, most everyone.

But mostly I was overwhelmed by what it meant to have killed something I loved, a dog in my case, the enormity of the sin, the weight of the burden. (I apologize to all those who have lost loved humans for going on about a dog. My fate was what it was. I can do no other than acknowledge it.) I was not a killer and never considered I could be, but I think it had always been the collectively responsible and ethical citizen in me that knew it would never cross that line. I had never realized the horrific personal consequences for doing so. In the course of all this, I discovered the ineluctable obligations that love entails, and how people can choose to sacrifice their lives for others.

For right or wrong, I came to feel that the responsibility for an animal is as great as for a child who, at least, is protected by human laws and will not likely be found guilty until proven innocent. I realized that any attempt on the part of an owner to defend his or her animal's behavior was automatically looked upon with suspicion and that it was easy for anyone for any reason to be disdainful of intelligence or plausible intention in considering the behavior of other species. It felt to me that a human adult would always be complicit in some degree and always somewhat responsible for what befell him or her, or if not, had at least the capacity to understand what was happening and perhaps defend him or herself. Not a dog. The dog came to represent to me the most abject of victims, as helpless as the most helpless child. A dog under attack by humans, I felt, was liable to find himself like the Jew in Nazi Germany or Christ-like in his innocence, that is, when the dog was indeed innocent. My ethical obligations in the face of such vulnerability became palpable to me. I think that St Francis knew what this was about, this similarity of animals to Christ.

During this time and while campaigning for a change of the dangerous dog laws, I volunteered through various groups to give aid to people whose animals they felt were being unfairly treated by the organizations designated to care for them. Some of the cases were excruciating. One involved a dog shot in the head by a humane society officer in front of the family for having run out of a gate left momentarily open. (The dog was being interned at home under the dangerous dog laws.) When I answered the phone, all I could hear was the screaming and wailing of a family in agony. Finally the story came forth. On another occasion, a dog owner became psychotic at the peremptory and, in my judgment, unwarranted killing of his two dogs the morning that a court order to desist had been obtained but not yet delivered. I testified for a homeless man whose dog, his only and longtime companion, was being taken away because of his breed, almost certainly to be euthanized.[21] This man had been arrested as a child for stealing food from neighborhood houses to give to the dog that his alcoholic father had staked out in his backyard and refused to feed. The dog had starved to death.

During this time I read books on death and bereavement. It consoled me and stirred my compassion to read of intolerable deaths, lost children, deaths of families by drunken drivers, poignant stories with special circumstances like the man who, cleaning his hand gun, accidentally shot his teenage daughter, his only child, in the forehead and immediately shot himself also in the forehead. I could understand instantly why he had had to kill himself. I also wondered how the wife could possibly tolerate the loss. Should he have shot her too or she herself?

Time helps. It helped to have the legal proceedings come to closure regardless of the outcome and after a period of time that I felt was painfully protracted and cruel, which, I came to appreciate, is common to every law suit defendant. The lessons I learned have stayed. All of them, I think, but without the passion and with more balance regarding the inevitability of human failings. The remorse and shame have also remained, more, though, in the form of uncompromising ethical guidelines than as raw emotions. A new dog was balm for my heart, and as I came to love him, I also came to feel that protecting him from people, when appropriate, would be more important than the other way round.

Coming back for the first time

I do not know how or why it happened. I do know when and through what events the beginning of a restoration occurred. It is only in retrospect that the significance of some matters is now understandable. Three years after the death, I do not know why I began to have an interest in writing another paper. This time it had to do with science and psychology. I intended to review the entire literature on neurobiology as it pertained to psychoanalysis and to offer some kind of collation of mind and brain with clinical implications. In the early 1990s, a thorough review of the literature was a demanding task but not yet impossible, which it became shortly after through the exponential rise of work in this field. I did what I proposed, and it was not a bad paper, offering especially a philosophical exploration for how one might even think about the impossible task of merging mind and brain, spirit and matter. In the writing, though, I found myself most drawn to the realization that symbolization as a prime example of subjectivity could not be localized in the brain. The irreducibles interested me more than the correlations and processes I could link and relate. Included among the imponderables that I took up were the mechanisms of emergence, supervenience, and complexity that now serve newer understandings regarding global brain events and, essentially, dynamic living fields. But most satisfyingly, it was what I now know was an uncontrived act of "negative capability" à la Keats that allowed me to think simultaneously and without a feeling of impossibility of the reality of both mind and brain. The conceptualization itself was not the most important issue nor was it the best fruit of the endeavor. In fact, it was the conceptualizing mind itself that had been in the way and had at last been exhausted over several months of thinking. What I felt finally, coming as if an epiphany, was a quiet but uncanny eureka-like experience and a release of tension after the months of struggle. The affect of the experience seemed to be both the solution and the reward, as did the realization, not a conception but rather an announcement, that reality could be seen, needed to be seen, as two simultaneous but absolutely different systems. I did not understand for several years that this was my first aware encounter with an experience of antinomy and the field dynamics of subjective life.

As I was preparing to write the paper on brain and mind, a supervisee gratuitously brought me a paper on immortality by a scholar little known outside of tight academic circles. It was the elaborated text of an invited talk delivered at the Harvard Divinity School in 1965 (Voegelin 1965/1990: 52–94). I do not know why I even looked at it, but when I did, I was captured. Here was a consummate scholar bringing language to experiences I had only heretofore felt and never identified nor labeled. It assumed the reality of transcendent experience as a matter of fact and called the demands "How do you know" and "How can you prove it" – "the smart idiot questions every college teacher knows." With this, the author says, "We have reached T. S. Eliot's Waste Land" (Voegelin 1965/1990: 54). The paper went on to discuss the case of an Egyptian man in the twentieth century BCE who is contemplating suicide ("Dispute of a Man, Who Contemplates Suicide, With His Soul"), and, in the predisposing personal and social conditions of that time, the author explores parallels with conditions in the twentieth century CE. Not until the writing of this piece did it occur to me how exactly parallel was the Egyptian's felt situation to my own, as I had experienced it three years before the immortality paper came to me. The Egyptian despaired of the society in which he lived and thought death better than life within it. Among his lamentations, there is this:

> To whom can I speak today?
> One's fellows are evil;
> The friends of today do not love
>   (Voegelin 1965/1990: 58–64)

The paper was remarkable to me also in that it had a language ample enough to explore the levels of both individual and collective consciousness for each époque.[22] It was the most honest and erudite work I had ever encountered. It assumed nothing, gave no *pro forma* primacy to authority, and built solely from the engendering experiences that, for example, give rise in the first place to the "class of experiences to which we refer to as the varieties of religious experiences," one symbol of which we call immortality. Moreover, the paper's syntax subtly avoided subject-object clarity such that the phenomena spoken about were laid out in reflexive sentences where they seem to simply appear in our awareness as existents, which I think is the actual nature of experience unprocessed by mind. Often I had to suspend my directed thinking only to let the ideas being presented beckon to me as if they were my own original thoughts, but I couldn't be sure they were mine or the author's or if I had actually even had a thought, so evanescent they were. I later learned to be more vigilant, more observant, more trusting. Shortly after, at a happenstance gathering at the house of the person who gave me the paper, I met the former personal secretary and literary heir of the author of the piece, the latter then dead for almost a decade. He had been told that I had recently read the paper. I started to say, "I can't believe . . ." He cut me off in mid-sentence. "Believe it," he laughed.

The next paper I read by Eric Voegelin (whose collected works run to thirty-four volumes) was "Reason, The Classic Experience" in which he reconstructs the origins of rational thought in the western world with its intrinsic transcendent dimension. Although originally otherwise, for us this is an expanded definition of reason that since the Enlightenment had been split into a utilitarian mode and such spin-offs as intuition, the imaginal, and the transcendent. In my immersion in this paper, I discovered the origins of the secular transcendent experience in the western world in pre-Socratic Hellas and in the dynamics of *Nous*, the third god after Kronos and Zeus, according to Plato, the first invisible god not representable by the senses. Of therapeutic value, I realized that a wholesome reason in the classical sense functions always, no matter what else it does, to locate us in the world and in existence. Here was a rationale, language, and historical precedent for the coexistence and simultaneity of, on the one hand, an ambient field of consciousness larger than our personal concerns and, on the other, the utilitarian everyday consciousness of the senses.

Most important, through his writing and his mind, Voegelin mysteriously taught me for the first time in my intellectual life to engage in what Harold Bloom calls strong reading, the approach to another's work as an equal such that the question being addressed by the author belongs equally to the reader. Both reader and writer have a right and responsibility to key on the source and not grant the written material primacy. I do not know precisely where and when I had come to a modicum of substantive ideas about immortality and the transcendent (they were more an aerie of intimations and feelings than ideas at the time), but I feel certain they were, in large part, an unexpected and unwitting product of the journey to darkness that I had taken over the preceding three years. For the first time then, I felt that life had returned to me. About twenty years before, I had had a dream of walking past a library and seeing a trail of smoke from smoldering books wafting out the window. I had no idea what this meant. I came to know.

The center of the circle and beyond

The tale of the circle, its worldly rim and its ineffable center, is a story of individual consciousness. It is a limited view of consciousness. Were the field of one's sensible being limited only to the personal center and its elaborations, it would be a solipsistic model, basically an expanded model of existential aloneness and loneliness. From time immemorial, either in the form of gods or feelings or, uniquely with Jung, demonstrable evidence in the form of synchronicity, humankind has had intimations of a larger world than we know through our senses, intimations that are easy for the hard scientist to discard as unreal because lacking empirical evidence.

For those who grant reality to the subjective and seek to know its structures, there once again comes a time to speak in terms of true tales, but the need for consensual objectivity seems greater in this instance because serious claims are being made for what truly constitutes ultimate reality in modern times for hard-minded, non-superstitious, scientistic people. In the name of appropriate respect for such serious claims, one seems disinclined to speak of tales, but tales they are, even though they pass by the name ontology.

In psychology, such ultimate considerations take us into what is called metapsychology,[23] or the foundational theoretical and philosophical underpinnings that support clinical and personal assumptions. Seen another way, the theory that thoroughly justifies a personal psychology must define the stuff of reality and the entirety of existence. In the Middle Ages, there were only two such comprehensive claims, one by the church, the other by Aristotelians, in other words, the champions of god and reason respectively. Whatever our terminology and whatever our pretensions, we are still in the middle of that larger struggle.

It is unusual for psychologists to advance an ontology, less strange for philosophers such as William James, who, not coincidentally I think, was also a psychologist. In his search for the essence of reality, James postulated that there is "only one primal stuff or material in the world, a stuff of which everything is composed" (James 1912/1996: 4). This stuff, which he chooses to name "pure experience," may be regarded from the point of view of objects, the things of the world, or from that of subjects, namely, the people whose consciousnesses know these things. By postulating "pure experience" as an overarching third, James strategizes to overcome the duality of body and soul or spirit and matter. For him, the ubiquity of the capacity for consciousness is so extensive that it is considered an intrinsic constituent of the primal stuff itself. Matter and mind are coextensive, consubstantial. All things of the world have some kind and degree of consciousness in the given of their being.

There are only two modern psychoanalysts whose work aspires to an ultimate vision.[24] They are C.G. Jung and W.R. Bion. James' conception is not far from Jung's implicit contentions. Jung's common substance, his ultimate ground, is the collective unconscious, which he confines to the human psyche, our only reality according to him, although he allows for the other-than-us noumenal world of Kant, the world of things in themselves that are forever beyond our knowing. Late in life Jung endorses the notion of the *Unus Mundus*, the world at the historically first instant of its discernment, a world which would comprehend all things, both observing consciousness and matter. But it is a world that cannot be proved to exist and is therefore metaphysical and off limits for psychological theorizing (Jung 1963/70: 539). For Bion, the ground of being is an entity that he designates simply as "O," which, curiously, he defines by essentially the same qualities that Aquinas attributes to God (Bion 1983/1995: 26; Clark 1995).[25]

The dynamics of consciousness

To bring in the operational aspect; that is, how the ground and personal consciousness interact, let us turn to yet another true tale, that of the Tohu Bohu, the biblical divine *prima materia*, from which God fashioned the world. In one model, Kabbalah envisions reality as four concentric spheres, each contained in the next larger sphere, each representing one of four levels of human life (Kaplan 1990: 21ff).[26] Beyond the fourth is the infinitely extensive Tohu Bohu, which, although seeming to exist outside the worlds, is in fact the substance from which they (the worlds) are made and remains always the enduring substrate. As such, the outer layer does not stand over and above the formed worlds as a transcendent realm like a heaven apart from earth. The divine Tohu Bohu as *Urstoff* and the world itself as creation are part and parcel of one another at all times. The world of the individual center and that of the ground of being by any name are ambient fields that are always present and always synchronic, that is, parallel. They may even be commingled.

Bion is more explicit than Jung about the relationship of the focused awareness and directed thinking of the personal field (K for knowledge in his lexicon) to the ground of "O." One cannot logically arrive at O from knowledge, cannot derive O from K. This is the deductive kind of abstraction that the Babylonians were predisposed to and underlies the founding of algebra. In contrast, knowledge constellates or crystallizes out of O in an acausal way, the only true abstraction according to Bion (1983/1995: 33). This is the logic, according to Zubiri, for which the Greeks and the ensuing western culture have as a talent and natural gift (Zubiri 1969/1970/1994: 29–30). The dynamics of the ground and its relationship to the personal field suggest that the proper use of focused reason is to be awake to, to discern, and to weigh what enters the psyche from the sentient ambient fields of being.

The complete laws that would explain the relationship of the personal field to the ultimate ground remain a perennial subject of speculation. Some say that the two fields are the same in essence, others that they are related but not the same. In one formulation, the question translates out as whether the irreducible core of an individual self is of the same substance as what we call god or whether we should call it all the collective unconscious. In another analogue of the same issue, it is the fourth century problem at Nicea of whether Christ and the Father are of the same substance (*homoousia*) or similar substances (*homoiousia*), the latter conundrum giving rise to the expression, "not a jot or iota (the Greek i) of difference." The issue corresponds to the distinction that various theoreticians seek to make between the big O and the personal O of Bion,[27] and the small self and the capitalized Self of Jung. The negotiations go on, and each individual has the onus of coming to his or her own decision. Is God the name we will call the deepest matrix in which we live and from which we are derived, agreeing to be bound by its laws, or will we call it something else, or not call it anything at all, each of which decision has its implications for how we situate, understand, and conduct ourselves in the world.

Death again

One might ask at this point what all of this has to do with death and just and unjust deaths. There are several axiomatic considerations that need to be underscored at this point. The first is that the ground and the personal experience of self qua center are ambient fields that can be directly experienced though never able to be described or proved to exist in the empirical ways of science and sense perceptions. The second is that the formation and qualitative nature of such fields are never created or arrived at through cognition or specific knowledge but only through experience in life and, alas, through suffering. A third is that there is a familiarity that one has with one's fields that is absolutely individual. One's knowledge of oneself is learned and enhanced only over time through personal experience attended by awareness, an awareness that may be either analogical, only on the fringes of formed consciousness, or more focused and supported by classical reasoning.

A fourth axiom is that effective learning other than as a polymath is enhanced by having a language for antinomy and paradox with which to dialogue with both oneself and, if one is fortunate, perhaps a few others. One should hope that one's analyst knows something of one's antinomian language.

The fifth and last consideration is that the road between the ground and individual consciousness is not a two-way street. Instead there are two different streets that interconnect the two realms, each one-way. As meaningful behavior occurs in personal life, the ground becomes strengthened in its turgor and enhanced in its complexity, constituting an ambient kind of learning at a metaphysical level, or, after Bion, in O. The ground does not repay the favor in the same currency. It seldom instructs us in didactic and explicit ways, even in times of greatest need when we often find that we receive nothing back in the way of instructions and are thrown back onto our all-too-human judgment. Instead, the ground, when properly cultivated, returns its boon by imbuing individual consciousness with a sense of deep security and well being or, otherwise said, with a sense better conveyed by the Greek term Dike, a concept which designates a cosmos in proper order and a word which translates into English as justice, as in a "just death."[28]

In the Judeo-Christian tradition, death came into existence because of original sin. Death was intended as a punishment in this story, and our deep tendency to think it so makes sense, for it answers to an alive, widely shared, and dominant cultural attitude. When I received my misdiagnosis on the phone in my office, two questions sprang to mind as soon as I hung up. The first was whether I had done anything wrong, the second whether I had to forgive someone I hated for cause whom I had no inclination to forgive. The answers came instantly from within in a kindly voice as if chiding a child: no, no, not at all.[29] In the development of a consciousness that would make for a "just death," one must come to grips with what I call the neurosis of death, which attitude, I think, is unavoidable in younger life when death is always unjust when it comes. Death is always personal, but it is also a dispassionate act of nature that divides humans from gods who are immortal. The tradition that affirms the impersonality of death predates Judaism and Christianity. It is again from the Greeks and first found in the single fragment that the earliest pre-Socratic philosopher left us. I speak of Anaximander. Below is a translation of the fragment, which is putatively the most ancient true tale in western culture. It comes in logos form that speaks to reason rather than as myth that speaks in images:

> The non-limited [gr. *apeiron*] is the original material of existing things; further, the source from which existing things derive their existence is also that to which they return at their destruction, according to necessity; for they give justice and make reparation to one another for their injustice, according to the arrangement of time.
>
> Anaximander of Miletus, fl. 560 BCE
> (Freeman 1983: 19)

Much speculation has been visited on this statement. For our purposes, please note that the word for justice is again Dike.

What I have described as the structures and axioms of consciousness presents us with a long and hard-earned way to be in the world, but one that offers not only some stability and constancy of self but also something about what it means to be a human being and to participate in the human condition. To have come to something of the above and to know it is, to my thinking, to be graced in all senses of the word. There is a kind of love that pertains simply to the wonder at existence itself and to the gratitude of being allowed to participate in it. And so, love is one boon of the work. As a second grace, to have found a language with which to explore the mysteries of life, even those that half kill you, a language whose intricacies and subtleties continue to grow, is to be in a firestorm of delight that feeds on itself. With regard to faith and especially for those for whom dying is difficult in its final throes or for those who, for instance, are taken sometimes so swiftly and unprepared that they have no time to mourn their lives, it is my experience that faith (and grace) often comes, when it does come, as an ethereal gossamer thread that, in its quiet subtlety, may be missed. One must pay equally subtle attention and tenderly try to recognize and welcome any hint of its felt presence. Its efficacy need not be dependent on any belief system.

All of the human fields including death, so far as we can imagine, are liminal ones beyond the threshold of what passes for ordinary life and, as in the Platonic myth of Er at the end of the *Republic* (Plato 1961: 834–844), death is where we are reduced simply to souls facing eternity. A rabbi friend says to me that when you are dying, your life will have been a mockery if you are not able to experience then the love and meaning that you experienced in life. He began to expand on his point. This presumes, I thought, that one has indeed experienced these things, and I agree that to have experienced them is to have truly lived. In agreement with him, I felt that this deathbed realization would likely predispose one to die a just death and to die with gratitude, even if one can only remember that one has indeed lived, whether or not one is not experiencing one's living blessings circa the time of death. As Said (2006) avers, and wisely I think, at death it is perhaps not fitting for the opposites to reconcile and for all to seem well; perhaps it is appropriately just the opposite, like in the difficult mixed strains of Beethoven's late quartets which do not simply sooth and also in the cacophony of John Coltrane's "A Love Supreme," his paean to God, which drives one dithyrambically closer to the divine anomie of Tohu Bohu rather than to a gentle bower.

Among that which constitutes and affirms having truly lived is also, of course, the exercising of classical reason, the logos that kindles the soul, the noetic exploration of existence, be it in the study of Bible or Torah or, perhaps as satisfying, in dialogue with a truly kindred and loved soul with a mind that also seeks. Aristotle coined the term "athanatizein" which, according to Eric Voegelin, translates as the act of immortalizing (Voegelin 1974: 88). It is the exercise of noetic mind in exploring as a participant the universe itself, the locus of oneself, one's sole and only abode of which one and one's consciousness is part. It is this logos-heavy activity that imparts an intimation of immortality. Voegelin was engaging in such meditative exegeses to the very end of his life, dictating his last paper to his personal secretary from his deathbed,[30] and proofing its final form the day before his death.[31] The paper is yet another powerful tour de force of intelligence and scholarship. Its title is "Quod Deus Dicitur," what God is said to be; that is, not what God her or himself is but the engendering experience that lies behind whatever we humans have chosen to call God (Voegelin 1985/1990: 376ff). It is not about theology and revelation although the title words are borrowed from Thomas Aquinas; it is about individual consciousness systematically seeking its source in its experiences in the world. Voegelin's wife chided him for watching himself die. He did not deny it. And so I said to my dear friend, the rabbi, "When one or the other of us is on his deathbed and the other there at bedside, do you know what we will be doing?" "No," said he. "We'll be talking like this." Exit laughing.

True exit

Laughter is not really the note on which I wish to end this meditation. It was only a trope I couldn't resist. More to the heart, in July 2006 Joseph Henderson celebrated his one hundred and third birthday. He stopped practicing as an analyst approximately a year before, when unpredictable lapses began to interfere with the work. Nonetheless, not a few people still come to talk with him, mostly in his living room and both as friends and covertly as clients. We find him still sage and affectively available but in a more muted, discontinuous, and less present way with more space between ideas. His memory span is shorter, his thoughts like little clouds dissipating in the middle of sentences. Recently, pondering a topic of our discussion of the moment, he wandered into a line of associations about an author he knew in Europe, now long deceased but clearly still alive for Joe who, as he spoke, was himself again in Europe. Still cognizant, though, of the multiplicity of levels on which he was dwelling, he quipped to me, "I'm inside out." Indeed. I found that all I had to do was spread wider the brackets around the person I know as Joe Henderson to find him still there, intact in his new way.

At present, I have some concern about saying goodbye to him, a very good use for consciousness, I have thought, especially when it involves two analysts with long and substantive ties. Certainly, it is our practice to terminate analyses with such due diligence. I want to talk with him about how he wants or hopes to say goodbye to the many people who are connected to him, but at the mention of the subject, no matter how delicately put (is delicacy really possible?), he suddenly jerks his head upright and stares straight ahead. He puts his chin in the air and, almost in caricature, clamps his mouth shut, and says nothing until the subject is changed. His constant attendant just laughs. She singsongs, "He won't talk about death. He says, every day is wonderful and don't talk about death," which, I think, is his contribution to the appropriateness, again à la Said, of leaving the end unfinished. A friend and colleague thinks Joe is deliberately hiding secrets about death. More recently, Joe did wax more forthcoming about death to a former analysand, who posed the question in terms of her own fears of dying. It seemed to me that he spontaneously became the analyst once more, telling of having almost died twice and reassuring about how fear passes. He said that he feels there is something beyond death but doesn't know what. Robust and clear on that day, he gave no indication that he was saying goodbye.

At the end of *Memories, Dreams, Reflections* in a chapter he himself wrote, Jung speaks of having come to an "unexpected unfamiliarity with myself" (Jung 1961/1963: 350) which is also, I think, a testimony to Said's vision of the imperfect end (Said 2006: 160). I have been a little incredulous that Joe would be so persistently and uncharacteristically unresponsive about something as important for humans as a considered leave-taking, but I have played and replayed my above "tell me, tell me" scene with him on several occasions and always with the identical outcome. It is true that I had never thought to put the question in terms of my needing help. I also like to think that he was in part more readily forthcoming because he was rising to an attractive woman in need.

A year or so ago, he told me of a dream he had had the night before. In it he is on the periphery of a small group of psychoanalysts in discussion. He hears one man ask with impatience, "Why do we have to keep talking about love since we have already talked about it?" In the dream Dr Henderson's reaction was immediate and trenchant: "Well, then talk about it again. Just keep talking about it." At the time I had ideas but no certain sense of the meaning of the dream. Since then, it has become apparent that there is a kind of love that emanates from Joe that is supported by his conscious behavior, an ambience which penetrates to individuals in the form of gentle regards, knowing smiles of recognition, and kind but also sometimes pertinent words of the professional. In a private moment at his birthday party, I told him I was writing about him. He thanked me. I also asked his permission to use the above dream. (I had asked before and received the same response.) "Yes," he said, "good." "In the final analysis," I remarked to this man of complex mind and eminent scholarship, "it seems that love is more enduring than logos." The next day I remembered that almost two decades earlier, in the pit of my despair when my dog died, it was he alone who had spoken of love. He had said, "I can see that you know how to love." At the time, I thought not.

When the last years of Jung's life are scrutinized, it seems that love also outstayed his particularly mighty logos. From all accounts he was devastated by his wife's death and there was concern "whether he would ever come back" (Bair 2003: 564). That was in 1955 at which time, after completing his three last and major works, he declared that his "task was finished." He had reached the "bounds of scientific understanding" (Jung 1961/1963: 221).[32] He gave over then to his intuition and feeling. In the later chapters of *Memories, Dreams, Reflections*, he speaks of death and particularly of intimations from dreams that life in some fashion goes on after death. He underscores that his speculation is founded on the meaningfulness to him of such unconscious material, and he waxes unapologetically and even more baldly metaphysical than ever before about the nature of life and world. From an earlier dream, he speculates that he may well be the meditation of a yogi who has Jung's own face and that

Jung will die when the meditation ends. Of course, like us, he knows that he "can do no more than tell stories – 'mythologize' " (Jung 1961/1963: 323, 299). A dream drags him out of private life one more time to orchestrate *Man and His Symbols*, but his own contribution to it is an unusually linear piece of writing without his accustomed complexity (Jung 1964: 18–103). That his logos is retiring corresponds for him with the rise of love or "eros" as the paramount force in the universe (although he never sanctions the "ideal of harmony" so often held by "feeling types": Jaffe 1971/1984: 112).[33]

Jung speaks for himself:

> Eros is a *kosmogonos*, a creator and father-mother of all higher consciousness. I sometimes feel that Paul's words – "Though I speak with the tongues of men and of angels, and have not love" – might well be the first condition of all cognition and the quintessence of divinity itself.
>
> (Jung 1961/1963: 353)

In contrast to Eric Voegelin's deathbed noesis, it comes to me that the difference between the authentic scholar/philosopher and the scholarly psychoanalyst may be whether the accent falls most heavily on logos or on love respectively, but it's a matter of accent only, for both may occasionally be found in ample measure in the same person.

But it is neither logos nor love, I think, that best captures the note on which life and this chapter may most appropriately end, at least in my opinion. The final note of a life, if consciously rung, can sound the attitude with which someone leaves, perhaps a matter of importance for some or at least a matter of some interest. This endnote is a conundrum of no small moment since a life in its entirety, deeply considered, is a wonderment and a mystery beyond description or comprehension. This pertains to every life, and so I want to say that to the extent I've had to make distinctions regarding better and worse deaths and, by implication, better and worse lives, I apologize for any appearance of having special knowledge about election in the face of death, the most unarguably democratic of all events, and I apologize especially to anyone who has come to this work with hope of finding understanding and solace regarding the unjust death of a loved one and found little or none. We may do our best to understand and better our lot, but there is too much that is simply out of our hands.

Returning to the subject of the final note, I want to share with you the amusement I found in the opening lines of the preface of May Sarton's book *Coming into Eighty*. This is May Sarton:

> I have loved W. B. Yeats for many reasons, not least because he changed his style radically in old age, writing perhaps his greatest poems after the age of eighty.
>
> (Sarton 1994: 11)

Never mind that Yeats died at the age of 74. I, too, have loved Yeats and, like Sarton, had also been fooled for some years, thinking he died at a greater age than he did because of the interest and poems that he had brought relatively early to the subject of death. Regarding his fate at the hands of death, Yeats might be said to have hedged his bets by having had various parting attitudes over the years. In one such version, he envisioned himself, like other artists (Shakespeare for one), remaining immortal in the form of a work of art:

> Once out of nature I shall never take
> My bodily form from any natural thing,
> But such a form as Grecian goldsmiths make
> Of hammered gold and gold enamelling
> To keep a drowsy Emperor awake;
> Or set upon a golden bough to sing
> To lords and ladies of Byzantium
> Of what is past, or passing, or to come.
> Sailing to Byzantium
> (Yeats 1956: 192)

Yeats was 62 when he wrote "Sailing to Byzantium." In "Lapis Lazuli," circa age 71, he envisages again an artifact that, although a human likeness this time, is, nonetheless, artifact. It has to do with a lapis carving of a mountain being ascended by two old men and a musician:

> . . . doubtless plum or cherry-branch
> Sweetens the little half-way house
> Those Chinamen climb towards, and I
> Delight to imagine them seated there;
> There, on the mountain and the sky,
> On all the tragic scene they stare.
> One asks for mournful melodies;
> Accomplished fingers begin to play.
> Their eyes mid many wrinkles, their eyes,
> Their ancient, glittering eyes, are gay.
> Lapis Lazuli
> (Yeats 1956: 293)

Sometime between the ages of 71 and 74 when he died, his vision seemed to grow less sanguine, more realistic, more accepting of his humanity, and more philosophical:

> Now that my Ladder's gone,
> I must lie down where all the ladders start,

In the foul rag-and-bone shop of the heart.
                    The Circus Animals' Desertion
                        (Yeats 1956: 336)

I have envisioned Yeats' ladder as the symbol for the platonic ascent to the transcendent or perhaps Jacob's ladder connecting heaven and earth. Either way, it stands for the meaning-making function that alone makes us human rather than animal only. In this variation, Yeats proposes that with age we return again to nature, to anomie, to entropy, to primal chaos, sans identity.

But this did not complete Yeats' array of visions. An avowed mystic, he engaged over time in a proleptic vision of what's to come and apparently had so mused during much of his adult life. Married late at age 52, he had been surprised and elated when his new wife was able to perform automatic writing which, although apparently authentic and beyond her will, dedicated itself to producing symbols as gifts for his work and visions. Moved by her productions, Yeats constructed, Gnostic-like, a detailed transcendental universe, spelled out in detail in his book *A Vision*. His system represented a continuation of the mystic explorations of his young adulthood in Dublin in the latter nineteenth century including his Theosophical studies and his fellowship in the Hermetic Order of the Golden Dawn (Hough 1984).

Of all the above, what combination of visions, what most consoling notion, we might ask, did Yeats choose to inhabit in his exit from life? In the final analysis, he, like I, seems to have concluded that the judgment of the awesome matter of a whole life best be left to the wisdom of eternity. Such suspension seems to me the most merciful stance, one of quiet and humble dignity after completion. Here is Yeats' final note carved in limestone for time without end, his epitaph:

Cast a cold eye
On life, on death.
Horseman, pass by!

Notes

1   Victor Turner was an anthropologist who lived from 1920 to 1983. Born in England, his career began at the University of London and moved to The University of California at Berkeley, then the University of Chicago, and finally the University of Virginia. His original anthropological work in the field was in Africa with the Ndembu tribe of Zambia and focused on initiatory rituals, which, for our purposes, are instances of substantive change in individual lives through structured and society-sanctioned processes. There is much that might be said of Turner, for he was an original thinker, but what I choose to say here pertains to the nature and process of change in both individuals and societies and follows largely from his book, *The Ritual Process: Structure and Anti-structure* (1969).

   Turner's study of initiation is in the tradition of the earlier work of Arnold van Gennep c. 1909 who also documented initiation rituals of young men in preliterate tribes and delineated in the processes a stage of separation from the society followed by a stage he called reaggregation or reincorporation. Following and extending this schema, Turner labels the initiate in the phase of separation as liminal, a word taken from the Latin, meaning threshold. Liminal people (he also calls them liminars) are ambiguous, stripped of worldly identity i.e. social roles, and no longer members of the society from which they have separated nor yet of that society to which they will again belong. In his examination of these rites, Turner differentiates out from one another the individual and the societal aspects of initiation. What he is seeking is not particularly and solely how individuals change but how whole societies change.

Turner postulates that communities at all times are composed of two synchronic moieties, both existing at the same time, one that he continues to call community and a second that he calls liminal and to which he assigns the Latin name *communitas*, which, of course, also means community. The first stratum, community, is characterized by a structured and hierarchical order. The person in community derives his identity from the role or roles he plays in the structures and institutions of the society. In contrast, the person in *communitas* defines himself *sub specie aeternitatis*, against the backdrop of eternity and outside of all institutional assignments. All he has is his essential humanity and his basic and unadorned human nature as identity. *Communitas* is composed of all those in a liminal state.

The above gives further meaning to Nietzsche's statement that "The living is merely a type of what is dead, and a very rare type" (Harrison 2003: 1).

2 Individuation has no "after" because, once attained, it does not end. What makes individuation special is that in addition to being rooted beyond contemporary societal roles, its state factors in a simultaneous awareness and acceptance of a present social identity with its ethical demands. Death remains a mystery that, at least from the point of view of life, is a pure liminal state without societal considerations, and as death approaches, one may think that the social identity of individuation may diminish to a point of non-existence for the dying person. This may be almost the case, but not entirely so, as seen, for instance, in the death of Tolstoy's Ivan Ilyich, whose struggle with his felt and failed obligations to life (e.g., family) continue to the very last breath. Of course, unlike in individuation, we have no knowledge of the society or *communitas*, if such exists, that we will be part of after our passage (if passage it be) through death.

3 That is, an overarching way of being and knowing in contrast to that of any of several more narrow cultural Weltanschauung or attitudes; namely, social, religious, aesthetic, or philosophical (Henderson 1984: 59ff.).

4 The mandala may, of course, be another. Individuation is a term of art in Jungian theory designating a culminating stage of a life hard fought and honestly and authentically lived. Its dynamics bespeak a more or less balanced tension of existence between immanent life and transcendent meaningfulness, the mundane and transcendent no longer experienced as naively separate poles. Raw and naive divisiveness yields to a living entente in a charged field, an ambience akin at its most benign to what Aristotle calls *eudemonia*, life under the tutelage of one's true spirit, known also as fulfillment or next best as contentment. Although intimations of individuation may appear in both symbols and feeling states at any period of life, individuation as a reasonably stable configuration almost always obtains only after years of struggle with the basic dominants of the human condition and the specifics of one's personal life, mediated or not mediated by formal psychoanalysis or therapy.

5 In Epicurean epistemology, prolepsis is one of three criteria of truth, the main one being sensation and another the emotions.

> *Prolepsis* operates in much the same way as the Stoic *katalepsis* [apprehension of an impression], except that the *prolepsis* is the result of a repeated apprehension of the same type of object, e.g. men, and hence is a universal concept, a kind of residual composite, e.g., "Man" based on many sensations of "men."
>
> (Peters 1967: 164)

I think of prolepsis as a potentially premonitory vision, one perhaps partaking of the prophetic with a greater (though not certain) claim to truth than intuition or imagination.

6 I was 64 when Dr Henderson was 100.

7 Notwithstanding the possibility that others outside that population may also find themselves in what I say and are welcome to do so.

8 Virtually all for whom I write have already attained to some definition of healthy aging. There are good books that address these issues; for example Vaillant (2002) for one. There is an original recent sociology work from Swedish academia that distinguishes a stage of very old age from old age. As my work on late aging strives for a dynamic understanding of the process, the author of this book employs instead a descriptive approach which lends itself to phenomenological assays and statistical assessment. It is of interest that his thesis and my ideas arrive at similar pictures of a period of very old age or, in my formulation, a late maturity which may come before very old age in the form of a seasoned individuation. He writes of changes in the relationship of people to the cosmos, including a loss of fear of death and a reassessment of life, a self-transcendence and a decentering of self interests, and a greater selectivity of contacts with avoidance of the superficial. A Transcendence not limited to traditional religion or spiritual definition figures large in his formulations and is distinguished from disengagement. This is an interesting study (Tornstam 2005).

9 All science another.

10 Either Schopenhauer or Feuerbach seem to be the originator of the phrase in its present usage, but the exact provenance is not clear.

11 This is Jung dealing with the ever evolving subjective: "Even though you add to my 'ultimate' an 'absolute ultimate,' you will hardly maintain that my 'ultimate' is not as good an 'ultimate' as yours." Speaking of the ego wending its way towards the "emptiness" of the center, Jung rationalizes a limit to the infinite round of inturning. At some point he postulates that the ego will be extinguished in the center itself and thus lose consciousness, hence the case for terminus expressions such as archetypes. It is as if the psyche fixing on archetypes could possibly think itself having reached the summit of the Matterhorn (or the bottom of the possible) when instead it has reached only the top of one of its shoulders, to borrow dream material Jung once cited regarding a patient (letter to Pastor Walter Bernet, 13 June, 1955: see Edinger 1996: 129). Further, *nota bene*: "The moment I touched bottom, I reached the bounds of scientific understanding, the transcendental, the nature of the archetype per se, concerning which no further scientific statements can be made" (Jung 1961/1963: 221).

12 The historical *Nous* as well as Bion's alpha function would present equally difficult problems with depiction, so too Bernard Lonergan's "understanding" (1957/1997). In sum, the problem would pertain to the human meaning-making function by any name.

13 Language of achievement, as used by Bion, denotes a language that signifies actual experience as opposed to a language of the senses and memory that pertains to knowing about experience. The latter is also called language of substitution because it substitutes for action (Bion 1983/1995: 125).

14 Jung's eschewal of the metaphysical because it has no empirical equivalents other than pure experiential states limits his laboratory to the sense-bound world which includes the image-dependent worlds of myth and symbol even if used indexically to point beyond themselves. It is this demurrer of the metaphysical that I take up in terms of Henderson's theory in "Thinking Individuation Forward" (Tresan 2007).

15 During the course of our work, my patient introduced me to Phillip Rieff's recently published *Triumph of the Therapeutic* (Rieff 1966), which he was reading for his own interest and as a student in a sociology graduate program. I did not read it and did not understand until much later that it was a critique of the psychoanalytic and psychotherapy establishment for having replaced the ancient traditions of ministering to soul and psyche with the utilitarian and secular values of modern life. Also popular at the time was Thomas Szaszs' antiestablishmentarian polemic against traditional psychoanalysis and therapy.

16 For those who may not know, Vince Lombardi was the longtime legendary coach of the Green Bay Packers professional football team. Leukemia is roughly the proliferation of immature white blood cells at the expense of all others, and the appearance of a helpful tutelary figure in the dream of a patient in therapy is thought to suggest that the therapeutic relationship is experienced as helpful.

17 The able James Hillman solved the issue for himself by cataloguing everything Jung had said about anima, grouping the sayings under ten different headings; e.g., "Anima and Contrasexuality," "Anima and Eros," "Anima and Feeling," etc. Moreover, he reframed the concept as a "personified notion." In these ways he masterfully sidestepped the traditional scholarly imperative to pluck out the one defining essence of an idea (Hillman 1985).

18 I am told that the cause was cancer, the onset acute and unexpected, and the course of illness short (Glenn Hughes, personal communication, 2006).

19 One can close up, obsess, collect bottlecaps, do whatever it takes to allay our fear. One can also detach from the body, taste the infinite and become God joining other schizophrenics in pushing a shopping cart down a city street. Or finally, we can as Martin Luther put it, "taste death as though it were present," kill off our illusions and admit that we are creature. Only then according to Kierkegaard can we see beyond to "absolute transcendence, to the Ultimate Power of Creation." One breaks the illusions of a cultural heroism, and through faith, aligns oneself with the infinite and in a sense a cosmic heroism (Blairon 2004).

20 Tolstoy's young adulthood is best summed up with his own words from his book *A Confession*:

> I cannot recall those years without horror, loathing, and heart-rending pain. I killed people in war, challenged men to duels with the purpose of killing them, and lost at cards; I squandered the fruits of the peasants' toil and then had them executed; I was a fornicator and a cheat. Lying, stealing, promiscuity of every kind, drunkenness, violence, murder – there was not a crime I did not commit. . . . Thus I lived for ten years.
>
> (Tolstoy 2001: Chapter II)

Later in life, Tolstoy formulated a unique Christian philosophy which espoused non-resistance to evil as the proper response to aggression, and which put great emphasis on fair treatment of the poor and working class. Tolstoy also gave a strong plea for Christians to reject the State when seeking answers to questions of morality and instead to look within themselves and to God for their answers.

At the age of 82, increasingly tormented by the disparity between his teachings and his personal wealth, and by endless quarrels with his wife, who resisted his attempts to renounce their material possessions, Tolstoy left his home one night. He fell ill three days later and died on November 20, 1910, at a remote railroad station. He was hailed as a uniquely powerful moral force throughout the world and a source of inspiration to many (Tolstoy 2002).

21 I testified by written affidavit.

22 The plight of the Egyptian contemplating suicide is addressed in a paper delivered at the annual meeting of the American Political Science Association Meeting, Eric Voegelin Society, 1996, in which Voegelin's analysis of consciousness with regard to the historical and the political is explored for its value for individual analysis (Tresan 1996).

23 For Freud, metapsychology, a word originally of his own invention, has idiosyncratic meaning in terms of the particular structures of psyche indigenous to his theory.

24 But there are other true tales of ultimate grounds. There is the noosphere of Pierre Teilhard de Chardin, the heraclitean world of *Nous* with an imminent and transcendent dimension, the Parmenidean world of Being, and arguably the potential space of Winnicott. On another front there is Einstein whose universe as time-space continuum is geometrical architecture without edge.

25 "O," according to Bion, is ultimate reality, absolute truth, the godhead, the infinite, the thing-in-itself, and experience.

26 The worlds are Asiyah (action), Yetzirah (speech), Beriyah (thought), and Atzilut (mind). A fifth is also advanced which is Adam Kadmon (will).

27 James Grotstein, personal communication, 2005, 2006.

28 When meaningful behavior on earth is no longer possible for a person, for whatever reason, be it dementia, illness, or depletion, then the ground is not fed, loses its vitality, its turgor, and its capacity to learn or evolve. The very tension of existence slackens and the sense of meaningfulness even at the affective level dissipates. Consciousness becomes a diffuse ambient field sans focus, self-awareness, or access to the world. One can see such process in the progression of, for instance, Alzheimer's. The most painful part for the person before oblivion often seems to be not so much the loss of memory and the power to focus *per se* but, through these, the loss of the ability to engage in meaningful and useful commerce with the world and to know one's functional self as one once did.

29 I did not know at the time that gratuitous forgiveness according to Judaism is meaningless and even a sin. What must precede it, if it is to be given, is the acceptance of a verdict of guilty by the offending party after which forgiveness can be meaningfully granted. Acceptance of guilt entails not only an owning up to responsibility but also evidence that the transgression and its effects have been understood. In that sense, an account such as I have written may be received by a transgressor either as a gift that could possibly enable the restoration of Dike or more simply as a gratuitous and unwelcome reminder of an inconvenient memory.

30 I am speaking of Paul Caringella, Voegelin's literary heir and Visiting Scholar at the Herbert Hoover Institution at Stanford where Voegelin's manuscripts are archived. It was, of course, Caringella who earlier said to me to "believe it." During the course of my writing this piece, he would doggedly address me as "my dying friend," his way, I think, to encourage me to finish, for he preferred we return to life sooner rather than later. I thank him for his attending and care.

31 The paper remained not quite complete although Voegelin gave instructions for its completion. In addition, his last intended book, *In Search of Order*, the last in a series of five, was only about one-third written (Voegelin 1987). What there was of it was published posthumously. Nonetheless, it is a very satisfying noetic exploration of reality and perhaps the most comprehensive of all his philosophical explorations.

32 Refer to note 11, which reads in part: "The moment I touched bottom, I reached the bounds of scientific understanding, the transcendental, the nature of the archetype per se, concerning which no further scientific statements can be made" (Jung 1961/1963: 221).
33 The exact quote reads:

> He could speak with biting scorn of the "ideal of harmony" that hovers before many people – they are often "feeling types" – because it is not in accord with the life and the truth of man. In the long run it cannot be kept up; sooner or later it comes to a disappointing end, turns into disharmony.
>
> (Jaffe 1971/1984: 112)

Acknowledgements

Extracts from "Lapis Lazuli", "The Circus Animals' Desertation", and "Under Ben Bulben" reprinted with permission of Scribner, an imprint of Simon & Schuster Adult Publishing Group, from *The Collected Works of W.B. Yeats, Volume 1: The Poems*, revised edited by Richard J. Finneran. Copyright © 1940 by Georgie Yeats; copyright renewed © 1968 by Bertha Georgie Yeats, Michael Butler Yeats & Anne Yeats. All rights reserved.

Extract from "Sailing to Byzantium" reprinted with the permission of Scribner, an imprint of Simon & Schuster Adult Publishing Group, from *The Collected Works of W.B. Yeats, Volume 1: The Poems*, revised edited by Richard J. Finneran. Copyright © 1928 by The Macmillan Company; copyright renewed © 1956 by Georgie Yeats. All rights reserved.

References

Bair, D. (2003) *Jung: A Biography*, Boston, MA: Little, Brown.
Becker, E. (1973) *Denial of Death*, New York: Free Press.
Bion, W.R. (1983/1995) *Attention and Interpretation*, Northvale, NJ: Jason Aronson.
Blairon, P. (2004) "Review of *Denial of Death* by Ernest Becker," (1973) in *California Literary Review*, http://www.calitreview.com/Reviews/denial_of_death_007.htm
Clark, M. (1995) *An Aquinas Reader*, New York: Fordham University Press.
Dickens, C. (1859/1974) *A Tale of Two Cities*, London: Peebles Press International.
Edinger, E. (1996) *The New God Image*, Wilmette, IL: Chiron.
Freeman, K. (1983) *Ancilla to the Pre-Socratic Philosophers: A Complete Translation of the Fragments in Diels, Fragmente der Vorsokratiker*, Cambridge, MA: Harvard University Press.
Giegerich, W. (2001) *The Soul's Logical Life*, Frankfurt am Main: Peter Lang.
Harrison, R. (2003) *The Dominion of the Dead*, Chicago, IL: University of Chicago Press. Quote from Nietzsche's *Gay Science*, para 109, p. 168.
Henderson, J.L. (1967) *Thresholds of Initiation*, Middletown, CT: Wesleyan University Press.
Henderson, J.L. (1984) *Cultural Attitudes in Psychological Perspective*, Toronto: Inner City Books.
Hillman, J. (1985) *Anima: An Anatomy of a Personified Notion*, Dallas, TX: Spring.

Hough, G. (1984) *The Mystery Religion of W.B. Yeats*, Brighton, UK: Harvester; Totowa, NJ: Barnes & Noble.

Hughes, G. (1996) "The Denial of Death and the Practice of Dying," paper delivered at "The First Interdisciplinary Multimodal Conference in Honor of Ernest Becker," at Skidmore College, Saratoga Springs, NY, co-sponsored by the Psychology Department at Skidmore College and the Ernest Becker Foundation, August 1996. A slightly later version, called "Tasting Death: Becker and Socrates," given as a lecture in 1998 at Seattle University, exists on audiotape (copies free).

Jaffe, A. (1971/1984) *Jung's Last Years*, Dallas, TX: Spring.

James, W. (1912/1996) "Does 'Consciousness' Exist?" in *William James: Essays in Radical Empiricism*, Lincoln, NE: University of Nebraska Press.

Jung, C.G. (1961/1963) *Memories, Dreams, Reflections*, ed. Aniela Jaffé, New York: Vintage.

Jung, C.G. (1963/1970) *Mysterium Coniunctionis*, 2nd edition, Princeton, NJ: Princeton University Press.

Jung, C.G. (1964) *Man and His Symbols*, London: Aldus.

Kaplan, A. (1990) *Innerspace: Introduction to Kabbalah, Meditation, and Prophecy*, Jerusalem, Israel: Moznaim.

Lonergan, B. (1957/1997) *Insight: A Study of Human Understanding*, Toronto: University of Toronto Press.

Peters, F. (1967) *Greek Philosophical Terms: A Historical Lexicon*, New York: New York University Press.

Plato (1961) *The Collected Dialogues of Plato*, ed. E. Hamilton and H. Cairns, New York: Bollingen Foundation.

Rayner, E. (1995) *Unconscious Logic. An Introduction to Matte Blanco's Bi-logic and its Uses*, London: Routledge.

Rieff, P. (1966/1987) *The Triumph of the Therapeutic: Uses of Faith after Freud*, Chicago, IL: University of Chicago Press.

Rothstein, E. (2006) "Twilight of His Idols" (Review of *On Late Style: Music and Literature against the Grain*, by Edward W. Said), *New York Times Book Review*, July 16.

Said, E. (2006) *On Late Style: Music and Literature against the Grain*, New York: Pantheon.

Sarton, M. (1994) *Coming into Eighty: Poems*, New York: W.W. Norton.

Tolstoy, L. (1886/1981) *The Death of Ivan Ilyich*, London: Bantam Classics.

Tolstoy, L. (1879–1882/1983) *A Confession*, trans. David Patterson, New York: W.W. Norton.

Tolstoy, L. (1879–1882/2001) *A Confession*, trans. Louise Maude and Aylmer Maude, http: //www.classicallibrary.org/tolstoy/confession/index.htm

Tolstoy, L. (2002) *Tolstoy (1828–1910): A Biography*, http://www.classicallibrary.org/tolstoy/index.htm (author unknown).

Tornstam, L. (2005) *Gerotranscendence: A Developmental Theory of Positive Aging*, New York: Springer.

Tresan, D. (1992) "The Anima of the Analyst: Its Development," in N. Schwartz-Salant and M. Stein (eds.) *Gender and Soul in Psychotherapy*, Wilmette, IL: Chiron.

Tresan, D. (1996) "An Analyst's Caveat: Therapy, Political and Personal – Voegelin's Analysis of Consciousness," American Political Science Association Meeting, San Francisco, August 30–31, 1996; Eric Voegelin Society, Twelfth Annual Meeting

Program, possibly archived at the Eric Voegelin Institute at Louisiana State University, Baton Rouge, LA.

Tresan, D. (2004) "This New Science of Ours: A More or Less Systematic History of Consciousness and Transcendence. Part I," *Journal of Analytical Psychology*, 49 (2): 193–216.

Tresan, D. (2007) "Thinking Individuation Forward," *Journal of Analytical Psychology*, 52 (1): 17–40.

Turner, V. (1969/1997) *The Ritual Process: Structure and Anti-structure*, New York: Aldine de Gruyter.

Vaillant, G. (2002) *Aging Well*, Boston, MA: Little, Brown.

Voegelin, E. (1965/1990) "Immortality: Experience and Symbol," Ingersoll Lecture on Immortality, delivered at Harvard Divinity School on January 14, 1965; *Collected Works of Eric Voegelin, vol. 12, Published Essays, 1966–1985*, Baton Rouge, LA: Louisiana State University Press.

Voegelin, E. (1974) *The Ecumenic Age*, Baton Rouge, LA: Louisiana State University Press.

Voegelin, E. (1985/1990) "Quod Deus Dicitur," *Collected Works of Eric Voegelin, vol. 12, Published Essays, 1966–1985*, Baton Rouge, LA: Louisiana State University Press.

Voegelin, E. (1987) *In Search of Order*, Baton Rouge, LA: Louisiana State University Press.

Winnicott, D.W. (1958/1975) *Through Pediatrics to Psycho-analysis*, New York: Basic Books.

Yeats, W.B. (1956) *The Collected Poems of W.B. Yeats*, New York: Macmillan.

Zornberg, A. (1995) *The Beginning of Desire: Reflections on Genesis*, New York: Doubleday Press.

Zubiri, X. (1969/1970/1994) *The Fundamental Problems of Western Metaphysics*, trans. J. Redonda, not in print. Entire text available on internet at http://www.catholicphilosophy.com/sys-tmpl/introduction1137/

Index

Cox, Harvey 88
Craighead, Meinrad 50–1
Crazy Horse (warrior and healer) 108
Crucifixion 65, 73
cultural complex 4
cultural unconscious 127
Cumont, Franz 91–2, 94

daimonios aner 160
dance, ritual 3
death 31, 34, 36–7, 180–3; and birth 44;
    difficulty of discussing 161; dreams of
    22; fear of 161, 170; and initiation
    103–4; just 180–2; a meditation on
    152–94; neurosis of 181; preparation
    for 151; prepubescent desire for 46;
    representation of 20; unjust 162–5, 180
The Death of Ivan Ilyich 167
deification mystery 94
Denial of Death 170–1
depression 91
depth psychology 89, 152
Descartes, René 159
Dike 181
directions: fifth and sixth 107; four
    cardinal 107
discovery, history of 155
domination, patriarchal 41
Douglas, Claire 7
drawing, initiatory 15–25
dreams 5–6, 17–18, 29, 33–4; of
    aggression 57; of aging 52; of altitude
    169; of analyst 68–9, 73; of apples 80;
    of architecture 90; of baptism 78, 81;
    of bears 35, 73–5; of birth 44; of biting
    animals 18–19; of black holes 73–4; of
    burning books 177; of Christ/the
    Messiah 66–9, 71, 74–8, 80; of
    cowboys 80; of the Crucifixion 66–7,
    70, 74, 81; of death 22; of doctors 79;
    of dreaming 71, 75–6; of gorillas 68;
    of hair 53, 60; of Henderson 74; of
    hunting 73; of Jews 76; of Jung 71–2;
    of love 184; of massage 54; of
    mountains 69–71; of music 67; of
    mustangs 80; of nakedness 54; of the
    Nile 75; of the penis 79; of pinball 164;
    of political leaders 72; of reindeer
    72–3; of rituals 59, 90; of running
    56–7; of self-adornment/grooming
    52–3, 59–60; of serpents/snakes 21–2;
    of shut doors 90; of the soul 90; of

sounds 66, 73–4; of speaking in
    tongues 78; of suspension 169, 172; of
    swimming 78; of temples 42; of
    urination 79; of whales 75
Duino Elegies 149
Dumuzi 146–7

Eanna (House of Heaven) 144
École Sociologique, Paris 3
Eliade, Mircea 91
Elijah 93, 95
emergence 8
Emmaus Road 78
enclosure 8
The End of History and the Last Man
    87
The End of Meaning and the Birth of
    Man 87
Enheduanna (Sumerian high priestess) 7,
    149–50
Enki (Mesopotamian god) 145–6
Er 182
Eranos Tagung 95
Erdoes, Richard 107
Erikson, Erik 86
Erishkigal (Mesopotamian goddess)
    144–7
experience, learning through 112–14

father figures 74
fear: of death 161, 170; of madness
    94
feminism, anti-male vengeance in 57
fertility 52
Fierz David, Linda 19
flesh sacrifice 109
flying saucers 88
Fordham, Michael 87
fossil-stones 109
four cardinal directions 107
Franz, Marie Louise von 7
Freud, Sigmund 4, 64, 93, 96–7
Friedman, Maurice 96–8
Fukuyama, Francis 87
fundamentalism 5

galatura 145
gender, issue of 41
Ghent, Emmanuel 64
Giegerich, Wolfgang 87–9, 91, 160
girls, sexualization of 9
Gnosis 85–90